Into the Twenties

Into the Twenties

THE UNITED STATES FROM ARMISTICE TO NORMALCY

Burl Noggle

UNIVERSITY OF ILLINOIS PRESS
Urbana   Chicago   London

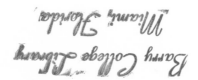

Library of Congress Cataloging in Publication Data

Noggle, Burl.
    Into the twenties; the United States from armistice
to normalcy.

    Bibliography: p.
    1. United States–History–1918–1921.   I. Title.
E766.N63   973.91'3   74–1388
ISBN 0–252–00420–5

FOR **Janie**

Preface

In traditional American historiography, shaped as it must be into topical and chronological arrangements, the decade of the Twenties, as subject and as period, follows immediately upon the heels of World War I. This practice can hardly be faulted except for the rapidity with which most historical accounts leap from the end of the war (Armistice, 1918) to the supposed inauguration of the Twenties—the election of Warren G. Harding in November, 1920. The only subject out of these two years that has been pondered and documented at any important length is Woodrow Wilson's trip to the Paris peace conference and his subsequent battle with the U.S. Senate over the treaty that he brought home from Paris. One or two other matters, such as the Red Scare of 1919–20 and the race riots of summer, 1919, have from time to time received good monographic treatment, but no one has thus far attempted to synthesize the numerous and discrete ideas and events that found life in the months following World War I and that spawned the phenomenon labeled "the Twenties." I have tried to create such a synthesis.

If verbose and involuted subtitles setting forth a book's fundamental claims were in fashion, I would propose something of the following for this one: "How the United States, having under the leadership of Woodrow Wilson fought and won a great war, sought to disengage its economy and society from the exigencies of war but instead, bereft of direction and leadership, stumbled for some two years through a trying time of demobilization, reconversion, race riots, and a frantic search for security at home and abroad from presumed enemies of the republic, and in the process surrendered to a state of mind that the war itself had already grossly stimulated, namely, a yearning for the national pieties and the political and economic conservatism personified by the Republican party's presidential nominee in 1920, thereby Harding and the legendary 'normalcy' of the Twenties resulting from America's engagement in and, more importantly, her disengagement from World War I."

More succinctly, I have tried to demonstrate how the United States, deeply involved in war in 1918, sought to demobilize after the November Armistice and step by step moved through a series of crises and readjustments that prepared the way for Harding's normalcy. The decade of the Twenties—with its intolerance and chauvinism, its search for psychic security, its falling away from whatever reform zeal the prewar Progressives had displayed, its ambivalence over centralization and rationalization of governmental and economic power, as well as its often exciting and innovative cultural and intellectual achievements—began to take form in the months after the Armistice. Harding, Coolidge, Hoover, and their colleagues in governing the American economy and society of the Twenties were more caretakers than innovators; they took command in March, 1921, of a country already predisposed to move in the direction in which they chose to go. The Twenties had, in large measure, already taken form before Woodrow Wilson rode down Pennsylvania Avenue for the last time as President of the United States and surrendered office to his successor. Wilson himself bore much responsibility for this. The care-worn face and racked condition of this great figure personified the state of the society that he bequeathed to his smiling successor.

I make no pretense of having exhausted the resources available on my subject, much less of having covered all the story. I could easily —and no doubt should—have given more attention to any number of subjects I either omitted or passed over lightly; for example, farmers and workers in chapter five, novelists and poets in chapter eight. Any one of the dozens of topics I did discuss, such as the work of the Reconstruction Research Division in the Council of National Defense, needs the book-length treatment it has not yet received. On the other hand, I have been gratified to find and to draw freely from any number of fine articles and monographs already done on certain topics relevant to my study. I have, above all, tried to identify and to establish an area for further historical study, and at the same time to modify the standard conceptualization of American history just after the war. The transition from Armistice to normalcy has been my concern, and I have ranged as broadly as my energies and curiosity allowed, drawing upon existing secondary studies and published government documents and other contemporary sources, as well as here and there digging into the personal papers of significant public figures. I have tried to set up a configuration of America after the war, to show the lasting impact and the residue of war within the nation in 1919–20, but at the same time to show a society taking form during these months that prefigured the decade ahead. I hope that the resulting narrative offers some freshness and cogency to students of the Twenties and that it will serve as an appropriate prelude to further studies of the decade by me and by fellow students of this myth-laden period sandwiched between Wilsonian and Rooseveltian America.

For carrying on portions of my research, the University Council of Louisiana State University granted me financial aid, which I hereby acknowledge. To those who have read the manuscript, warmest thanks. The dedication is to my most essential reader—and raison d'etre.

B.N.
Baton Rouge

Contents

I

Armistice

At 11 A.M. (Paris time), Thursday, November 11, 1918, the Great War came to a stop. The Armistice had not been easy to reach. Early in October the German government had asked President Woodrow Wilson "to take steps for the restoration of peace." Through October and into early November the President had maneuvered his fellow Allies and the defeated Germans into accepting an armistice on Wilsonian terms. Both the Allies and the Germans entered the Armistice understanding that Wilson's Fourteen Points of January, 1918, along with his subsequent statements of principles, would provide the basis for peace negotiations soon to begin in Paris.[1]

These negotiations, as well as the peace treaty itself, would have enormous import for the future. But on November 11, 1918, rejoicing over the moment exceeded concern over the future. Four days after the Armistice began, the American Expeditionary Force newspaper in France, *Stars and Stripes*, described the reaction among American doughboys on the western front: "At the eleventh hour on the eleventh day of the eleventh month hostilities came to an end from Switzerland to the sea. Early that morning from the wireless station on the Eiffel Tower in Paris, there had gone forth through the air to the wondering, half-incredulous line that the Americans held from near Sedan to the Moselle the order from Marshal Foch to cease firing on the stroke of 11." At the hour, "the cannons stopped, the rifles dropped from the shoulders, the machine guns grew still. There followed then a strange unbelievable silence as though the world had died. It lasted but a moment, lasted for the space that a breath is held. Then came such an uproar of relief and jubilance, such a tooting of horns, shriek-

---

[1] *United States Army in the World War, 1917–1919*, X: *The Armistice Agreement and Related Documents* (Washington, 1948), 3 and *passim*; Ray Stannard Baker, *Woodrow Wilson, Life and Letters*, VIII (New York, 1939) ; Arno J. Mayer, *Politics and Diplomacy of Peacemaking: Containment and Counterrevolution at Versailles, 1918–1919* (New York, 1967) ; Harry R. Rudin, *Armistice, 1918* (New Haven, 1944).

1

ing of whistles, such an overture from the bands and trains and church bells, such a shouting of voices as the earth is not likely to hear again in our day and generation."[2]

Not every doughboy rejoiced on the stroke of eleven. Some of them were still fighting, and some of them died, even after the hour. The German armistice delegation had crossed the French lines on the night of November 7, but the war continued. The French and the Americans prepared for an offensive to begin on November 14; meanwhile, AEF Commander John J. Pershing, distrustful of the Germans and hoping for a harsher armistice than the one Wilson was proposing, ordered his American forces to keep pressuring the Germans. At 5:10 A.M. on November 11 a German delegation signed the Armistice agreement in Marshal Foch's railroad car parked in the forest of Compiègne. At the time Americans held some 20 percent of the western front (eighty-three miles). By the time word of the Armistice reached that front, some attacks were already underway. In the 2nd and 89th Divisions, advance units did not receive word until after eleven and continued fighting.[3]

Among the Americans, reaction to the Armistice was sometimes subdued. Sergeant Elmer F. Straub, from Indiana, noted in his diary that when news of the war's end arrived, "the fellows had a smile on their faces but there was not any rejoicing to amount to anything. We sat around a fire talking it over until 2:30 and then we had a stable formation." Another American's diary entry for November 11 read: "No excitement at first. . . . Disappointed in selves. Wanted to be tremendously moved—and weren't." Private Horace Baker of Greenwood Springs, Mississippi, recalled his emotion: "Now I knew that the war was over, and in the depths of my soul fervently I murmured, 'Gott sei dankt!' " Why he thanked God in German he never fathomed.[4] Other Americans, less meditative, wanted to "fire the last shot." In one artillery battery, long ropes were fastened to the lanyards of four guns, and on signal 200 men on each rope cheered and

[2] *Stars and Stripes*, November 15, 1918, 1.

[3] James G. Harbord, *The American Army in France, 1917–1919* (Boston, 1936), 529–30; Edward M. Coffman, *The War to End All Wars: The American Military Experience in World War I* (New York, 1968), 355–56; Bullitt Lowry, "Pershing and the Armistice," *Journal of American History*, LV (September, 1968), 281–91.

[4] Elmer Frank Straub, *A Sergeant's Diary in the World War*, Indiana World War Records, III (Indianapolis, 1923), 219; "Anonymous," *Wine, Women, and War: A Diary of Disillusionment* (New York, 1926), 260; Dixon Wecter, *When Johnny Comes Marching Home* (Cambridge, 1944), 257–58.

pulled in unison. Contrary to orders, some fraternizing with the enemy took place. In the 124th Machine Gun Battalion, 33rd Division, a lieutenant allowed two of his men to cross no man's land for an exchange of talk and souvenirs with the Germans. Other doughboys responded in other ways. In a base hospital where Captain Charles L. Bolte was recuperating from a chest wound, a man entered the ward and announced that the war was over. The lieutenant in the bed next to Bolte made the only comment: "What the hell do you know about that?"[5]

In Paris a thousand church bells pealed at eleven o'clock, and 1,200 guns fired a salute to victory. Planes swooped over the city, dropping flowers. The streets became avenues of rejoicing throughout the day and all through the night. News of the Armistice reached New York before dawn, and a giant searchlight on the Times Building began playing its beam over the city. Sirens and church bells began to sound. Workers coming off the night shift joined milkmen, policemen, and "denizens of all night coffee stands" to form the nucleus of a crowd that quickly filled Times Square.[6] From the White House on November 11, Wilson announced the Armistice: "Everything for which America fought has been accomplished. It will now be our fortunate duty to assist by example, by sober, friendly counsel and by material aid in the establishment of just democracy throughout the world."[7] The Great War, the World War, the war to make the world safe for democracy, the war to end all wars, was over. The world, wrote a *New York Times* columnist later, "had been sown with graves and drenched with blood. Victory was bought at a cost that staggered humanity. But liberty was saved and the future of civilization assured."[8]

This was pride and even complacency. But in retrospect poignancy

[5] Wecter, *Johnny*, 257–58; Coffman, *War to End All Wars*, 356.

[6] Harbord, *American Army in France*, 530–33; Wecter, *Johnny*, 261–62. Ecstatic though it was, celebration of the Armistice in the United States was inhibited by recollection of a false armistice four days earlier, when Roy Wilson Howard of the United Press filed a premature cablegram and the nation exploded with delirium. See *U.S. Army in the World War*, X: *Armistice and Related Documents*, 46–47, for analysis of the origin and dissemination of the rumor. Arthur Hornblow, Jr., "The Amazing Armistice: Inside Story of the Premature Peace Report," *Century Magazine*, CIII (November, 1921), 90–99, is an account by an army intelligence officer at Brest, France, from which Howard dispatched his message to America.

[7] Baker, *Wilson, Life and Letters*, VIII, 580.

[8] *New York Times, Current History, The European War*, XVII, (New York, 1920), xvi.

and irony and naivete arise as well from this celebration of victory. Even before President Wilson left Washington for Paris and the peace talks, even before the first AEF units left France and headed for demobilization centers at home, some signs of the coming times appeared. On the first Sunday after the Armistice, on a day that many states and cities decreed a day of thanksgiving, the mayor of New York ordered police to make sure that henceforth, in view of "the horrors and outrages of unrestrained mobs abroad," the Red Flag be banned from display on any occasion. In Winston-Salem, North Carolina, a mob in search of a Negro broke into a hardware store to get guns and assaulted the jail where he was held. Local authorities, supported by a tank corps of federal troops, managed to hold the jail and protect the prisoners; but in the rioting several men died, including white officers. Elsewhere Negroes were less fortunate. During 1918 sixty-four of them died at the hands of lynch mobs.[9] The Red Scare of 1919, the race riots of 1919, the chauvinism and hysteria that would rage in the months ahead—these were rooted in the country's experience with war, though not until peace proved to be as difficult as war did these darker phobias and tensions erupt as responses to the perplexities of demobilization and (as the current expression ran) "reconstruction."

Even before demobilization and reconstruction began, however, the terrible impact of World War I stood readily apparent to anyone who cared to contemplate the awesome results. In the two decades after the war—until another one distracted them—Americans wrote much about the Great War, recalled its agonies, analyzed its origins and effects, drew presumed lessons from its history, and made it sometimes into legend, sometimes into myth.[10] Increasingly of late, historians have begun to appreciate the revolutionary nature of the war, demonstrating its role in the growth of the American economy, in centralization of federal power, and in the destruction of older strands of thought and values. One historian writes: "World War I was the first important and intensive phase in a fairly continuous development, indeed as a harbinger of the present, an auspice of what the country has become today. One might say that it was for

---

[9] Wecter, *Johnny*, 263; *Crisis*, XVII (February, 1919), 180–83.

[10] Warren I. Cohen, *The American Revisionists* (Chicago, 1967). Joseph J. Waldmeir, *American Novels of the Second World War* (The Hague, 1969), 39–57, contains a discussion of the literary response to the war by novelists in the Twenties and Thirties.

the United States the beginning of the twentieth century, the era of American leadership in a world of wars and international crises, of the global economy, the leviathan state, the mass society, and the age of anxiety."[11]

Much of this was, of course, unclear in 1918 or even a decade later. But as soon as the war was over, studies of its costs began. The *Times* calculated that Treasury Department disbursements since April 1, 1917, including loans to the Allies, had exceeded normal outflow by $22,589,986,000. By mid-1920 Secretary of War Newton D. Baker had fixed the costs at $13,730,395,576.73.[12] In the Twenties the Carnegie Endowment for International Peace sponsored a massive study of the war. Many of the planned volumes never appeared, but one that did appraised "the costs of the World War to the American people." Its economist author, John Maurice Clark, estimated the net cost of the war to the United States up to June 30, 1929. It came to $37,573,960,113.69.[13] Clark had calculated not only the expenses of the wartime period itself, but also continuing costs such as interest on debt and Veterans' Bureau expenses. He also estimated government revenue accruing from sale of army and navy surpluses after the war, though he found the salvage on this material to be "only a small fraction of what had been spent."[14] As for human life, some five million

[11] Charles Hirschfeld, "The Transformation of American Life," in *World War I: A Turning Point in Modern History*, ed. Jack J. Roth (New York, 1967), 65. See also William E. Leuchtenburg, "The New Deal and the Analogue of War," in *Change and Continuity in Twentieth-Century America*, ed. John Braeman *et al.* (New York, 1966), 81–143, for the claim that "World War I marked a bold new departure," and that much New Deal thought and action drew upon World War I for inspiration and example. For the impact of the war on the entire world, Geoffrey Barraclough's statement is representative: "From a distance of fifty years it is more obvious than ever that the First World War—far more than the Second—was the great turning-point of modern history." "Goodbye to All That," *New York Review of Books*, II (May 14, 1964), 3.

[12] *New York Times*, January 1, 1919, 1:3; *War Department Annual Report, 1920* (Washington, 1921), 18–19. The whopping difference between the *Times*'s figure and that of Baker was evidently due to the latter's bookkeeping. Baker took into account the unexpended balance of appropriations by the Treasury, as well as income from sales of surplus War Department property and other recoveries.

[13] John Maurice Clark, *The Costs of the World War* (New Haven, 1931). For comment on the series, see John Higham *et al.*, *History* (Englewood Cliffs, N.J., 1965), 50; James T. Shotwell, *The Autobiography of James T. Shotwell* (Indianapolis, 1961), 134–55; and Shotwell's *Annual Report of the Director of the Division of Economics and History, Carnegie Endowment for International Peace* (March 22, 1922).

[14] With all due respect to the economist's (or perhaps the accountant's) art, one may question the validity of any such attempt at determining the cost of the war.

persons were in the armed forces of the United States at one time or another during the war. The surgeon general of the United States in 1925 estimated that over 50,000 of those had died on the battlefield or from wounds received there. Writing five years later, Clark found it impossible to estimate with any precision the "total loss of life chargeable to the war" but made a guess that it was no less than 160,000 and possibly exceeded half a million.[15]

Clark was aware that even these shocking figures could not convey the magnitude of the war for the United States and for the world. It was, he wrote, "impossible to canvass all the effects of the war." It was a great calamity, though with all its tragedy we had not felt enough of it "to make us appreciate what the rest of the world has borne and suffered."[16] All we could be sure of, he concluded, was that "nothing has remained untouched by the war. Everything that has happened has happened differently because of it."[17]

If the intangibles were beyond measure, the death count and the return of the dead from France in 1919 and 1920 were grimly clear. But when the *Antigone* arrived in port on August 7, 1920, with 1,575 bodies on board, and the *Princess Matoika* docked a month later with 1,280 coffins in hold,[18] nearly 190,000 survivors had already come home from Europe and been demobilized through a process often brilliant in execution but just as frequently unfortunate in economic implications.

The very word "demobilization" was new in 1918, though its essential meaning was clear enough: the reverse of "mobilization." The

---

Clark himself was perfectly aware of this and called attention to the intangibles of the war. Nevertheless, it is revealing of the mentality on the war—and on the status of economics—that an economist would attempt, that the Carnegie Endowment would support, and that Yale University Press would publish a sober study of the war's costs and detail them down to the last cent.

[15] These figures include not only battle casualties but also deaths occurring after the war due to wartime injuries and illnesses. For example, some 48,000 to 78,000 war-caused deaths occurred after the war and, as of 1931, were "still occurring . . . at a heavy but diminishing rate, at present about 3,000 annually." Clark, *Costs of the War*, 181ff.

[16] *Ibid.*, 289–90. By comparison, Britain lost 947,000 men; the French, 1,385,000; the Russians, 1,700,000; and the Germans, 1,800,000.

[17] Clark, *Costs of the War*, 289–90.

[18] *New York Times*, August 8, 1920, 22:5; September 5, 1920, 19:4. Newspapers in the months following the war periodically carried casualty lists, such as losses by universities, losses by army divisions, losses by states, and even, from time to time, statistical summary charts. See, for example, *New York Times*, May 4, 1919, II, 2:4; May 11, 1919, IV, 8:1; and February 8, 1920, 6:3.

intricacy and the scope of that mobilization, as well as a patriot's uncritical pride and satisfaction with it, are suggested in the following passage from a 1921 publication on demobilization coauthored by Benedict Crowell, who was director of munitions, 1917–20:

[At the front] boys in our own khaki wriggled, charged, fought, plunged ahead all the morning [of November 11]. Behind these outpost men were the AEF, two million strong. Behind the AEF, in America, was a training and maintenance Army nearly as numerous. . . . Behind the [Army] were twenty-five million American men . . . registered [and ready to] join the current that led, if necessary, to the supreme sacrifice.

The foundation on which rested this human edifice was industrial . . . —seven million Americans delving in the earth for ores, chemicals, and fuels, felling the forests, operating the cranes . . . slaughtering the beeves, fashioning the garments . . . and accomplishing the million separate tasks necessary to the munitioning of the Army. And . . . behind both the military and the industrial armies was . . . perhaps the greatest force of all— . . . one hundred million Americans who . . . in one way or another put forth effort that did not flag until victory came. Such was America in a war that truly threatened her existence. America invincible.[19]

Just how this giant process of mobilization for war was to be reversed and how it was to relate to still another postwar process—reconstruction—was a national conundrum.

The word "reconstruction" had become commonplace by November, 1918.[20] Everyone, it seemed, talked about it. Nobody in a position of real power and influence had done anything about it. Insofar as one can measure or gauge the national consciousness, it was, in 1918, preoccupied with war—with winning it and ending it. Yet the war and the aftermath of war were inseparable matters, and many people knew it. Throughout 1918 increasing numbers of pundits and public officials wondered about the "postwar world." The war was a terrible, jolting war, and as it drew nearer to a climax, one saw people groping for their bearings. Albert Bushnell Hart, Harvard historian, wrote in October, 1918: "The trend of the political organization of mankind in 1918 is as different from that of 1914, as 1914 was . . . from 1814 or from 1514. . . . The world is uncouth, dishevelled, possessed of evil spirits, full of woe, wrath, and putridity . . . a world in which two and two make three or five . . . but never four." Out of this

---

[19] Benedict Crowell and Robert Forrest Wilson, *Demobilization: Our Industrial and Military Demobilization after the Armistice, 1918–1920* (New Haven, 1921), 2–3.

[20] For extended discussion of reconstruction, see pp. 31–83 below.

"frightful confusion" the United States, like the world, was "re-making." Changes in the United States in a year and a half of war, Hart observed, had been as great as those of a century and a quarter preceding 1917. The federal government, in function and accretion of power, had especially undergone "tremendous adjustment." We knew what we had become, wrote Hart, but "we know not what we shall be, [though] it is easy to see that the United States is a new country."[21]

Reconstruction, then, had already begun—the United States had been remade by the war. But reconstruction in another sense was the commoner thought: once the war was over, what then with the United States, its economy, its social structure, its mission, and its direction? If only to bolster their wartime resolves and to rationalize the awful act of war, scores and scores of Americans entered the Armistice yearning for and expecting an upsurge of reform and progress. Having presumably made the world safe for democracy, they must now sustain and intensify that democracy. The United States did not end World War I in a fit of reaction. Events of 1918–21 would embitter many men, destroy many illusions, and prepare the way for much of the reaction prevalent in the Twenties. But the war itself did not destroy the prewar Progressive movement. Many Americans moved from war to peace with high hope and lofty resolve. No one before the war or during it expressed any more yearning for continued progress than did Owen R. Lovejoy, president-elect of the National Conference of Social Work, in a 1919 address to that body: "The war has taught us the value of certain policies, among them cooperation and the practical utility of sacrifice. . . . Shall the giant [now] fall down before the task of utilizing the power of united effort and of unselfish sacrifice in order to make this a country of opportunity for all people?" In war, nothing had been too good for the army. Now the task was to show that "there is nothing too good for the homes, the villages, the institutions, the laws, the liberties and the country."[22]

Such aspiration could hardly be faulted. But just how, and by whom, should society be led toward this better condition? By November, 1918, President Wilson had planned virtually nothing in the way of a domestic program of reconstruction. Preoccupied (his critics would say obsessed) with the coming peace conference, he provided

[21] A. B. Hart, "The New United States," *Yale Review*, n.s. VIII (October, 1918), 1–17.

[22] Owen R. Lovejoy, "A War Program for Peace," National Conference of Social Work, *Proceedings* (1919), 664.

no program of his own and encouraged none from his administration.[23] Even the army seemed surprised when it suddenly faced the problem of demobilizing its men.

Preparations for military demobilization got underway about mid-October, 1918, when a War Department committee began drawing up tentative plans. Two questions immediately arose. First, were soldiers to be demobilized by military units, and as quickly as possible, regardless of the occupational and industrial needs of the country; or by industrial skills so as to avoid a glut on the labor market? Second, was the army to take them home before releasing them, thereby avoiding the danger of a labor surplus congregating near the large cities, or would several major mustering-out centers make for an easier and more effective demobilization?[24] Doughboys themselves sometimes recognized the problem. "Beginning to think of *apres la guerre*—dreadful problem of living," wrote a young AEF officer a few days after the Armistice. "Down to earth and job, after voyage on the coat-tails of Fate."[25]

The job was only part of the problem. As U.S. Army Chief of Staff Peyton March noted, the army, in planning for demobilization in 1918, had no American precedent worth following and few European examples to emulate. At the end of the Civil War, for instance, desertions had been common, men leaving trains at the point nearest their homes rather than waiting for mustering out. As a result their records were incomplete, and their subsequent claims for pensions and compensation filled the courts for years. The army wanted to avoid duplicating this problem in 1918. Mobilization in the Spanish-American War was so meager compared to World War I that 1899 provided no models for 1918. France and Italy planned demobilization by length of service, those longest in the army leaving first. This was inapplicable in the United States—or so thought the War Department. American participation in the war had been so brief that General March could find no valid distinctions in length of service. In any case, the men who had served longest were usually in supply services and were needed to help demobilize the remainder of the army and to serve the army of occupation in Germany. The British government

[23] See pp. 48ff. below.
[24] E. Jay Howenstine, Jr., "Demobilization after the First World War," *Quarterly Journal of Economy*, LVIII (November, 1943), 91–105; Peyton C. March, *The Nation at War* (Garden City, N.Y., 1932), 310–14.
[25] Wecter, *Johnny*, 5.

9

tried demobilization by occupation and soon had a near mutiny on
its hands. The U.S. Army, then, had little to go on and little to choose
from. It was either demobilization by occupational class or by military
unit. The army chose the latter, though not without first opting for
the former and then, in a certain panic, stumbling toward the most
expeditious solution it could find.[26]

When the War Department's demobilization committee began its
work in October, it copied portions of the elaborate British plans
that had been in preparation since the summer of 1917. Then suddenly came the Armistice, and at once massive pressure arose to get
Johnny home. His family wanted him back, but more than sentiment
was at work. Economic pressures set in as well. The needs of the
economy were, at least in theory, to influence the rate and process of
demobilization; but the slower the demobilization, the greater the
expense to the federal government. On November 11 the war was
costing the United States about $50,000,000 a day. Every day's delay
in implementing demobilization added to the burden of taxation
required to help maintain that army.[27]

On November 12 Secretary of War Newton D. Baker admitted that
"no plans had been finally formulated," but he noted that a scheme
worked out by the Labor, War, and Navy Departments and the War
Industries Board would go to President Wilson in a few days. Under
this plan Baker expected that demobilization would "be carried out
largely on a basis of the ability of trades and occupations to absorb
[the returning men]." He thought that, as "a matter of justice," men
longest in the service should leave it first, but "the industrial situation" would probably modify this principle.[28] Thus on the day after
the Armistice Baker expressed the quandary that the army faced—
but that neither he nor the army had to face for long.

The nearest thing to a plan that Baker possessed at this time had

[26] Peyton March, "Demobilization," *National Service* (April, 1919), 201–6; March,
Nation at War; Howenstine, "Demobilization after the War"; Edward M. Coffman,
The War to End All Wars: The American Military Experience in World War I (New
York, 1948), 155; Paul Barton Johnson, *Land Fit for Heroes: The Planning of Brit-
ish Reconstruction, 1916–1919* (Chicago, 1968), 360–61; *War Department Annual
Report, 1920,* 153–55; Winston S. Churchill, *The World Crisis, 1918–1928: The
Aftermath* (New York, 1929), 40–54.

[27] Crowell and Wilson, *Demobilization,* 5.

[28] Howenstine, "Demobilization after the War," 93; *New York Times,* November
12, 1918, 24:1; Daniel R. Beaver, *Newton D. Baker and the American War Effort,
1917–1919* (Lincoln, Nebr., 1966).

come from the army's committee on classification of personnel, and more particularly from a civilian member of the committee, Robert C. Clothier. Clothier, who had made a detailed investigation of British demobilization plans, recommended that Baker imitate them— discharge by trade and occupation, not by military unit. This would require exhaustive analysis of industrial conditions to determine just what skills were needed where. Such data, however, should have been collected and evaluated long before the Armistice. There were organizations on both the local and national level, such as community labor boards of the U.S. Employment Service, which could have supplied at least some of this information, but the plain fact was that the War Department, like the bulk of the Wilson administration, had made no plans for peace at home. George Peek of the War Industries Board had, just before the Armistice, begun to think of plans comparable to the one that Clothier presented to Baker. Felix Frankfurter of the War Labor Policies Board felt much the same way, though not until November 22 did he propose to Secretary of Labor Wilson a schedule for demobilization that would first release farmers, cattlemen, and others in agricultural work, and then six other occupational groups down to the last category—"men of independent means"—a class "clearly less important than the first six." Provost Marshal General Enoch H. Crowder proposed that the 4,684 selective service boards throughout the country handle demobilization, on the principle that nobody would know better how to reintegrate a soldier into the community than his friends and neighbors who had taken him from it.[29]

None of these proposals, of course, had been adopted by November 11. But Secretary Baker had to make an early decision—or at least a statement. On November 15 he announced that his department would work closely with the Labor Department and the War Industries Board in carrying out demobilization, doing so with full regard for its economic impact. Such a scheme never got off the ground. The very next day, November 16, Chief of Staff Peyton March issued orders for mustering out the first 200,000 men upon the basis of military units. The orders were to be carried out in two weeks, and

[29] James R. Mock and Evangeline Thurber, *Report on Demobilization* (Norman, Okla., 1944), 127–28; Coffman, *Hilt of Sword,* 155; John Lombardi, *Labor's Voice in the Cabinet: A History of the Department of Labor from Its Origins to 1921* (New York, 1942) ; Wecter, *Johnny,* 306.

once "the machine" of demobilization was in "full operation," said March, "we expect to release thirty thousand men a day."[30]

Just how and why March took practical command of demobilization and began to implement his military principle over Baker's industrial plan is not clear. The General did, in fact, have a good case. After the Armistice he analyzed the demobilization options and measured them by one standard: that demobilization be carried out "in the promptest, fairest and most efficient manner." Industrial demobilization presented too many problems. To analyze the occupational priority of every individual soldier would unduly delay his discharge. Mustering out by occupational skill would possibly riddle some of the service and administrative units needed to demobilize the rest of the AEF. If local draft boards did the job, the army would have to supply each of them with military personnel to prepare discharge papers and service records, as well as facilities for housing and feeding them and providing medical examinations and possible hospitalization before discharge. March also objected to demobilization through local draft boards on the grounds that "it would make parades impossible."[31]

Although by late November military demobilization had, for the moment, prevailed over industrial demobilization, in the months to come the War Department would mitigate its plans in face of mounting criticism from labor interests aroused over a growing labor supply and from city fathers complaining about the congregation of unemployed veterans in metropolitan centers during the winter of 1918–19.[32] But the occasional gestures toward industrial demobilization did not occur until the vast machine of military demobilization had begun pouring the AEF back into the country.

[30] *Official U.S. Bulletin*, November 16, 1918, 6; Beaver, *Baker*.
[31] Howenstine, "Demobilization," 95–96; Coffman, *War to End All Wars*, 156–57; Mock and Thurber, *Demobilization*, 126–33; March, *Nation at War*, 321.
[32] March, *Nation at War*, 316–17, 326–27.

II

Demobilization

They began to come home in November. A week after the Armistice, Pershing released all American troops in Europe except 200,000 men needed for the American army of occupation that was already moving across the frontier into Germany and settling into its quarters at Coblenz on the Rhine. At the time the AEF contained 81,800 officers, with 1,037,000 men in the advanced combat areas and 855,600 men in the rear, together with 47,700 civilian workers and 35,000 prisoners of war, the latter being used as laborers. Scattered through the AEF were 45,000 saddle horses, some 30,000 trucks, nearly 8,000 cars, and 13,700 motorcycles. The AEF was operating some 450 locomotives and 3,300 railroad cars along about 7,400 miles of railways. Its weapons included 1,400 pieces of heavy artillery, 1,890 pieces of field artillery, 1,362,000 rifles, 68,000 machine guns and automatic rifles, 240 tanks, nearly 2,000 airplanes, and 219 balloons.[1] Most of the equipment, animals, vehicles, and weapons would remain in France to rust, die, or be sold in a huge salvage operation by the AEF. The men, however, except for the modest few who were to remain abroad as students, as exiles, or as husbands of French or English wives, wanted to come home, and the army wanted to bring them.

The problem was shipping. Of the 2,000,000 men in the AEF, over half had crossed the Atlantic in foreign ships, most English. At the end of the war the British government, wanting to return Australians and other troops of the Empire to their countries and also eager to restore its foreign commerce, immediately withdrew its tonnage from service by Americans. So did France and Italy. The great "bridge of ships" on which the AEF had moved to Europe disappeared, as 2,000,000 Americans in Europe looked for transportation home.[2]

[1] James A. Huston, *The Sinews of War: Army Logistics, 1775–1953* (Washington, 1966), 385–86.

[2] Paul Barton Johnson, *Land Fit for Heroes: The Planning of British Reconstruction, 1916–1919* (Chicago, 1968), 251–56, 356; Huston, *Sinews of War,* 391ff.;

On Armistice Day, American troop ships had a one-way capacity of 100,000 to 150,000 men, though many of these ships needed repairs. Without additional ships, it would take over a year to bring the AEF home. The army and navy began to scrape up the needed shipping. The army converted cargo carriers into troop ships. American shipyards, congested with construction on new vessels ordered by the Emergency Fleet Corporation, stopped their wartime construction and by April, 1919, had equipped fifty-eight of the fastest and largest cargo ships with bunks and galleys and turned them over to the Embarkation Service. This wartime agency, headed by Brigadier General Frank T. Hines, merged in December with the Inland Traffic Service to form the Transportation Service which, under Hines's direction, handled the Atlantic crossing from Europe.[3]

Meanwhile, the navy installed bunks and other facilities on fourteen battleships and ten cruisers to provide a total capacity of 28,600 troops. The Allied Maritime Council apportioned all confiscated German ships equally between Britain and the United States (on the basis of tonnage), giving the United States the larger vessels because it had the large harbors to accommodate them. The largest ship in the world, the German *Imperator*, became the U.S. transport *Leviathan*. Soon after the Armistice ten other German ships stood ready for use. From the Allies and from a few neutrals the Transportation Service chartered thirty-three passenger ships. By June, 1919, the transportation fleet reached its maximum limit—174 vessels with one-trip accommodations for 419,000 troops. Larger by forty ships than the entire fleet of American and Allied troop ships available to the United States before the Armistice, it could have carried the entire AEF in five trips, with room to spare.[4]

Embarkation began from France in November when 26,000 men came home. The process peaked with almost 350,000 returning in June, 1919, and by the end of August, 1919, only 40,000 American

---

Benedict Crowell and Robert Forrest Wilson, *Demobilization: Our Industrial and Military Demobilization after the Armistice, 1918–1920* (New Haven, 1921), 6; Stephen Wentworth Roskill, *Naval Policy between the Wars*, I: *The Period of Anglo-American Antagonism, 1919–1929* (New York, 1968), 102ff., 204ff.

[3] Roskill, *Naval Policy*, 30ff. The first ship to be converted was the *Buford*. During the Red Scare in 1919–20, it would be dubbed the "Soviet Ark" when it carried 249 aliens and reputed Reds into exile in Europe.

[4] Coffman, *Hilt of Sword*, 159; Huston, *Sinews of War*, 391–92; Crowell and Wilson, *Demobilization*, 6, 30–37.

troops remained in Europe, all of them either logistical units or remnants of the American occupying forces in the German Rhineland.[5]

At home demobilization took place even more rapidly.[6] The army discharged over 600,000 men in December, 1918, even before many AEF troops had begun to arrive. By March, 1919, over 1,600,000 officers and enlisted men had received discharges. By then only 300,000 of the AEF had reached the United States, but the demobilization centers were empty and ready to receive them. By June 30, 1919, over 2,600,000 enlisted men and 128,436 officers had been mustered out, and on January 1, 1920, only 130,000 men, mainly regular army, stood under arms maintaining the token occupation force in Germany or elsewhere carrying on normal peacetime duty of the regulars. By April 1, 1920, the U.S. Army contained less than one-eighth of 1 percent of those Americans who had enlisted for emergency duty during World War I. Navy discharges had proceeded just as rapidly. Within a year after the Armistice, the navy released some 400,000 men and the marines about 50,000. Four days after the Armistice, Secretary of the Navy Josephus Daniels ordered all ships and stations to release from active duty, at the earliest possible date, all members of the naval reserve force and all men who had enlisted for the duration. In subsequent orders he released some of the regular navy as well. At its peak in 1918 the navy (including the Coast Guard) contained just over 530,000 men. By November, 1920, it was down to 127,809. The Marine Corps by then contained just under 20,000, in comparison to its wartime peak of nearly 75,000.[7]

Rapid and efficient though it was, this massive demobilization had

[5] John Maurice Clark, *The Costs of the World War* (New Haven, 1931), 53–54; *War Department Annual Report, 1920* (Washington, 1921), 151ff.; James R. Mock and Evangeline Thurber, *Report on Demobilization* (Norman, Okla., 1944), 134.

[6] On Armistice Day itself, several thousand new enlistees were on their way by train to basic training camps, having taken their induction oath that morning. Within an hour after the Armistice these troop trains had turned around, and by nightfall the new inductees were home again. Crowell and Wilson, *Demobilization*, 46.

[7] *Ibid.*, 50; Russell F. Weigley, *History of the United States Army* (New York, 1967), 396; *War Department Annual Report, 1920*, 155; Mock and Thurber, *Report on Demobilization*, 136ff.; Clark, *Costs of War*, 53–54; *Annual Report of Secretary of the Navy . . . 1919* (Washington, 1919), 173; *Annual Report of Secretary of the Navy . . . 1920* (Washington, 1920), 220–21. In returning men from Europe, the navy gave first priority to members of the Naval Reserve Force, second to those who had signed for the duration, and third to regular four-year men. Ordinarily, seamen with the shortest time left to serve went home first.

not occurred without delays, provocations, and frustrations. By late November a new version of George M. Cohan's "Over There" had sprung up in the military hospitals near Bordeaux: "And we're going back for it's over over here."[8] But either because it was over, or because they were not going back soon enough, the AEF began to grumble and discipline began to crack. Within three weeks after the Armistice, fifty-one new military police companies were organized and kept busy. Paris and the embarkation ports began to collect AWOL's. In the spring of 1919 barracks graffiti included: "Lafayette, we are *still* here." Men grumbled about the YMCA ("the YMCA went over the top / They thought they heard a nickel drop"), preferring the Salvation Army with its free doughnuts and coffee and more modest publicity, and the Red Cross, which, as one soldier wrote, "is what the YMCA advertises itself to be."[9] Feuds broke out between officers and enlisted men. In barracks-room ballads of the AEF, the brass hats "were mocked, damned, charged with every shortcoming from cowardice to sexual impotence."[10] A marine corporal, convalescing in postwar Paris from his wounds, wrote: "A city for officers only, now. Every place an enlisted man wanted to go in, there was a sign up, For Officers Only. I hope the next war will be for officers only." In 1919, when the Graves Registration Service began laying out American cemeteries in France, complaints soon reached the U.S. Senate that bodies of officers were put in metal coffins and segregated from those of enlisted men. On the other hand, officers had complaints peculiar to themselves. When they reached port in the United States, at the foot of the gangplank many of them were presented demotions, as the War Department reduced stars to eagles, eagles to oak leaves, and double bars to single ones. To make matters worse for these returning heroes of the officer class, the army for a while took away their Sam Browne belts. The symbol of caste in the AEF was this diagonal across-the-shoulder leather strap attached to a broad belt at the waist. Cherished by many an AEF officer, it was an object of hatred among enlisted men. Evidently because of a barrage of post-Armistice criticism against wartime conditions and the special privileges that officers had enjoyed, army regulations forbade use of the belt in the United States. In 1921, however, when

[8] *Stars and Stripes*, November 29, 1918.
[9] Quoted in Dixon Wecter, *When Johnny Comes Marching Home* (Cambridge, 1944), 275–76.
[10] *Ibid.*, 276.

Pershing became chief of staff, one of his first orders directed that the belt be worn at all times outside of quarters.[11]

Discipline and morale were minor problems compared to logistics. The AEF in November, 1918, had no camps or ports in France suitable for immediate use as embarkation centers. But within a week following the Armistice the U.S. Quartermaster Service chose Brest, Bordeaux, and St. Nazaire as ports of embarkation, with Brest as the major outlet. At Brest the army soon built "the largest installation for the embarkation of passengers the world had ever seen."[12] Midway between Paris and the Biscay coast of France, at Le Mans, the army during the war had established an enormous assembly area, a transfer point for troops coming off ships and on the way to the front. It now turned the process around, and Le Mans became an assembly area for troops bound for the embarkation ports. Traveling by rail from the front or from Paris, American troops moved into Le Mans by the thousands. From just after the Armistice until late spring, 1919, the camp sustained a transient population always over 100,000. Le Mans was vast. "There was," wrote two Wilson administration officials, "nothing like it in the United States. A man could walk briskly for an hour in a single direction at Le Mans and see nothing but tents, barracks, drill fields, and troops."[13]

From Le Mans the troops ordinarily went by rail directly to the embarkation ports. The camps built at the three major embarkation ports were themselves large and busy centers. Camp Pontanezen at Brest, the largest of the three, accommodated 80,000 men. Pontanezen, "a complete American city set down amid the quaint roads of old Brittany," contained barracks, theaters, stores, libraries, restaurants, hospitals, and churches. At Le Mans or at the embarkation port itself, the men underwent medical examinations, received the care of dentists and barbers, and, if necessary, acquired a new outfit of clothing. "In 1919 we brought home the first American army that had ever fought in a great war and returned in anything but rags."[14]

[11] *Ibid.*, 276–77, 300; Coffman, *Hilt of Sword*, 163.

[12] Crowell and Wilson, *Demobilization*, 11–12. Some doughboys left France from Marseilles, Le Havre, and other cities, but most of them went on board ship at Brest, Bordeaux, or St. Nazaire, though each of the latter two handled one-fifth or so of the traffic that passed through Brest.

[13] *Ibid.*, 21.

[14] *Ibid.* For an intimate account of his unit's stay at Brest, written by a young sergeant who would become a historian, see William L. Langer, *Gas and Flame in World War I* (New York, 1965), 104ff. For a grimmer tale, see Arthur W. Little, *From Harlem to the Rhine: The Story of New York's Colored Volunteers* (New York,

If he came home well clad, the doughboy also came home deloused. The louse, euphemized as "cootie," gained national fame during World War I. One inspection revealed that 90 percent of American troops at the front were infested with the pesky parasite. Every embarkation port in France contained a section known as the "dirty" camp, another as the "clean." Troops arriving at the port first entered the dirty camp for a delousing bath, then settled into the clean one to await transportation home. If pressed to do so, Bordeaux could cleanse, delouse, equip, and otherwise prepare 180,000 men a month for the voyage home.[15]

In late spring, 1919, Le Mans closed. On June 30, Bordeaux closed as a port of embarkation. St. Nazaire ceased operations on July 26. Brest was the last to close in the fall. By then the AEF no longer existed in France.

The runs across the Atlantic were usually routine. Not a man lost his life on the return home. Some troops came back in finer style than they had gone over. Many men brought European wives with them, and army regulations said that husband and wife must travel first class. Transports arriving in the United States docked either at Boston, at New York (more specifically at Hoboken, New Jersey), at Newport News in Hampton Roads, or at Charleston, South Carolina. New York and Newport News received the largest number. The oil-burning *Great Northern* set the record for all crossings. She left Hoboken on June 24, 1919, a few days later arrived at Brest and took on some 3,000 troops, and was back in Hoboken twelve days, five hours, and thirty minutes after leaving there. She also held the record of eighteen transatlantic cycles, at an average of twenty-three days each. In New York the Red Cross met the doughboy at the foot of the gangplank and offered him a snack. The commanding officer at the port reported that, after much experimenting, he found the doughboy's favorite food to be frankfurters and sauerkraut.[16]

Each doughboy, as he left the army, kept a complete outfit of clothing along with varied equipment, such as his toilet kit, which included a trench mirror and a safety razor. The army had introduced thousands of Americans to this little razor and thereby changed the shaving habits of a generation. The doughboy's duffel bag bulged

---

1936), which describes the discrimination and brutality experienced at Brest by this famous Negro unit.

[15] Crowell and Wilson, *Demobilization*, 23.

[16] *Ibid.*, 38–40, 54; Wecter, *Johnny*, 300.

with souvenirs. The demand for German Iron Crosses had become so great that "Germans had been constrained to manufacture them for the overseas trade." By early 1919 the exchange value of one Iron Cross was quoted as having fallen to one cake of American soap. "A joke of the trenches said that the French might be fighting for freedom, but the Yankees were fighting for souvenirs."[17]

The army could have paid off the troops at the debarkation ports, given them a travel allowance provided by Congress, and been freed of all further responsibility. But the War Department was afraid to turn hundreds of thousands of ex-soldiers loose on the big city with bonuses and back pay in their pockets. Besides, the War Department could transport the men home at much less than five cents a mile. Therefore, to protect the men from the presumed evils of the big city, to save money, and to avoid undue concentration of surplus labor, the War Department often shipped the troops by rail to points near their homes. Many men, however, did receive their discharges in the debarkation ports or camps far from home, though as they turned away from the disbursing window with money in hand, they often met a Red Cross or YMCA worker urging them to buy a ticket at once and leave for home on the first train.[18]

Before they left the army, thousands of troops took one last march through the streets of New York or Philadelphia or Washington or Chicago—or lesser cities. All told, nearly 200,000 troops marched in more than 450 victory parades, ranging from brief processions of a single company to great spectacles in New York and Washington. On February 17, Harlem's famous black regiment, the 15th New York Infantry, marched for seven miles up Fifth Avenue, then into Harlem itself and up Lenox Avenue. There Jim Europe's band struck up "Here Comes My Daddy Now." Jim Europe, "the most celebrated bandmaster in the AEF," had come through the war unscathed, but he would be murdered three months later and would be buried in Arlington Cemetery dressed in the pleated silk shirt and striped vest of his jazz band.[19]

[17] Wecter, *Johnny*, 311.

[18] Crowell and Wilson, *Demobilization*, 50–52. As added inducement the U.S. Railroad Administration offered veterans a special travel rate of two cents a mile if they bought a ticket within twenty-four hours after discharge. See William G. McAdoo to Newton D. Baker, November 20, 1918, Letterbook 64, Container 500, William Gibbs McAdoo Papers, Division of Manuscripts, Library of Congress.

[19] Wecter, *Johnny*, 303; *Crisis*, XVII (April, 1919), 293, 295; Little, *From Harlem to the Rhine*, 357–62. The 370th Infantry, "the only regiment in America . . . Colored

Other black Americans had served and returned, too. Some 350,000 to 400,000 black troops served in World War I. Less than 50,000 of them were combat troops, the remainder serving in labor battalions, depot brigades, and other units where the army, operating from a segregationist and racist position, put them. When the war ended there were some 250,000 of them in France, chiefly in service battalions. During the Christmas season Robert R. Moton, successor to the noted black leader Booker T. Washington as principal of Tuskegee Institute, visited some of the black troops. Moton drove by car for 1,000 miles from Laon down through Alsace and Lorraine, talking with the men of the 92nd Division and with three regiments of black Americans brigaded with French troops. In keeping with his position as Washington's successor, Moton talked accommodation to the troops. He told them that both black and white Americans would welcome them home, and he stressed the importance of the black soldier's going home in "a manly, yet modest, unassuming manner." In less than a year all black troops in the AEF had been returned home, though their homecoming did not result in the welcome that Moton had anticipated. No blacks served in the Rhineland army of occupation.[20]

Until the army of occupation came home, and until the U.S. Army had disposed of its enormous surplus properties in Europe and had tried to strike a cash balance with the Allies for war material bought and sold—until then, demobilization by any definition was not ended. In accord with the Armistice, the German armies began to pull out of France and Belgium on Tuesday, November 12. American and Allied armies then moved forward into the evacuated areas.[21] On November 17 the great line of Allied and American troops, strung out from the English Channel to the Swiss border, began a coordinated advance toward the German frontier. In the American zone the newly formed Third Army, now labeled the American army of occupation,

---

from the colonel down to the last buck private," received a tumultuous welcome when it returned home to Chicago and marched down Michigan Avenue. See Howard A. Phelps, "The Return of the 'Black Devils,'" *Half-Century Magazine*, March, 1919, 11.

[20] *Stars and Stripes*, January 3, 1919; Robert Russa Moton, *Finding a Way Out* (Garden City, N.Y., 1921), 250–65; Wecter, *Johnny*, 303; Rufus E. Clement, "Problems of Demobilization," *Journal of Negro Education*, XII (Summer, 1943), 533ff.; *Negro Year Book*, 1921–22, pp. 188–93.

[21] The forces detailed for occupation of Germany included the Second British Army; the Fifth, Eighth, and Tenth French Armies; the Third American Army; and a part of the Belgian army.

200,000 strong, marched toward the Rhine flanked by the French on their right and the English on their left. Moving some twelve miles per day, the Americans crossed the German frontier at 5:30 A.M. on December 1, 1918. As they moved eastward, a great stream of released prisoners, both Allied and American, passed them moving westward, many of them in cast-off German uniforms. Well ahead of the main American occupation army moved an advance guard, followed by engineers who repaired roads and bridges, cleared mine fields, and inspected water reservoirs. Coblenz, built by the Romans where the Moselle flows into the Rhine, was the American destination.[22] On the afternoon of December 8, American cavalry patrols reached the Rhine. On Friday the thirteenth, in the fifth week of the Armistice and in a dismal rain, Americans crossed the river and occupied the bridgehead assigned to them. The "March to the Rhine" had ended. The "Watch on the Rhine"—occupation slogan mocking the German patriotic war tune—had begun. By terms of the Armistice the American and Allied armies would remain in Germany until a peace treaty had been signed.[23]

The American Third Army eased into Coblenz without band and without fanfare. "We're just going in sort of casual like," said one American. The body of troops rode into the city on a German troop train manned by German engineers, firemen, and conductors. Twenty-four hours after they entered Coblenz, *Stars and Stripes* reported that the Americans were "completely at home there. They haunted the candy stores and the beer halls, they went to the movies and the opera, they submitted nervously to the attentions of German barbers, they stared into the neat, bright shop windows all gay with

[22] The Americans were to occupy the city, as well as a bridgehead of 30 kilometers radius on the east bank (the city lying on the west side of the river). The British were to hold Cologne and a corresponding bridgehead to the north on the Rhine, while the French established another bridgehead at Mainz to the south of the Americans.

[23] For detailed study of the American and Allied occupation, see Ernst Frankel, *Military Occupation and the Rule of Law: Occupation Government in the Rhineland, 1918–1923* (London, 1944); Report of [Colonel Irvin L. Hunt] the Officer in Charge of Civil Affairs, Third Army and American Forces in Germany, *American Military Government of Occupied Germany, 1918–1920* (mimeo ed., Coblenz, 1920); and a series of essays and documents in *American Representation in Occupied Germany, 1920–21,* I–III, compiled by the Assistant Chief of Staff, G2, American Forces in Germany (mimeo ed., Coblenz, 1922–23); Henry T. Allen, *My Rhineland Journal* (Boston, 1923) and *The Rhineland Occupation* (Indianapolis, 1927), a memoir-history by General Allen, who commanded American occupation forces from July 2, 1920, to February, 1923.

Christmas cards, and they sauntered along the lamplit streets taking lessons in German from Lena and Gretchen." Soap, they found, would buy them "anything" from the Germans. Supply officers, finding their kitchens and wagons stripped of soap, placed supplies under triple guard. After some 200,000 Americans had spent an uneventful first week "in undisputed possession of a well-ordered countryside," *Stars and Stripes* marveled at the occupation: "Surely there was never such another military occupation." Off-duty Americans crowded into "jolly and bright" cafes, one of them run by a German aviator named Wahl, who had once flown with barnstorming Americans back home. Billeted in German homes, the Americans often enjoyed soft beds, hot suppers, and German cleanliness.[24]

Early in the occupation the venereal disease rate dropped to a remarkable low, due perhaps to an anti-fraternization order issued by the American command. An official army of occupation report for the week of December 25 marked "a new low record in disease incidence in the history of the American Army." As late as February 5, the rate in the occupation army was 14.8 per thousand, compared to 32.2 per thousand for the entire AEF at the same time. But then, as fraternization rose, so did the VD rate. So did marriages by Americans to German girls. During the first six months of occupation, 140 Americans applied for permission to marry Germans. Thereafter the number increased. Between October 1, 1919, and January 1, 1922, the Third Army received 1,527 applications for marriage. It approved about half of them.[25]

Not all Americans found life in occupied Coblenz compatible. Neither did some Germans. As the occupation went on, thousands of AWOL's went into hiding in Germany. Those who spoke German were especially difficult to track down. They simply left their units, changed into civilian clothes, and dropped out of sight of other Americans. During the first ten months of occupation, friction between American soldiers and German civilians led to numerous convictions, but the Germans received a significant share of them. Six Americans were convicted for homicide, two for manslaughter, five for rape and

[24] *Stars and Stripes,* December 13, 1918; December 20, 1918; and January 3, 1919; Ernest Peixotto, *The American Front* (New York, 1919), 226–30; *U.S. Army in World War I,* XI, 202ff.; Wecter, *Johnny,* 286.

[25] *Stars and Stripes,* January 17, 1919; March 14, 1919; Hunt, *American Military Government,* 206–7; *New York Times,* July 4, 1919, 9:1; *U.S. Army in World War I,* XI, 204; *American Representation in Occupied Germany,* II, 41–49, and III, 238–41.

five more for attempting it, six for nonsexual assault upon German women, eight for burglary, eight for robbery, twenty for larceny, and twenty-three for assault with deadly weapons. During the same ten-month period, some 9,700 Germans were convicted of offenses against American soldiers or for breaking military rules. The most frequent convictions were for such actions as selling alcoholic drinks, theft of U.S. government property, practicing prostitution while diseased, and using insulting language toward the U.S. Army.[26]

As spring, 1919, approached amid rumors of severe peace terms from Paris, civilian food shortages, and political unrest in Germany, the resentment began to focus on the Americans and their intervention. Men and women crowded soldiers off the sidewalks, and in cafes waiters treated them with insolence. Meanwhile, either as cause or effect of such attitudes, Americans billeted in German homes frequently humiliated their hosts by playing the role of conqueror to the hilt. Brawls broke out between American soldiers and young demobilized German soldiers, due to drinking or to jealousy over German girls. Nevertheless, when rumors arose that the Americans were pulling out of the Rhineland to be replaced by French troops, Germans in the area "invariably asserted" their preference for the Americans.[27] By late spring, 1919, *Stars and Stripes* no longer intoned the solemn "Watch on the Rhine." Rather, the army now spoke casually—and a little wearily—of "The Rhine, the Rhine, the Yankee Rhine."[28] Though their numbers steadily decreased, there were Yankees on the Rhine until February, 1923. Until the Germans signed the peace treaty, the Americans were to remain at Coblenz in force. Germany signed the treaty on June 28, 1919.[29] Pershing dissolved the Third Army on July 2 and turned over remaining occupation forces to Major General Henry T. Allen, who commanded a force of some 16,000 men in December, 1920, reduced to 1,200 by the end of 1922. These came home in January, 1923. When Allen himself

[26] *U.S. Army in World War I*, XI, 206–12; *New York Times*, August 21, 1919, 15:6; Hunt, *American Military Government*, 212–15; and Wecter, *Johnny*, 287.

[27] *American Representation in Occupied Germany*, I, 26, and II, 40ff.; *U.S. Army in World War I*, XI, 204–7; and *Foreign Relations of the United States, 1922* (Washington, 1938), II, 214ff.

[28] See, for example, *Stars and Stripes*, May 30, 1919, 7.

[29] Thereafter the Americans and the Allies remained in occupation of their German bridgehead under terms of the Rhineland Agreement, a document put together at Paris in the days preceding the June 28 treaty ratification. For the text of the agreement and for discussion of its provisions, see Frankel, *Military Occupation*.

left Coblenz by train on February 19, it was cold and raining. "The doughboys long since returned to civilian life would have thought the weather appropriate."[30]

American demobilization in Europe required more than evacuation of the AEF and the army of occupation. At Armistice, the army had on hand in France vast quantities of supplies. One estimate valued the surplus on November 11 in the United States at $2,000,000,000. In Europe the surplus totaled $1,330,000,000 over and above what the army expected to return home and outside of what it would consume while still in Europe after the war. These figures covered only the inventory to November 11. The war industry still had weeks to go before it could finally come to a stop; before all production for war finally ceased, hundreds of millions more accumulated. In February, 1919, the War Department established the U.S. Liquidation Commission to supervise liquidation and settlement of all army contracts and properties in Europe. Except for 850,000 tons of artillery, road-making machinery, and other heavy equipment (which it shipped to the United States), the army sold its holdings in Europe, mostly to France. The French government agreed to pay $400 million in bonds for much of the surplus property. The Portuguese government bought a large quantity of army shoes. The Czechs took 10,000 army overcoats. Estonia bought 3,000 tons of army bacon. The French government bought American suspenders valued at $22,000. Most of its supplies the Army sold at cost of manufacturing, plus the expense of transporting the material to Europe.[31]

Surplus sales in the United States were more complicated. No other government made a bulk purchase as the French had made in Europe, and the surplus in the United States was much greater. To avoid disrupting private business as much as possible, but at the same time to dispose of the surplus, the War Department transferred material to other federal departments where feasible. The remainder it began to sell to the general public in the summer of 1919. War Department catalogs went out to postmasters all over the country. The postmaster was to receive orders and payment and send in con-

[30] Edward M. Coffman, *The War to End All Wars: The American Military Experience in World War I* (New York, 1968), II, 245; Allen, *Rhineland Journal*, 570. With dissolution of the Third Army, the staff and troops remaining in Germany were officially designated as the American force in Germany. Allen, *Rhineland Occupation*, 130.
[31] Crowell and Wilson, *Demobilization*, 242ff.; Huston, *Sinews of War*, 395–96; Clark, *Costs of War*, 54ff.

solidated requisitions. This cumbersome method quickly broke down, and the War Department set up surplus stores over the country and sold goods directly over the counter to the customer. According to the catalog's listing, the customer could buy any kind of food, from "Apples, evaporated," to "Vinegar"; among general supplies he could choose from "Arctics, cloth top," to "Whips, artillery." The price was usually well below the market average.[32]

The army took its greatest loss in disposing of surplus buildings and land. Within a year after the Armistice, the department had disposed of fourteen National Guard camps, three embarkation camps, sixteen training camps, four flying fields, four hospitals, and various buildings for a total of $4,215,000. The original construction cost of the National Guard camps alone had been about six times this much. Camp Beauregard in Louisiana, which had cost $4,300,000, brought $43,000 in "salvage recovery." Up to March 1, 1920, the War Department disposed of surplus property which had cost it $2,600,000,000. For this material the government received $1,633,000,000. In the meantime, War and Navy Department contracts were cancelled or otherwise settled, as were contracts with the Allies for supplies, obligations for railroad transportation, and the interminable exigencies of war.[33]

No demobilization of any kind at any speed would have pleased everybody. When the War Department in November quickly abandoned its hurriedly contrived plan for industrial demobilization, it aroused not only the ire of labor spokesmen worried about a labor surplus, but also criticism from employers wanting particular men with particular skills back in the plant, office, or mine. On the other hand, military demobilization, faster though it was, did not move rapidly enough for mothers, wives, and others wanting Johnny home at once. Members of Congress, besieged by constituents' complaints, passed along criticisms to the War Department. As early as January, 1919, however, General Peyton March thought that his decision to demobilize by military unit had been justified. Presenting comparative figures on British and American demobilization, he showed the sluggishness of the British system and noted the mass mutinies in the British army, revolts evidently provoked by the presumed favoritism shown to men in certain occupations and industries. In

[32] Crowell and Wilson, *Demobilization*, 272–85; Huston, *Sinews of War*, 396–97.
[33] Huston, *Sinews of War*, 396–97; Clark, *Costs of War*, 54–98; Crowell and Wilson, *Demobilization*, Ch. 18.

England, Winston Churchill entered the War Office on January 15, 1919, and in five days abandoned the industrial system in favor of military demobilization. British demobilization, the product of long and careful planning, had failed. General March, devising an American plan within days after the Armistice, had done well by comparison.[34]

Yet American demobilization had its shortcomings. Some of the economic consequences would become clear in 1919–20 as the nation entered its reconstruction. More elusive but perhaps more important than economics was the state of mind that the American ex-soldier came home with—though no system of demobilization could have coped with this force. The American doughboy's hatred for the war he had fought was clear enough. The postwar slogan coined by troops in France awaiting shipment home, "From Hell to Hoboken," neatly summed it up. His attitude toward politics and affairs of state was harder to fathom. In March, 1919, from "every part of France and Germany where American soldiers are stationed," reported *Stars and Stripes*, delegates came to Paris and organized the American Legion. In time this body would form a potent interest group of ex-doughboys. In Paris that early spring of 1919, the 500 organizers were not united even on a name. Among the titles proposed were American Crusaders, the Legion of the Great War, Veterans of the Great War, Society of the Great War, and the one they finally adopted. Later, in the United States, the very first American Legion conventions would demonstrate the political consciousness of the Legionnaires, though even then the members seemed to be concerned mostly with three things: reunions, patriotism of a sort, and bonuses or other advantages for the ex-doughboys.[35]

For the most part, the individual soldier's political or social consciousness must go undocumented, though Dixon Wecter made a reasonable guess when he wrote of the returning doughboy: "Statesmanship he did not understand; domestic politics was apt to bore

[34] E. Jay Howenstine, Jr., "Demobilization after the First World War," *Quarterly Journal of Economy*, LVIII (November, 1943), 91–105; Coffman, *Hilt of Sword*, 156; Winston S. Churchill, *The World Crisis, 1918–1928: The Aftermath* (New York, 1929), 40–44.

[35] *Stars and Stripes*, March 21, 1919; Richard Seelye Jones, *A History of the American Legion* (Indianapolis, 1946); William Gellermann, *The American Legion as Educator* (New York, 1938). For further discussion of the American Legion after the war, see p. 120 below.

him. . . . He preferred baseball."[36] A few soldiers ran for political office soon after the war, stressing their wartime service, and won. In August, 1919, Kentucky elected the first World War I soldier to Congress, a Republican lawyer from Lexington named King Swope. To Wecter, the doughboy came home with a divided mind. "The war, he felt, had been a grim struggle for survival against the Hun, but talk about saving the world for democracy had been mostly bosh. . . . If the need arose, he would fight again . . . but he would gag at the sugar-coating of idealism. He was now a man, serious beyond his years. Some of the old provincial innocence of Americans in 1917 had perished as a casualty of the struggle."[37]

Whatever they thought about the war, some doughboys found a home in the army and remained in it, though by 1921 the U.S. Army had become only a shadow of its wartime might. Debate over the size and function of a peacetime naval and military force began as soon as the war ended. Not until June, 1920, did Congress, with passage of the National Defense Act, finally establish a peacetime army. Shortly after the Armistice, Chief of Staff March gained temporary approval from President Wilson and Secretary of War Baker for his proposal: a peacetime army of 576,000 men, expandable in case of war to double its size, the additional forces coming from reserves to be formed through a proposed system whereby all qualified males should take three months of compulsory training during their nineteenth year. Relegated to third place behind this regular army and its reserve would be the National Guard.[38]

Senator James W. Wadsworth (Republican, New York), chairman of the Senate Military Affairs Committee, introduced the March-Baker bill in January, 1919, and began holding hearings on it. The bill was meanwhile introduced into the House by S. Hubert Dent, Jr. (Democrat, Alabama). Opposition was intense. Perhaps King Swope, the freshman ex-doughboy Republican from Kentucky, summed up the majority view: "Everybody had a bellyfull of the damn Army." Percy E. Quincy of the House Military Affairs Committee said it another way: "They propose that outrage in time of

[36] Wecter, *Johnny*, 370.

[37] *Ibid.*, 378.

[38] Coffman, *Hilt of Sword*, 173ff.; Weigley, *U.S. Army*, 396–97; Bernard Boylan, "Army Reorganization 1920: The Legislative Story," *Mid-America*, XLIX (April, 1967), 115–128; Jim Dan Hill, *The Minute Man in Peace and War: A History of the National Guard* (Harrisburg, Pa., 1964), 289–315.

peace. My goodness think of it."[39] Inconclusive hearings continued for months. Pershing arrived in New York in September and received tumultuous welcome in a parade down Fifth Avenue and then in another one down Pennsylvania Avenue in Washington. Between October 31 and November 5 he testified before the Wadsworth Committee. Already the committee had heard from Colonel John M. Palmer, a member of Pershing's original general staff. The two professionals offered an alternative to the March bill. Both Pershing and Palmer had come to doubt the doctrine of Emory Upton, the nineteenth-century strategist whose emphasis upon a large army of highly trained soldiers had long influenced U.S. Army policy. Palmer suggested a small regular army, ready to serve in any emergency short of mass mobilization, and one whose primary function would be to train the citizen army that must be the nation's reliance in any major war.[40]

Palmer's testimony—along with Pershing's—was influential, and Palmer helped shape final legislation, though congressional debate continued into the spring of 1920. General William ("Billy") Mitchell and other airmen pressed their congressional supporters for a separate air force rather than an army air service. National Guard supporters wanted larger appropriations and a more distinctive relation to the army, one analogous to the Marine Corps's relationship with the navy. Economizers and anti-militarists wanted to reduce the army to the minimum. Others wanted to abolish all universal military training. A bill finally emerged and on June 4, 1920, Wilson signed the National Defense Act. The regular army was cut to 280,000 men. The civilian National Guard received larger control over its own affairs. An organized reserve was to receive periodic instruction from the regular army. The air service, created in 1918 by executive order, gained congressional approval as a branch of the army coordinate with the infantry, cavalry, and other traditional units.[41]

[39] Coffman, *Hilt of Sword*, 188; *Cong. Rec.*, 66 Cong., 1 sess. (August 28, 1919), 4476.

[40] Weigley, *U.S. Army*, 399; Coffman, *Hilt of Sword*, 189ff.; *War Department Annual Report, 1920*, 5ff.; U.S. Congress, Senate, Subcommittee of the Committee on Military Affairs, *Hearings on Army Organization*, 66 Cong., 1 & 2 sess. (1919–20), 2 vols. Palmer's views on the postwar debate are conveniently found in his *America in Arms: The Experience of the United States with Military Organization* (New Haven, 1941), 165–90.

[41] *New York Times*, January 29, 1920, 1:7; February 5, 1920, 2:6; February 6,

Congress reduced this regular army to 150,000 men in 1921 and to 137,000 a year later. During the Twenties and Thirties the U.S. Army "may have been less ready to function as a fighting force than at any time in its history. . . . As anything more than a small school for soldiers the Army scarcely existed."[42]

Neither did the navy. At the end of the war, the U.S. Navy ranked second only to Great Britain's. During 1918 the Navy Department drew up plans for even further development, including twelve more battleships and sixteen more battle cruisers. In December, 1918, the navy presented to Congress a proposed three-year program of expansion. Wilson supported it, as of course did Secretary of the Navy Daniels. Wilson wanted to use the expansion program as a bargaining tool with Great Britain. If the British would support the League of Nations, Wilson would consider a general reduction in armament, one that would keep the American and British navies on an equal basis. Evidently Wilson did agree to suspend the three-year expansion program when the British agreed to enter the League. Meanwhile, voices in Congress began expressing opposition to even a navy comparable to Great Britain's. Talk arose of "militarism" at home and a "naval race" with Britain that could lead to war. Other congressmen talked of economy. A reaction against "navalism" developed and sustained itself through 1919–20. By the winter of 1920–21, the reaction was building toward the mood that produced the Washington Disarmament Conference of 1921–22. In 1921, after establishing the navy's personnel strength at 137,435 men, with officers in a fixed proportion of 4 percent, Congress appropriated enough money to pay only 106,000 men.[43]

And so by 1921, as Woodrow Wilson prepared to leave the White House and Warren G. Harding to enter it, the military force raised to fight the Great War had been demobilized, a peacetime army and

---

1920, 14:1; Burke Davis, *The Billy Mitchell Affair* (New York, 1967), 49ff.; Hill, *The Minute Man*, 293ff.; Weigley, *U.S. Army*, 399–400; I. B. Holley, Jr., *Ideas and Weapons* (New Haven, 1953), 149ff.; 41 *Stat.* 759ff.

[42] Weigley, *U.S. Army*, 403; *Report of the Secretary of War, 1922* (Washington, 1922), 13. These figures do not include the U.S. Army Reserve enrollment or that of the National Guard—though neither of these fared any better than the regular army at the hands of Congress.

[43] Harold and Margaret Sprout, *Toward a New Order of Sea Power: American Naval Policy and the World Scene, 1918–1922* (Princeton, 1940), 48–60, 100–118; Donald W. Mitchell, *History of the Modern American Navy from 1883 through Pearl Harbor* (New York, 1946), 252; Roskill, *Naval Policy between the Wars*, I, 213–33.

navy had been created, and (except for the remnant along the Rhine) there were no American doughboys left in Europe.[44] The two million who had by then come home were, along with the rest of the nation, still undergoing what was commonly labeled "reconstruction." This was, if anything, more nettlesome than "demobilization."

[44] After the Armistice a ghoulish debate arose in the United States over whether the bodies of Americans killed in France should be shipped to America for reburial or should remain in the cemeteries in France where the AEF had interred them. The War Department agreed to allow either choice, guaranteeing that the graves in France should be "maintained and kept beautiful forever by the American government." Thousands of bodies were returned to the United States; thousands more remained in France. For a chart showing the names and locations of American cemeteries in France, and the number of burials there, see Crowell and Wilson, *Demobilization*, 88.

III

"We Have an Opportunity to Do Great Things"

Reconstruction Proposed

Well before the Armistice, even before the war's outcome was certain, talk about a new and better postwar world grew common. Perhaps this anticipation of a brighter future was, in part, a catharsis of the suspense and suffering. Yet with the end of the war, the nation's exhilaration was not merely over the peace, blessed though that was, but also over the new society that countless Americans now began to contemplate. The future was open, full of potential. Reaction, disillusionment, even despair—these would develop in time. But such a mood did not prevail in November, 1918, or for months afterward. A common mood at war's end was that of hope, of eagerness, over the future. Not war but the war's aftermath produced the weariness and apathy associated with normalcy. Warren G. Harding's presidency and the Twenties of legend were, in considerable measure, products of reconstruction, coming into view in 1921 but not in 1918.

In 1918, as the AEF began to demobilize and thoughts of peace replaced those of war, one editor phrased the common mood succinctly: "We need no longer work for the right of self-determination for the peoples of the earth. That is won. . . . Militarism is dead, unless we are so incredibly stupid as to revive it. . . . The Atlantic Ocean is the new Mediterranean, and while trade winds blow its waves shall be consecrated to freedom." But a question remained: "The war is won. Under what device can we consolidate its gains, eliminate its evils, capitalize for the programs appropriate to peace the social enthusiasms which it has generated?"[1]

Optimism was abundant that such a device was at hand. In late November at a New York "Conference on Demobilization and the Responsibilities of Organized Social Agencies," chairman Felix Adler issued a call to action. "We should be courting disaster if we thought we could create all things anew, [but] I feel that . . . the hour has

---

[1] "American Ideals Triumphant," *Survey*, XLI (November 16, 1918), 185.

come when we have an opportunity, such as has never existed before in this country, to do great things." Adler would sustain in peace the "high wave of service" that the country had manifested in war. He spoke hopefully of "sick insurance," of slum eradication, of a "war against prostitution." He would fight disease, not just for the individual and his welfare but "in order that we may have a sound nation. We have been wishing for the health of individuals . . . but can't we make this *nation* sound? Can't we make a healthy *people*?" Adler, a prewar Progressive, had lost none of his optimism. If anything, the war had strengthened his hope and extended his vision from betterment of individuals to betterment of society and even the world. With the Great War won, America's purpose now, in peace, was to move mankind further along toward its achievement of "the perfect man," a "fairer and more beautiful and more righteous type than any . . . that has yet existed."[2]

For Adler, the war had demonstrated the nation's potential for "service." For another old Progressive, Donald Richberg, it had pointed a different moral and left him less optimistic over the potentials of reconstruction. Yet even Richberg entered the Armistice with a sense of hope. Richberg, who along with his Chicago law partner Harold Ickes had supported Theodore Roosevelt's Progressive ticket in 1912, would in the Twenties and early Thirties establish a reputation as an expert in labor legislation. During the war he expressed his concern over organized labor's future. To Chicago meatpacker Ogden Armour he wrote, "I believe in America's war heart and soul. I believe that all humanity will move forward many strides after its terrible suffering is ended. But I also know . . . that one of our greatest menaces at . . . present is the selfish stupidity of some of our so-called captains of industry who, even in this time of national need . . . cling to their outworn notions of class interests." Richberg, who insisted that he was "not a Socialist or anarchist [but] a college-bred, hard-working lawyer," wanted to see an end to "oppression of work-

---

[2] "A New Purpose," *Survey*, XLI (December 7, 1918), 288–89. By 1918 Adler was a veteran crusader against exploitation of children, serving from 1904 to 1921 as chairman of the Child Labor Committee. Clarke A. Chambers, *Seedtime of Reform: American Social Service and Social Action, 1918–1933* (Ann Arbor, 1967), a fine study of social service organizations that survived the war or that developed during the Twenties, reveals Adler's enthusiasm at war's end but then his and his colleagues' growing concern as many of their hopes did not materialize. See also Allen F. Davis, *Spearheads for Reform* (New York, 1967), 227ff., for comments on social work after the war.

ers." He wanted Armour and "every other large employer of labor" to proclaim their support for "unionization of labor." By Christmas, 1918, Richberg had begun to doubt that a war for democracy in the world was leading to greater democracy at home. The war had been fought "by all the people and . . . not by any class or for the benefit of any class." But already, in peace, "the short-sighted capitalist class whose arrogant methods create class consciousness and organize class antagonisms, the ass who brays over his dinner table about the follies of 'the working class,' " was "recruiting his army" for a "world war over industrial control." American workers were not yet "fully class conscious." They still hoped to become "the capitalist of tomorrow." But as "reactionary politicians, financiers, and employers" continued to protect their own class interests, they were arousing an "embittered army which, once in the field, can in thirty days destroy every personal and property right which the class conscious capitalist holds so dear." If the "Caesars and Napoleons" of American society and industry continued in their "vain and stupid" ways, the country would "go through the agonies of revolutionary reconstruction, in order that, having helped to make the world safe for democracy, we may save democracy for the world."[3]

As Richberg himself insisted, he was no socialist or anarchist. He was, instead, a most moderate (and articulate) Roosevelt Progressive, who hoped through such moderate reconstruction as unionization of labor to save the American capitalist from his own shortsightedness. The war had been a just war, but if the nation was, "upon the war ruins," to build better "houses of government," it must "be dedicated to the service of men as human beings, not to . . . any particular social or industrial class. . . ."[4]

If Richberg represented one Armistice version of a Roosevelt Progressive, William Gibbs McAdoo and Franklin K. Lane voiced two versions of the wartime Democracy of Woodrow Wilson. McAdoo's rhetoric—if it was even that—never approached Wilson's level. As Secretary of the Treasury and then as Director of Railroads during the war, McAdoo contemplated the end of the war and the "readjust-

---

[3] Richberg to Ogden Armour, December 3 and 14, 1917, Container 1, Richberg Papers, Division of Manuscripts, Library of Congress. Arthur M. Schlesinger, Jr., *The Coming of the New Deal* (Boston, 1959), contains comments on Richberg before and during the New Deal; see also Richberg's own *Tents of the Mighty* (New York, 1930) and *My Hero* (New York, 1954).

[4] Richberg, "Christians and the World at Peace," *Life and Labor*, December, 1918, copy in Container 5, Article File, Richberg Papers.

ments" afterward in prosaic terms. Three days after the Armistice, McAdoo wrote, "It has been the most tragic time in the history of the world but I hope there will emerge from it the realized vision of genuine liberty and democracy for all the responsible people of the world." A week later he noted: "If we keep our heads . . . and act as intelligent people should act, we [can gain] all the great things America entered the war to accomplish. . . ."[5] This was the upper limit of the McAdoo eloquence, and even here the reference to intelligent people was a clue to his sober caution. Meanwhile he concentrated—and with admirable efficiency—upon more mundane matters.

On November 14, 1918, he declared, "The collapse of our enemies necessitates instant reconsideration of the financial problems before the government. . . . The prompt enactment of a Revenue Bill is imperative." In June, McAdoo had been prepared for "a long war and an increasing military program" and had estimated expenditures for the fiscal year 1918–19 at $24,000,000,000. Now he hoped for a reduction to $18,000,000,000. Federal expenditures must continue for the army and navy for "salaries and wages of war establishments." Too, the United States must continue to advance credit to European governments "for purposes growing out of the war." But foreign loans must remain minimal, importers must pay cash for U.S. exports, and at home the administration must reduce "war and excess profits taxes" and offset this reduction by raising corporation and individual income taxes.[6] A week later he deplored talk of canceling Allied debts to the United States and even asked Attorney General Thomas W. Gregory to stifle ("with propriety") advocacy of the idea from a civilian organization working under Gregory's authority.[7] Meanwhile, in his other role as Director of Railroads, McAdoo, though he would soon resign the part, began to grapple with the problem of railroad demobilization, finally coming to advocate continued federal control

[5] McAdoo to William Jennings Price, November 14, 1918; McAdoo to Captain Charles A. Lyerly, November 20, 1918, Letterbook 66, Container 500, William Gibbs McAdoo Papers, Division of Manuscripts, Library of Congress.

[6] McAdoo to Furnifold Simmons, November 14, 1918, Container 213, McAdoo Papers.

[7] McAdoo to Attorney General T. W. Gregory, November 19, 1918, Letterbook 64, Container 500, McAdoo Papers. McAdoo referred to a remark by A. M. Briggs, chairman of the board of directors of the American Protective League, who had declared: "Every true American would rejoice if on the day peace is declared President Wilson tears up and throws to the four winds every bill we hold against our allies."

for a five-year period during which a scheme could evolve for returning the roads to private ownership.[8]

Thus McAdoo, while uttering the conventional rationale for war and its possible benefits for the future, tended to mind his fiscal business and to seek a return to lower federal expenditures and eventually to less federal intervention in the economy. By 1920 he would be seeking, however discreetly, the Democratic presidential nomination. Perhaps for this reason he would be—again discreetly—criticizing his father-in-law Woodrow Wilson for preoccupation with the peace treaty and neglect of reconstruction problems at home. But at war's end McAdoo seemed to have few notions of just how to attain the "great things America entered the war to accomplish," except through financial retrenchment.

His cabinet colleague, Franklin K. Lane, had scarcely more vision. Lane did strain to come up with at least one fresh scheme, though even that one—settlement of ex-doughboys in rural areas—smacked of nostalgia for the agrarian past.[9] Offering the preface to a collection of essays on *American Problems of Reconstruction,* Lane warned: "The one danger of any period of reconstruction is . . . in letting go the old before the new is tested. . . . [To] reject tradition, to despise the warnings of history is to drive without a chart into a Sargasso Sea." But Lane did not anticipate such a future, since to him the American people were "the safest and sanest people on earth. There is no danger whatever of their rushing headlong down a steep place into the sea."[10]

Lane's oceanic metaphor could not conceal the banality of his outlook. Even William Jennings Bryan offered more breadth, though Bryan, too, seemed tied to old programs and old rhetoric. His Nebraska paper, *The Commoner,* urged "immediate reeducation of the army and navy to a reasonable peace footing," and immediate cancellation of "all unnecessary army and navy contracts." All three levels of government—local, state, and national—should at once begin public works programs to provide jobs for ex-servicemen. The federal, state, and municipal governments should own and operate railroads,

[8] See Ch. 5 below for discussion.

[9] See pp. 74–75 below for discussion of Lane's soldier resettlement program.

[10] Elisha M. Friedman, ed., *American Problems of Reconstruction: A National Symposium on the Economic and Financial Aspects* (New York, 1918) ; Lane's foreword reprinted as "The Purpose of Reconstruction," *Survey,* XLI (November 2, 1918), 120.

telephone and telegraph lines, and merchant marines. The "special interests should not again be permitted to shift the burdens of war upon the people in the form of protective tariffs." The real producers of the country should be protected against packing house combines, grain elevator combines, and other such trusts and monopolies. A constitutional amendment should provide for the initiative and referendum. With such a program, and with Prohibition and woman suffrage in sight, the country could hope for "domestic welfare."[11]

Both the style and substance of the Bryan program would have been familiar to an old Populist.[12] Within a year or so after the war's end, even Populist disposals would seem revolutionary in many circles, but in late 1918 there were schemes more advanced and elaborate than Bryan's.

Algie Simons, an old prewar Socialist who had opposed the war until America entered it but then became a superpatriot condemning all antiwar Socialists as pro-Germans, wrote an entire book on reconstruction. Simons thought that "the problems of peace call for a greater crusade than the one that rallied millions to the battlefields to crush autocracy." Insofar as they were "suitable," he said, "all the enthusiasms, institutions, material and persons mobilized to win the war should now be mobilized to fight ignorance, poverty, disease, and social injustice."[13] The war, wrote Simons, had destroyed a

[11] Charles W. Bryan (associate editor and publisher, *The Commoner*), quoting W.J.B. in Circular Letter, December, 1918, Container 216, McAdoo Papers.

[12] Lawrence W. Levine, *Defender of the Faith, William Jennings Bryan: The Last Decade, 1915–1925* (New York, 1965), 150–51, notes that Bryan's views at war's end were "in line with the New Freedom philosophy upon which the Democratic party had campaigned in 1912 and from which Wilson had often deviated. . . . Bryan's fight for the adoption of these reforms was waged as a part of his concerted effort to prevent postwar reaction from setting in."

[13] Algie M. Simons, *The Vision for Which We Fought: A Study in Reconstruction* (New York, 1919), preface. On Simons's changing view toward the war, see James Weinstein, *The Decline of Socialism in America, 1912–1925* (New York, 1967), 122–23, 129–30; and Kent and Gretchen Kreuter, *An American Dissenter: The Life of Algie Martin Simons, 1870–1950* (Lexington, Ky., 1969), 163ff. The Kreuters portray Simons transferring his loyalty from socialism to nationalism. Simons had worked long and hard to reform American life through socialism; when the party failed to take a stand for war and against Germany, he decided it was time to transfer allegiance. The United States, through war, could cleanse the world of militarism and class rule. As the war progressed Simons even saw it working to bring about reform at home. American radicals, he felt, must work in concert with these measures of war and extend them when the war ended. *The Vision for Which We Fought* took form during the last year or so of the war, though by the time the book appeared (February, 1919) the vision, in Simons's estimate, had evaporated in the United States. Simons turned elsewhere for fulfillment—to a career in scientific management.

"whole social system," and the world was now beginning to glimpse the growth of a new society. The war had "revolutionized industry and all the social structure built upon industry."[14] To win the war, America had catalogued and classified all industry. It had created an administrative machinery that said "to each mill, shop, mine, farm, and railway: 'There is your place. Fall in.' " The old incentive for private profit gave way to that of "social service."[15] Flushed with the war's success, Simons rhapsodized over the country's mobilization for "service" and the enduring consequences of this. The war, he felt, had "almost abolished the old form of competition." Federal activity "wiped out all competition as foolish, wasteful and obstructive of good service. There is to be an end of comparative advertising, duplicate trains, rival ticket and freight offices." Such things were now "relics of the political economy of pre-war times . . . fossils in the legislative strata."[16] To Simons, the industrial capitalist who ruled the nineteenth century had "committed suicide in the great war." Power was now passing to labor, as the government, in order to organize production for war, organized the producers. In fact, "viewed from any of a hundred different points," the federal government was "the great organizing force . . . toward which all else is oriented, the nucleus about which all social life is turning." Never again would government be "the harsh repressive instrument . . . the source of fat plunder. . . . It will hereafter be something to use for the common good, to serve the common ends, to defend the common interest, and produce and distribute the common wealth."[17]

Simons was laying down an ideal program more than he was anticipating a certain future. As he wrote privately to an old Socialist comrade in November: "We are going to be in for merry hell all over the world. The Bourbons and the Bolsheviks are working together to prevent any constructive . . . reconstruction. The Bourbons want the unemployed so they can smash the unions. The Bolsheviki want a panic so they can raise hell. It looks like both would get what they want, which will be tough on the rest of us."[18] Even in his published *Vision*, Simons admitted that the task of reconstruction was "the

14 Simons, *Vision*, 1.
15 *Ibid.*, 18–26. Simons later qualified this judgment by noting that the war had "temporarily at least partially removed the element of private gain" (p. 35).
16 *Ibid.*, 27–28.
17 *Ibid.*, 36–37, 73–79.
18 Simons to Charles E. Russell, November 26, 1918, vol. X, Charles E. Russell Papers, Division of Manuscripts, Library of Congress.

greatest mankind has ever attempted. . . . We have built up a marvelous machine for socializing joy, work, and national defense. We cannot afford to lose this machine."[19]

Without advocating the socialist commonwealth that Simons proposed, other analysts of reconstruction also sought to maintain for peace much of the wartime "machine." The National Municipal League, in a late November "Conference on American Reconstruction Problems," called for continuation of most federal controls that had developed during the war. For example, the U.S. Employment Service, the Food and Fuel Administration, and the War Industries Board had proved their value and efficiency. "Every effort should be made to preserve the nucleus of these valuable agencies [so] that we may achieve some part of that efficiency in peace." Such wartime innovations as federal housing for industrial workers should now become permanent government functions. The Labor Department's Bureau of Industrial Housing should even broaden its program to include educational work and research on industrial housing problems. The Public Health Service should work to influence "moral and health conditions" in peace as it had for soldiers and industrial workers during the war. "In short," the League concluded, "we, as a people, during the next few months must vigorously hold the ground we have gained during the war."[20]

The National Catholic War Council also proposed holding onto wartime innovations. In February, 1919, the Council issued the "Bishops' Program of Social Reconstruction," so labeled because it appeared under the signature of the four bishops who then constituted the administrative committee of the NCWC, although the document had been written by Father John A. Ryan, veteran advocate of social reform.[21] The bishops (Ryan) wanted Congress to continue and

[19] Simons, *Vision*, 195.

[20] Platform of the NML, reprinted in *Survey*, XLI (November 30, 1918), 266. For basic information on the NML, see Mel Scott, *American City Planning since 1890* (Berkeley and Los Angeles, 1969), 145–46.

[21] The administrative committee consisted of Peter J. Muldoon, bishop of Rockford; Joseph Schrembs, bishop of Toledo; Patrick J. Hayes, bishop of Tagaste; and William T. Russell, bishop of Charleston. After the committee read Ryan's work, "they were impressed to the point of making it their own and issuing it over their signature." John Tracy Ellis, ed., *Documents of American Catholic History* (Milwaukee, 1956), 611–29. This volume reprints the Bishops' Program, along with an informative introductory note by Father Ellis. For Ryan's own recollections about the document, see his memoir *Social Doctrine in Action* (New York, 1941), 143–58. Ryan, *Social Reconstruction* (New York, 1920), is a series of lectures explicating the program.

strengthen the war-born U.S. Employment Service and the National War Labor Board. The wage level that labor reached during the war should not be lowered. Cities should carry out housing programs begun during the war by the federal government. Wartime price fixing should end, but cooperative stores could offer an effective solution to "extortionate prices." States should enact minimum wage laws and should provide for comprehensive insurance against illness, invalidism, unemployment, and old age—the insurance funds to be raised primarily by the industry in which a man was employed. The right to collective bargaining, widely upheld during the war, should never again be challenged.

Upton Sinclair, who found the report "amazingly radical," called it a "Catholic miracle." Stephen C. Mason, president of the National Association of Manufacturers, protested to Cardinal Gibbon that it was "partisan, pro-labor union, socialistic propaganda." In 1929 a committee of the New York Senate investigating seditious activities described it as the work of "a certain group in the Catholic Church with leanings toward Socialism."[22] The program was hardly this radical. As Ryan explained, he hoped through these proposals to sustain the existing system and forestall a "collectivist organization of industry that would mean bureaucracy, political tyranny, the helplessness of the individual . . . and in general social inefficiency and decadence." To prevent such a calamity, the weaknesses in the current American system must be overcome. The Ryan program sought to nullify those weaknesses.[23]

The Bishops' Program illustrates the range of reconstruction schemes that emerged with the end of the war. By January, 1919, reconstruction conferences were providing forums for an even richer variety of plans and panaceas. On December 2 the Reconstruction Committee of 100 met in New York. A week later the New York Academy of Political Science held a labor reconstruction conference. The American Public Health Association met in Chicago on December 11–13 and discussed reconstruction. On December 16 a Re-

[22] Ryan, *Social Reconstruction*, 13; Ellis, ed., *Documents of American Catholic History*, 611.

[23] Ryan, *Social Reconstruction*, 234–35. This Catholic program did not differ essentially from that of a great many Protestant statements issued after the war. See "The Churches and Reconstruction," *Survey*, XLI (December 21, 1918), 375, for a report on a reconstruction conference held by twenty-seven Protestant denominations. For resolutions on reconstruction passed in May, 1919, by the Federal Council of the Churches of Christ in America, see *Survey*, XLI (July 5, 1919), 548.

construction Conference of Governors convened at Annapolis. On December 3 over 5,000 businessmen representing 400 industries met at Atlantic City in a Reconstruction Congress of American Industries. Pronouncements on reconstruction had become a national fad.

One group of public-spirited citizens, with Paul Strayer as its spokesman, even proposed formation of "study groups" among "all classes and in all communities throughout the nation" to discuss and formulate plans for reconstruction. "Through tragedy and panic," a point had been reached in human progress when, with resolute thinking, a "new world order" could be established. "We must," they wrote, "build a new world or this war will have become murder on a colossal scale." If the nation should blunder into reconstruction, it would blunder through it. Leadership was imperative, but if in every community throughout the land a group of men and women of good will should organize and make a thorough study of reconstruction, the leadership would develop. The study group listed "immediate problems" that needed attention, such as jobs for returning veterans, the status of women who had found new jobs and new liberties during the war, and "prevention of the wave of drunkenness and vice which usually follows war." More enduring problems also called for attention: how to increase production and distribute wealth; the question of government controls; prevention of war. The Strayer group included elements of the prewar Social Gospel movement, as well as figures prominent in the YMCA and YWCA during the war. Although their stated goals were broad, they were, by their own account, aiming at "universal peace and good will" and "the Kingdom of God."[24]

More secular but not much less comprehensive in its views was the Conference on Social Agencies and Reconstruction, held in New York on November 29–30, 1918. Its committee on a national program, after several months' work, offered proposals for federal legislation affecting education, civil rights, probation, health, country life, conservation, labor, housing, pensions, public works, and the budget. "It is obvious," said the committee, "that the future welfare of other nations, as well as our own welfare, depends . . . upon the strength, the prosperity, and the resourcefulness of the American nation. . . .

[24] See *Study Outline in the Problems of Reconstruction Period* (New York, 1918). Besides Strayer, who was president of the Presbyterian Social Service Commission and chairman of the final revision committee that drew up this outline, the Strayer group included Walter Rauschenbusch, Raymond Fosdick, Henry Sloane Coffin, and "specialists of the YWCA and YMCA."

For food and raw materials, for financial credit, for transportation facilities at sea, for progress in science and the arts, for the maintenance of international obligations, the world will inevitably look to us as never in the past." This implied no superiority on America's part but was "the inevitable result of circumstances." The committee proposed new and expanded insurance programs, and even suggested a new cabinet post, "Secretary of Insurance, Compensation, and Pensions." It proposed more federal aid to education and a "standardizing and unifying" of the "whole educational system" under a plan that would safeguard the freedom and responsibilities of the states. "Freedom to think and the possession of something to think with," they said, "are the most precious gifts of fathers to sons." The committee would restore the civil rights that wartime brutality and censorship had all but destroyed. Beyond this, "Negroes as well as white citizens and aliens" were entitled to protection from mob violence. The committee supported a federal anti-lynching law, and in all measures for social reconstruction would "scrupulously" include provisions for blacks. The Public Health Service, the U.S. Employment Service, the Labor Department's Bureau of Housing—these the committee would retain and strengthen.[25]

At least one black leader could have agreed with the committee's provisions for Negroes. In the early spring of 1919, W. E. B. Du Bois, who since the death of Booker T. Washington was undoubtedly the most prominent figure in Black America, made a trip to Europe. There he learned of the gross prejudice shown to American blacks in the AEF. No one needed to tell him of the black experience in America, but evidently the trip to Europe caused him to explode with anger in an editorial in *The Crisis,* the NAACP magazine he edited. "We are returning from war. . . . [We] fought gladly and to the last drop of blood for America, a nation that represents and gloats in lynching, disfranchisement, caste, brutality, and devilish insult." America, "this country of ours, despite all [that] its better souls have done and dreamed, is yet a shameful land." For fifty years it had lynched two Negroes a week. It had never really tried to educate its Negroes, wanting them only as "servants, dogs, whores, and monkeys." Yet this country was the Negro American's fatherland, and it was right for him to fight for it. But "by the God of Heaven," said Du Bois, "we are cowards and jackasses if now that war is over,

[25] See "Social Reconstruction," report on the Conference on Social Agencies and Reconstruction, *Survey,* XLI (June 7, 1919), 402ff.

we do not marshal every ounce of our brain and brawn to fight a sterner, longer, more unbending battle against the forces of hell in our own land."[26]

Such reconstruction aspiration, arising from despair and expressed in militant terms, was uncommon. More conventional was the social worker's more impersonal sociological survey. Social workers and Social Gospel pioneers were understandably predominant in reconstruction conferences and prolific with reconstruction proposals. It was the nature of their professions or their ideology. But reconstruction proposals sometimes came from other directions and other ideologies. Even before the war ended, Elisha M. Friedman, statistician in the War Finance Corporation, initiated and edited a symposium, *American Problems of Reconstruction*. Europeans, noted Friedman, had built up an extensive literature on reconstruction; Germany had established an Imperial Office for Transition Economy, while England had a Ministry for Reconstruction. Even neutrals such as Spain and the Scandinavian countries had committees at work.[27] Encouraged by his former employer Eugene Meyer, Jr., financier and wartime director of the War Finance Corporation, as well as by economist Irving Fisher and New York banker Frank Vanderlip, Friedman set to work gathering information that might provide the basis for a national plan of reconstruction.

Friedman had "great hope in some big central public service body to carry out Reconstruction." He proposed that a "small body of enterprising economists" study foreign plans for reconstruction and then establish a committee which, as an official government agency, would plan and direct reconstruction at home. Friedman was concerned more with immediate problems arising from the "transition out of a state of war" than he was with "any general attempt to alter fundamental conditions" of the economy—that is, with convalescence of wounded soldiers, demobilization of the army and civilian war workers, prevention of postwar unemployment, and other adjustments to peace. But he also proposed study of broader and more enduring problems. The nation needed a "national labor policy" which would maintain, in peace, the wartime harmony between labor and management; it needed a study of foreign trade to recommend means for extending it; it needed to study fluctuations of prices to determine whether or not wartime controls on prices and distribution might

[26] W. E. B. Du Bois, "Returning Soldiers," *Crisis*, XVIII (May, 1919), 13–14.
[27] Friedman, ed., *American Problems of Reconstruction*.

continue in peace.[28] Reconstruction of a nation, wrote Friedman, "cannot be treated piecemeal. It is an organic problem and can be approached only as a unit." The nation needed "that degree of coordination which can come only with a central authority to deal with the problem."[29]

Friedman's association with Eugene Meyer and Company, his contacts with Frank Vanderlip, and his selections of contributors to his symposium suggest that he was speaking for the rationalization—and centralization—of the economy that major financial and industrial interests had so avidly worked for before the war.[30] But for Friedman and his contributors, writing near the end of the war, it remained to be seen what plans or leadership in this or any other kind of reconstruction would emerge from Washington.

Talk of reconstruction was common enough. What was not common was an underlying unity or direction for the talk. As *The Survey* commented in appraising a Rochester meeting of the National Municipal League, "reconstruction" at the conference took on a variety of meanings. To some speakers "the term meant a spiritual regeneration," but to others it signified "new roads and a large mercantile fleet." Some spoke of it as "having to do with a national program for a period covering at least a century," while others were impatient to solve problems of the next two months.[31]

If there was no pattern to the reconstruction talk, there was a spectrum. Two contributors to a symposium on reconstruction expressed the two extremes. The old iconoclast Thorstein Veblen wrote, ". . . there can be no return to the *status quo ante*." The nation, he explained, needed a "revision of . . . the present system of vested interests, and of the scheme of equities within which that system is now working at cross purposes with the common good." George Roberts of the National City Bank, New York, noting that some people expected "an overturning of the existing order after the war," ridiculed the idea. "They think that the relations between capital and

[28] *Ibid.*, 5–9.

[29] *Ibid.*, 22.

[30] The contributors included such men as Charles M. Schwab, chairman of Bethlehem Steel Corporation; George W. Perkins, director of U.S. Steel and partner in J. P. Morgan & Co.; and E. R. A. Seligman, professor of economics at Columbia University and member or chairman of numerous economic commissions and committees.

The attempt by major corporate interests to rationalize the economy through increased federal regulations is lucidly expressed in James Weinstein, *The Corporate Ideal in the Liberal State, 1900–1918* (Boston, 1968).

[31] "A City Set on a Hill," *Survey*, XL (November 30, 1918), 241.

labor will be very different." As a rule, said Roberts, "those who hold this view have always held a sentimental belief that the wage-earning class was 'exploited.' " Banker Roberts preferred to believe that "the entire community gains by the accumulation of wealth, no matter who owns it, and that comparisons and deductions as to the common welfare drawn simply from the ownership of wealth are fallacious." Roberts did not anticipate any change toward more "arbitrary management and distribution."[32]

Replace the existing system with a new one that would provide for the common good, or return to the *status quo ante* which presumably did the same—somewhere at these extremes or between them most students of reconstruction plotted the future. To aid them in their study, teachers and publishers began to assemble relevant material. The publication department of the Russell Sage Foundation ran an advertisement labeled "Your College and Reconstruction" which read: "Do you want your college to have the necessary equipment when problems of reconstruction are being worked out by her teaching staff?" Students and teachers would need "accurate information and scientific facts," and these the Sage Foundation's book could supply.[33] Early in 1919 (when it was too late to do much good) teachers were even preparing study guides and bibliographies, drawing especially on British reconstruction plans and literature.[34]

By early 1919 everyone, it seemed, had developed a view of reconstruction. Every major interest group, each of the conventional factions in national politics, any number of professional pundits—all had declared themselves.[35] The citizen had spoken, though if his

[32] Thorstein Veblen, "On the General Principles of a Policy of Reconstruction," in National Institute of Social Sciences, *Reconstruction after the War* (Alexander, N.Y., 1918), 37–46; and George Roberts, "Financial Reconstruction after the War," *ibid.*, 68–75.

[33] *Survey,* XLI (November 30, 1918), 276.

[34] See "Peace and Reconstruction: Preliminary Bibliography," prepared by the National Board for Historical Service, in *The Historical Outlook,* X (March, 1919), 151–67; and "Some British Reconstruction Views," *ibid.* (February, 1919), 95–111.

For an intriguing version of reconstruction thinking as expressed by "a group of Pennsylvania educators" and designed for use in elementary schools, see "Bobbie after the War," *The Historical Outlook,* X (March, 1919), 138–44. "What is meant by reconstruction, Dad?" asks Bobbie. Dad's answer is loquacious and full of current clichés, but it demonstrates an attempt to grapple with basic problems such as hunger in Europe and unemployment in the United States.

[35] The views discussed or cited thus far in this chapter could be lengthened indefinitely to include, for example, Samuel Gompers's postwar program for labor— see *New York Times,* December 2, 1918, 7:1; and Ronald Radosh, *American Labor*

government was listening, it was difficult for it to determine just what he wanted. Perhaps because of this uncertainty, Congress itself was divided over reconstruction. This inaction may explain why a current of anxiety over reconstruction began to appear as early as January, 1919. Novelist and essayist Herbert Quick, for one, commenting on the war and the tardy development of a reconstruction policy, declared: "The old world order has exploded like a bomb." In the war, democracy had become "the Golden Apples of the Hesperides, the Holy Grail, the Sepulchre of Jesus." Democracy had won, but unless Congress and the President soon acted, the nation would face "an era of dreadful depression, labor disturbances, agitations, eruptions." To date, reconstruction measures introduced in Congress "slumbered in committees." Quick had faith in what he labeled "Greater Englishry," the "tried democratic methods" of the United States and Great Britain, which he preferred to the "short cuts and new governmental inventions of Eastern Europe." Anglo-America's "slow, evolutionary compromising method" was best. Nevertheless, Quick now pleaded for a "vigorous and correlated national policy on reconstruction."[36]

Such a policy could develop only through initiative from Washington. But, as of January, 1919, neither Congress nor Wilson appeared disposed to provide the nation with a program.

---

and United States Foreign Policy (New York, 1969), 268–303; or John D. Rockefeller's "After-War Creed Offered to the Reconstruction Congress of the U.S. Chamber of Commerce," *New York Times,* December 6, 1918, 13:1; or the glum judgment of Oliver Morris, editor of *The Nonpartisan Leader* in Saint Paul, Minnesota, that "flushed with a military victory as we are, most of us will forget the liberal doctrines on which we told the world we were fighting, that we will enter into another era of good old Republican 'prosperity' with a full dinner pail, and that most of us will get busy scrambling for dollars and world trade, letting fanciful doctrines about a league of nations and disarmament go glimmering." Morris to Amos Pinchot, November 26, 1918, Box 36, Amos Pinchot Papers, Division of Manuscripts, Library of Congress.

[36] Herbert Quick, *From War to Peace: A Plea for a Definite Policy of Reconstruction* (Indianapolis, 1919), preface, 12–16, 271–78.

IV

The Wilsonian Dismantling

Writing during World War II and hoping to find lessons from the past to apply to the postwar reconstruction that lay ahead, two students of the World War I period found that in 1918–19 Congress "neither attempted to lead the people out of the wilderness in this time of crisis . . . nor appointed a committee or agency to correlate the reconstruction that had . . . evolved."[1] Between May 16, 1918, and January 31, 1919, eleven resolutions and bills introduced in the two houses of Congress proposed formation of committees on reconstruction. Not one resolution or bill passed.

One of the earliest attempts to plan for congressional action came on January 4, 1918, when Senator Wesley L. Jones (Republican, Washington) submitted a resolution authorizing the President to appoint a commission to study problems growing out of the war. Referred to the Senate Finance Committee, there it died. On April 5, 1918, Congressman George B. Francis (Republican, New York) spoke on reconstruction. Having found that at least twelve other countries had established official agencies to prepare for the transition from war to peace, he suggested that the American government do the same. Again Congress failed to act. A significant gesture toward congressional action came on September 27. On that date Senator John W. Weeks (Republican, Massachusetts) introduced a resolution calling for a joint congressional committee on reconstruction. Six senators and six representatives, evenly divided between the two major parties, were to investigate a specified number of problems and make recommendations for legislation. The scope of the Weeks proposal was all but limitless: the committee was to study such things as reemployment of discharged veterans, the role of women in the nation's labor pool, federal loans to private enterprise,

---

[1] James R. Mock and Evangeline Thurber, *Report on Demobilization* (Norman, Okla., 1944), 205.

disposal of surplus government supplies, reconversion of the nation's railroads to private control, foreign trade, price fixing, land allotment to veterans, federal loans to farmers, and "in general all matters arising during the change from the activities of war to the pursuit of peace." The Weeks resolution, authored by one of Wilson's most severe wartime critics, not only proposed a nearly boundless territory for Congress to explore; it also would have placed reconstruction entirely in the hands of Congress. Predictably, Weeks stirred up a Democratic response.[2]

Less than a week after Weeks made his proposal, Senator Lee S. Overman (Democrat, North Carolina) offered a counterproposal which, along with the Weeks plan, illustrated the partisanship that permeated reconstruction. Overman offered a bill to create a five-man federal commission on reconstruction, to be appointed by the President with the consent of the Senate.[3] Like Weeks, Overman proposed a broad field of inquiry for his committee, but its locus of power was more significant than its scope. Overman, who thought reconstruction was an executive and not a legislative function, was proposing to give Wilson authority over reconstruction. On the eve of the November congressional election, over a month before the Armistice, Democrats and Republicans began to wrangle over reconstruction.

Shortly after the election, which gave the Republicans a majority in Congress,[4] a caucus of forty Republican senators adopted a resolution aimed at gaining for their party absolute control over all reconstruction legislation. Their action, reported the *New York Times*, "sounds a note of warfare upon any attempt by the Democrats to undertake what the Republicans characterize as state socialism in the reconstruction work." The *Times*'s reference to state socialism may have reflected an honest judgment, though no Democrat had

---

[2] *Cong. Rec.*, 65 Cong., 2 sess. (January 4, 1918), 558; (April 5, 1918), 5077–79; (September 27, 1918), 10838–41. *Survey*, October 12, 1918, 48–49, contains a succinct outline of the Weeks resolution, alongside one of the Overman bills mentioned below. For Weeks's opposition to Wilson, such as his attempts from the very beginning of the war to curtail Wilson's authority, see Seward W. Livermore, *Woodrow Wilson and the War Congress, 1916–18* (Seattle, 1968).

[3] *Cong. Rec.*, 65 Cong., 2 sess. (October 3, 1918), 11030–31.

[4] Voicing the more common view, Seward W. Livermore, "The Sectional Issue in the 1918 Congressional Election," *Mississippi Valley Historical Review*, XXXV (June, 1948), 34, calls the election a "Democratic disaster," though he qualifies such a sharp estimate in his *Wilson and the War Congress*, 246–47. David Burner, "The Breakup of the Wilson Coalition of 1916," *Mid-America*, 45 (January, 1963), 18–35, argues that "the nation as a whole repudiated neither Wilson nor the Democratic Party in 1918."

yet prepared any program that could legitimately carry such a definition. Congressman Meyer London (Socialist, New York), on the other
hand, had offered something closer to a socialist proposal. On October
4 he called for a "joint congressional committee on reconstruction,"
to be made up of six Republicans, six Democrats, and one Socialist,
to prepare and recommend legislation for nationalizing basic industries, communications, and transportation, for reclamation of arid
and swamp lands, for encouragement of farmer's cooperatives, and
for establishment of a national system of obligatory education.[5]

Reconstruction, as it actually developed, would not remotely approach London's proposals. The meaningful conflict over reconstruction legislation was not between state socialism and some imagined
laissez-faire alternative. Instead, in the months to come after the war,
Congress did not even decide between the Weeks and the Overman
proposals for coping with reconstruction. Congress neither established its own unified control over reconstruction nor granted control
to a presidential body, though individual congressmen introduced
hundreds of proposals to deal with reconstruction. The second session
of the 65th Congress, the "War Congress," ended on November 21,
1918. But a third session, which lasted from December 2, 1918, to
March 4, 1919, brought forth several reconstruction proposals. And
on May 19, Wilson called the newly elected 66th Congress into special
session. This "Reconstruction Congress" would finally deal one by
one with such basic matters as railroad regulation, a national employment service, and price reductions. The countless debates that
such matters engendered and the specific laws that gained passage
revealed a basic congressional conservatism on reconstruction. One
by one, Congress abolished or diminished powers over the economy
that the government had assumed during the war. The so-called Reconstruction Congress never implemented those reconstruction vi-
sions that arose during and just after the war.[6]

This congressional inertia was due largely to the lack of leadership
by the President. As the war came to an end, the White House was
strangely negative about domestic reconstruction. Between 1913 and
1916 Wilson had supported enactment of an impressive array of

[5] *New York Times*, November 20, 1918, 1:1; *Cong. Rec.*, 65 Cong., 2 sess. (October
4, 1918), 11151, 11377.

[6] For discussion of these matters in more detail, see pp. 57–83 below. For a convenient index to activity by the 65th Congress, see Leo F. Stock, "Summary of the War
Legislation of the Sixty-fifth Congress," *Historical Outlook*, X (October, 1919),
401–19.

legislation. In 1917 he had led the country into war, and, before he left office in 1921, he would drive himself to the edge of martyrdom pursuing his vision of a "just and lasting peace." But while he planned and worked for peace in the world, the United States stumbled leaderless into a reconstruction process at home that made a shambles out of most post-Armistice enthusiasms for reform and that eventually produced the reaction, chauvinism, and disillusionment that gained notoriety in the Twenties.

Wilson began to receive reconstruction advice well before the war ended. As early as October, 1917, Elisha Friedman of the War Finance Corporation recommended to him a committee on reconstruction. In September, 1918, when E. A. Filene of the U.S. Chamber of Commerce suggested a reconstruction commission to him, Wilson replied, "I have had in mind the formation of such a commission . . . but have not satisfied myself as to the personnel of it or . . . instructions which should go to it." Wilson was aware of reconstruction commissions "on the other side of the water," but he thought they had already "gone very far afield" and he doubted the usefulness of such "roving commissions." He dissuaded the Chamber of Commerce from appointing a commission because he thought "it would be very hurtful to have a number of competitive and class schemes for reconstruction after the war." Senator Weeks's proposal of September 27, to create a congressional committee on reconstruction, Wilson found most distasteful. He disliked this congressional gambit to wrest control of reconstruction from him. On the other hand, he also disliked the alternative Overman bill. As he informed Overman, it "made the scope of the inquiry too great for any single commission to compass."[7]

Two days before the Armistice, War Industries Board chairman Bernard Baruch proposed a reconstruction meeting in Washington of representatives from the State Councils of National Defense. Wilson forced cancellation of the talks after Secretaries Baker and Houston advised him that the subject "had not been sufficiently thought out." Then immediately after the Armistice the Chamber of Commerce made public its earlier request to Wilson that he establish a reconstruction policy. The Chamber hoped that "all government departments" would follow "certain common principles" in adjustment of all wartime contracts. On November 15 the *New York Times*

[7] Mock and Thurber, *Report on Demobilization*, 108; Wilson to Filene, September 7, 1918, in Ray Stannard Baker, *Woodrow Wilson, Life and Letters*, VIII (New York, 1939), 390; Wilson to Overman, October 5, 1918, *ibid.*, 451–52.

reported that "official circles" thought Wilson would soon announce his plans "for the great era of after-war reconstruction." Most officials agreed there was "no reason for economic disturbances" if a "comprehensive program [could be] adopted without delay." According to the *Times,* the opinion "most widely expressed . . . in Washington" held that certain wartime agencies such as the War Industries Board and the Food and the Fuel Administrations would continue to function for six to eighteen months to "insure proper readjustment." Wilson seemed to suggest this himself on November 18 in a letter to Anna Howard Shaw, chairman of the woman's committee of the Council of National Defense. Wrote Wilson: "I doubt if I shall appoint a new and separate Reconstruction Commission. I have been trying to get the work in hand through existing instrumentalities."[8]

By December 2, on the eve of his departure for the peace conference in Paris, where he would try to reconstruct the affairs of the world, Wilson rejected any such ambition for reconstruction at home. Addressing a joint session of Congress, he said: "So far as our domestic affairs are concerned, the problem of our return to peace is [one of] economic and industrial readjustment." In achieving this, Americans did not want to be "coached and led. They know their own business, are quick and resourceful at every readjustment . . . and self-reliant in action. Any leading strings we might seek to put them in would speedily become hopelessly tangled because they would pay no attention to them and go their own way." All that he and Congress could do, said Wilson, was "to mediate the process of change here, there, and elsewhere, as we may."[9]

In October, 1917, Wilson had thought it "much too early to contemplate the creation of a committee on reconstruction." Having rejected all proposals for a reconstruction program as being premature or too extensive, he declared in his December, 1918, message to Congress: "From no quarter have I seen any scheme of 'reconstruction' emerge which I thought it likely we could force our spirited businessmen and self-reliant laborers to accept with due pliancy and obedience." Eleven days after he delivered this speech, Wilson was in France "ready to draft reconstruction plans for the world."[10]

[8] *Ibid.,* 576; *New York Times,* November 14, 1918, 1:1; November 15, 1918, 4:2; Mock and Thurber, *Report on Demobilization,* 109.

[9] Ray Stannard Baker and William E. Dodd, eds., *The Public Papers of Woodrow Wilson* (New York, 1927), I, 312–13.

[10] Wilson to Joseph Tumulty, October, 1917, in Baker, *Wilson,* VII, 300; final quotation from Mock and Thurber, *Report on Demobilization,* 110.

The contrast between Wilson's plans for the world and his plans for the nation may point up a relationship rather than a paradox. Wilson's very ambition in Paris may explain his negative policy at home. By rejecting any further aggressive controls over the economy, and by his flattering references to American businessmen, he may well have been hoping to divert Republican criticism from his peace-without-victory plans in Europe. As between the two major parties, the Republican had wanted unconditional surrender and now wanted a harsh peace in Europe. Wilson possibly hoped to buy support for his treaty aims in exchange for minimal reconstruction policy at home.[11] Ironically, if this was so, it meant that Wilson had misread much American "business" thought, and it, in turn, misunderstood his goals in Europe. American business—at least substantial portions of it—wanted much more central direction than Wilson chose to give it in the reconstruction period.[12] Meanwhile, Wilson's very aim in Europe was to preserve a system in which American capitalism would thrive and endure.[13]

Such interpretations may ascribe too much prescience to Wilson and grant him a more reasoned and synthesized view of affairs than he—or anyone—could possibly have had. As Arthur S. Link suggests, Wilson may simply have concluded "that the machinery of [war] mobilization was so powerful that it was unsafe to permit it to exist any longer." Wilson's "great fear," says Link, was that "conservative businessmen would gain control of the machinery, if not in the immediate future, certainly after he went out of office."[14] Whatever his reasoning, Wilson did not say much about reconstruction at all. The treaty and the League possessed him. The contrast between his plans for the peace treaty and his neglect of reconstruction sharply reveals his order of priorities. Wilson did virtually nothing during or after

[11] Arno J. Mayer, *Politics and Diplomacy of Peacemaking: Containment and Counterrevolution at Versailles, 1918–1919* (New York, 1967), 131.

[12] James Weinstein, *The Corporate Ideal in the Liberal State, 1900–1918* (Boston, 1968), shows the growing acceptance of federal regulation by business and industrial leaders in the period before and during the war. Gerald D. Nash, *United States Oil Policy, 1890–1964: Business and Government in Twentieth Century America* (Pittsburgh, 1968), is a good case study of this development in one major industry. On the general theme during World War I, see Paul A. C. Koistinen, "The 'Industrial-Military Complex' in Historical Perspective: World War I," *Business History Review*, XLI (Winter, 1967), 378–403; and Robert D. Cuff, "A 'Dollar-a-Year-Man' in Government: George N. Peek and the War Industries Board," *ibid.*, 404–20.

[13] Mayer, *Politics and Diplomacy of Peacemaking, passim*, but see pp. 3–30 for a clear statement of this view.

[14] Arthur S. Link, "World War I," in John A. Garraty, *Interpreting American History: Conversations with Historians* (New York, 1970), II, 137.

the war to plan for reconstruction. But in September, 1917, over a year before the war ended, he sponsored creation of The Inquiry, a group of scholars who were to prepare the American program for peace.[15] As it turned out, Wilson made little use of their elaborate preparations. Even in his postwar foreign policy he relied mostly on his own resources and personal vision. These gifts, at least, he took to the Paris conference. But there his vision came to focus on a single overpowering aim. As his biographer has noted, "for Wilson, planning for postwar reconstruction meant creating the League of Nations."[16] While Wilson worked for the League in Paris, his administration at home groped for a reconstruction program.

The lack of presidential initiative or even a central reconstruction board in November, 1918, meant that each existing government agency either did nothing about reconstruction or, at best, attempted what it had the power and interest to do. The result was often chaos, with agencies working in isolation from one another but for this very reason often implementing programs at cross-purposes with one another. One office did try to bring some order and direction to this turmoil—the Reconstruction Research Division in the Council of National Defense. On August 29, 1916, eight months before America went to war against Germany, Congress created the Council, an advisory board consisting of the Secretaries of War, Navy, Interior, Agriculture, Commerce, and Labor, and an advisory commission of seven "experts." The council was to coordinate industries and resources for national security and welfare, and as such it became "the largest interdepartmental unit under the government."[17]

On May 6, 1918, Grosvenor B. Clarkson, secretary of the council and its advisory commission, proposed creation of a reconstruction agency. "It is elementary," said Clarkson, "that after the war America will not be the same America. Already she has in many directions broken with her past and she is being hourly transformed." To Clarkson, only a proper "readjustment and reconstruction" after the war would justify the nation's participation in it. As a beginning, he recommended that the CND gather literature on the subject of reconstruction and begin to study it. The council agreed. Then some two

[15] Lawrence Gelfand, *The Inquiry: American Preparation for Peace, 1917–1918* (New Haven, 1963).

[16] Link, "World War I," in Garraty, *Interpreting American History*, II, 138.

[17] U.S. Council of National Defense, *Third Annual Report, 1919* (Washington, 1919), 11.

weeks later Clarkson drew up an elaborate memorandum on reconstruction material available in Washington and a resumé of reconstruction organizations in other countries. On June 10, 1918, the CND recommended to President Wilson that he designate the council "as the agency to coordinate studies of reconstruction problems" and to suggest methods of procedure for dealing with them. Nine days later Wilson approved the idea and encouraged the CND to make further studies.[18]

Clarkson at once began to organize what he called a "small reconstruction research staff." This group drew up charts outlining reconstruction problems and projected programs for various federal agencies. Whatever the value of this material, it found few if any users at the war's end. But Clarkson continued his operations. On February 3, 1919, Clarkson, by then himself director of the CND, reorganized his original study group into the Reconstruction Research Division and named Herbert N. Shenton of Columbia University as chief.[19] The RRD soon built up charts of federal bureaus involved in reconstruction; it established contact with thousands of state and local organizations interested in reconstruction; it kept a digest of state reconstruction news; it gathered and studied reports on foreign reconstruction; it maintained a clipping bureau to collect, review, digest, and cross-index news items, editorials, pamphlets, and books on reconstruction; it compiled annotated bibliographies and memoranda; and it held conferences with various government agencies. By early 1919 it began to release at noon every day a *Daily Digest of Reconstruction News*, circulating it to all official departments of the government.[20]

The RRD was not a policy-making body and was not intended as one. Conceived as a great information center on reconstruction, it collected and disseminated tons of data, evidently to little avail. When the RRD dissolved on April 1, 1920, it had in no discernible way implemented a national program of reconstruction, though its charts and compilations provide a useful index to the reconstruction process, such as it was, that did unfold.

One of the RRD's most revealing compilations indicates the general

---

[18] *Ibid.*, 17–18; and U.S. Congress, Special Committee Investigating the Munitions Industry, *Minutes of the Council of National Defense* (December, 1916–February, 1921), 74 Cong., 2 sess. (1936). Senate Committee Print no. 7, pp. 239, 240, 247–48.
[19] U.S. Council of National Defense, *Third Annual Report, 1919*, 18.
[20] *Ibid.*, 22–26.

nature of reconstruction activity on the state level. As reflected in this volume, "readjustment and reconstruction" in the forty-eight states fell into three broad categories: "Americanization," aid to ex-servicemen, and public works programs. The term "Americanization" bristled with ideological connotations but in this context referred primarily to an educational goal, that of teaching immigrants and illiterate natives to read and write English. This knowledge, in turn, would facilitate indoctrination, and it is obvious that "Americanization" in the states in 1919 usually meant more than merely a humane concern over literacy—though that was there, too.[21] Aid to veterans extended from simple information services to rehabilitation programs, bonuses, employment agencies, and free schooling. Public works programs as a means of converting the economy to peacetime, of providing jobs for veterans, and of maintaining the community spirit of wartime were popular topics of discussion, though nobody did much about them. However it was to occur, reconstruction was a pervasive topic in state legislatures. Committees and councils on reconstruction formed in practically every state. In Oregon, for instance, a state reconstruction congress which met in Portland for a three-day session in January, 1919, called for special payments to veterans by the federal government, federal appropriations of land to veterans, a road-building program in Oregon, and extensive use of the U.S. Employment Service in finding jobs for veterans.[22] In Alabama the governor appointed a postwar "council of defense" to coordinate Alabama's reconstruction activity with that of other states and the federal government. The council was to develop an interest in health, sanitation, welfare, recreation, and social activities "and in maintaining the spirit of organized community life brought about during the war."[23] The Alabama legislature appropriated $5,000 for expenses.

The Alabama appropriation, pitiable though it was, mocked the failure of Congress or the Wilson administration to even formulate a program, much less to appropriate money, for "reconversion and reconstruction." In the face of widespread pleas for retaining wartime

21 U.S. Council of National Defense, Reconstruction Research Division, *Readjustment and Reconstruction Information*, II: *Readjustment and Reconstruction Activities in the States* (Washington, 1919). For discussion of Americanization programs in 1919, see pp. 116–20 below.

22 *Ibid.*, 277.

23 *Ibid.*, 6–7.

boards and the wartime level of federal regulation, Wilson and the Congress, either from disinterest or conviction, allowed agency after agency to expire, and the machinery of wartime mobilization disintegrated.

During 1917 and 1918, as the more or less permanent departments and boards in the government took on new functions and powers, an emergency establishment developed alongside them. Between them, these permanent and emergency organizations numbered in the thousands. A 1918 publication, *Handbook of Economic Agencies for the War of 1917*, listed nearly 3,000 separate agencies involved one way or another in wartime mobilization. The very names suggest the breadth of that mobilization. The Alimentary Paste War Service Committee, organized in September, 1918, by the National Association of Macaroni and Noodle Manufacturers under direction of the U.S. Food Administration, maintained restrictions on macaroni and noodle production. The Bolts, Nuts, and Rivets War Service Committee, organized in April, 1918, and representing 98 percent of this industry, took charge of allocating government requirements for bolts. The Chalks and Crayons War Service Committee, appointed in October, 1918, represented the four manufacturers of chalk and crayon in the United States. Seventeen committees represented cotton alone.[24]

While boards such as these tried to control production, others tried to control thought and behavior. The American Protective League, formed in March, 1917, as an auxiliary of the Justice Department, claimed at Armistice time some 250,000 members, with branches in all large towns and cities, who volunteered to help uncover "every activity, disloyalty, draft evasions and other illegal activities." The Army Department contained a Patriotic Promotion Section, organized in July, 1918, to inspire a "proper patriotic spirit among workers on construction jobs."[25]

On the federal level there were at least ten major committees concerned with women, ranging from the Women in Industry Service of

[24] *Handbook of Economic Agencies for the War of 1917* (Washington, 1918). A useful guide to World War I agencies is Waldo G. Leland and Newton D. Mereness, comps., *Introduction to the American Official Sources for the Economic and Social History of the World War* (New Haven, 1926).

[25] Joan M. Jensen, *The Price of Vigilance* (Chicago, 1968), is a comprehensive history of the APL. William Preston, Jr., *Aliens and Dissenters: Federal Suppression of Radicals, 1903–1933* (New York, 1966), 88–117, contains a copiously documented chapter on the government's use of the army to suppress dissent during the war.

the Labor Department to the Committee of Women Physicians, General Medical Board, CND.[26] Most important of all were such powerful agencies as the War Industries Board, the War Labor Policies Board, the U.S. Food Administration, and the U.S. Railroad Administration. Once the war ended, some of these boards had little reason for continued existence. But no matter what kind of readjustment and reconstruction the country was to experience, many of the boards still had functions to perform after November, 1918. Grosvenor Clarkson's RRD issued a chart of "Official Agencies Created for War Purposes" on November 15. Exclusive of those in the War and Navy Departments, the list included over fifty agencies, such as the Bureau of War Risk Insurance, the U.S. Employment Service, the National Research Council, the U.S. Grain Corporation, and the U.S. Shipping Board. Two weeks after issuing its chart on these agencies, the RRD issued another one on "Readjustment Activities of Federal Agencies." Many of those listed on the chart of November 15 showed up again, alongside a cryptic summary of the agency's reconstruction functions. Whether such activity was the stated goal of the agency itself or whether it merely represented a suggestion from the RRD is not clear from the chart itself. In either case, the chart indicates a vast range of reconstruction activity that dozens of government agencies might have undertaken in November, 1918. Merely to list some of the proposals is to reveal the enthusiasm for social and economic reform that prevailed after the war, at least as expressed by the RRD, and the possibilities for reconstruction in the United States. Among more than 100 reconstruction topics, the service listed such items as: continuation of public housing; standardizing of wage scales and "bringing about a more nearly equal parity of wages"; education and employment for returning servicemen; reclamation of arid, swamp, and cut-over land; development of "attractive community life"; and "continuance of efforts in repression of prostitution and sale of liquor."[27] The readjustment and reconstruction that occurred, however, was minuscule in comparison to the program blocked out by the RRD in its little boxes in December, 1918. Whether this program would

[26] *Handbook of Economic Agencies for the War of 1917* contains a handy list of these women's organizations. A wartime study is Ida Clyde Clarke, *American Women and the World War* (New York, 1918), which surveys federal, state, and private organizations and includes a "directory of leading women's organizations doing defense work."

[27] U.S. Council of National Defense, *Third Annual Report, 1919*, following p. 160.

have been more beneficial to the nation than the scheme of things that actually developed is, of course, conjectural. What did transpire, however, is subject to some documentation.

A great many of the federal agencies created during the war, and which might be used to regulate the economy afterward, were scheduled to expire at "the end of the war" or after "the period of the existing emergency" or following the "declaration of peace"—the phrases in wartime legislation varied and sometimes raised difficulties, but the temporary status of the wartime agencies was clear enough. Within and around many an agency at war's end swirled a controversy: should it continue in existence and, if so, what was its function? Some of these agencies did gain permanent status, though often under a new name. Others quietly died. Several expired only after turmoil and debate in Congress and the public press.

The War Finance Corporation underwent an odd transformation, but one that gave it continued life and that illustrates how World War I agencies sometimes fed into the New Deal of the Thirties. Created by Congress on April 5, 1918, the WFC was to provide credit for industry and enterprise necessary to the war and to supervise issuance of securities. The Victory Liberty Loan Act of March 3, 1919, authorized the WFC to advance $1,000,000,000 to American exporters and American banking houses to finance exports of domestic products. This authority the WFC exercised until May, 1920, when it suspended operations. But on January 4, 1921, Congress, trying to cope with a current agricultural depression, directed the corporation to resume activity and to help finance agricultural exports. In 1929 the WFC again dissolved, but through the work of Eugene Meyer and other World War I members of the corporation it gained new life in 1932 in the form of the Reconstruction Finance Corporation, designed to cope, however inadequately, with the Great Depression that had settled in. Already, even before the New Deal amply extended the practice, "the institutional procedures and techniques that had been developed under the stress of World War I were transmitted to a new generation which found itself faced by another serious crisis."[28]

---

[28] Gerald D. Nash, "Herbert Hoover and the Origins of the Reconstruction Finance Corporation," *Mississippi Valley Historical Review*, XLVI (December, 1959), 468. See also Leland and Mereness, *Official Sources*, 423; Eugene Meyer, Jr., to William G. McAdoo, November 18, 1918, Container 213, William Gibbs McAdoo Papers, Division of Manuscripts, Library of Congress. On the influence of World

The history of the Bureau of War Risk Insurance reveals an, evolution in federal insurance and welfare policy for American servicemen. Originally designed to help maintain foreign commerce of the United States, the bureau came into existence on September 2, 1914. At that time it was to provide insurance for U.S. vessels whose owners could not receive adequate insurance elsewhere. An amendment of June 12, 1917, provided for insurance of merchant seamen against loss of life or injury due to war, as well as compensation to them if they became prisoners of war. An amendment of October 6, 1917, vastly enlarged the bureau's activity, granting it a division of military and naval insurance, which offered policies against death or total permanent disability to all American men on active military and naval service and to all women in the Nurse Corps, as well as other benefits such as hospital insurance and monthly allotments to the families of enlisted men. By an act of August 9, 1921, Congress converted the BWRI into the Veterans' Bureau, independent of the Treasury. On July 3, 1930, a new Veterans Administration absorbed the Veterans' Bureau as well as the Bureau of Pensions and the National Home for Disabled Volunteer Soldiers. This action consolidated all medical, hospital, and domiciliary services for U.S. war veterans and administration of disability compensation and government life insurance programs.[29]

Several other World War I agencies, like the BWRI, gained permanent status under a new name. For example, the Women in Industry Service, established in July, 1918, became the Women's Bureau in June, 1920. But most bureaus went the way of the Division of Negro Economics. This agency, established on May 1, 1918, to promote cooperation between black workers and white employers and white workers, organized committees of black and white citizens in localities where racial problems arose and conducted educational campaigns to promote racial harmony. The division expired in January, 1921, though some of its activities were presumably to endure in the Department of Labor.[30]

The U.S. Shipping Board, born just before the war, survived the

War I upon the New Deal, see Gerald Nash, "Experiments in Industrial Mobilization: WIB and NRA," *Mid-America*, XLV (July, 1963), 157–74; and William E. Leuchtenburg, "The New Deal and the Analogue of War," in *Change and Continuity in Twentieth-Century America*, ed. John Braeman *et al.* (New York, 1966), 81–143.

[29] Gustavus A. Weber and Laurence F. Schmeckebier, *The Veterans' Administration* (Washington, 1934); Leland and Mereness, *Official Sources*, 37–38; "Soldiers and Sailors Insurance Law," *Survey*, XXXIX (October 13, 1917), 39–40.

[30] Gustavus A. Weber, *The Woman's Bureau* (Baltimore, 1923); Leland and

war only as a thorny economic and political problem. Established in September, 1916, the board was originally a promotional and regulatory agency, one set up to guide and stimulate American naval and commercial shipping. After the country entered the war, the board quickly became more—"a board of directors for a great constructing and operating enterprise."[31] Through its acquisition and construction of ships, and often by commandeering enemy vessels, the board and its wartime auxiliary, the Emergency Fleet Corporation, soon raised a formidable fleet. The EFC even came to control housing near shipyards and street and interurban railways necessary for transporting shipyard workers. On November 21, 1918, the Shipping Board owned, managed, or chartered some 1,300 vessels. Construction and acquisition slowed down after the Armistice, though the board continued to receive ships manufactured under wartime contracts until 1922. By then the board had acquired over 2,300 ships. In the meantime, however, it had begun to sell ships, yards, materials, and houses. In June, 1920, the Merchant Marine Act confirmed the direction of congressional thinking on the subject of government ships: the board was to be liquidated as soon as possible and in the process encourage private interests by selling them ships built or acquired by the board, by lending money for construction to American citizens, by granting mail contract subsidies, and by establishing special water rates for American shipping. The board failed to stimulate postwar maritime trade, partly because most of the board's ships were inadequate for the fierce rivalries that the industry suffered. As of January, 1921, the Shipping Board was still operating over 1,100 vessels and was running up a deficit of about $15 million per month. The question of American shipping and the role, if any, of the Shipping Board in the American maritime industry would plague the Harding administration and even its successors.[32]

In contrast to the Shipping Board's fate, several of the most active

Mereness, *Official Sources*, 249–50, 254–55; and U.S. Department of Labor, Division of Negro Economics, *The Negro at Work during the World War and during Reconstruction* (Washington, 1921).

[31] Darrell Hevenor Smith and Paul V. Betters, *The United States Shipping Board: Its History, Activities and Organization* (Washington, 1931).

[32] *Ibid.*; James G. Randall, "War Tasks and Accomplishments of the Shipping Board," *Historical Outlook*, X (June, 1919), 305–10; E. S. Gregg, "Failure of the Merchant Marine Act of 1920," *American Economic Review*, XI (December, 1921), 601–15; Robert K. Murray, *The Harding Era: Warren G. Harding and His Administration* (Minneapolis, 1969), 280–93; Paul Maxwell Zeis, *American Shipping Policy* (Princeton, 1938), 125–41.

wartime agencies expired quickly after the war ended. The U.S. Food Administration, organized on a volunteer basis in May, 1917, gained official status on August 10, 1917. Designed to encourage production of food while conserving its supply and controlling its distribution, the Food Administration was a brilliant success, and its director, Herbert Hoover, wanted to apply some of its principles to postwar foreign policy. Hoover had been willing to exercise food controls during the war but felt that with the Armistice all justification for federal regulation at home had ended. Controls "necessary to enable the prosecution of the war," said Hoover, became in peace "a strangulation of initiative and would burden the country with bureaucracy." At the same time, Hoover would, if necessary, use federal power to dispose of the nation's great surplus of food at war's end and avoid "financial difficulties to our farmers and the public at home." Both to get rid of the surplus and to save Europe from what he called "anarchy," Hoover went to work as Allied Food Administrator in Europe. Often this work resulted in humane salvation, though just as often Hoover wanted to use food as a weapon in U.S. foreign policy: feed the nation's supporters and imitators and use the threat of deprivation against its enemies, especially the Russian Bolsheviks, to make them behave—according to Hoover's standards. Meanwhile, at home congressional food policy was less ambitious. After the Armistice, the Food Administration's activities were greatly curtailed, and by July, 1920, except for one or two minor boards, the Food Administration had ceased to exist.[33]

The Fuel Administration disappeared even sooner. Established in August, 1917, to regulate production, distribution, and use of coal, natural gas, and other fuels, the Fuel Administration had planned a gradual removal of controls over the oil industry after the war. Within the industry itself, the *Oil and Gas Journal* reported much support for continuation of the wartime "cooperation" between government

[33] Hoover, quoted from his introduction (written in 1920) to William C. Mullendore, *History of the United States Food Administration, 1917–1919* (Stanford, 1941). On the work of the FA during the war, see *ibid.*, and Albert N. Merritt, *War Time Controls of Distribution of Foods: A Short History* (New York, 1920). On food relief programs after the war, see Frank M. Surface and Raymond L. Bland, *American Food in the World War and Reconstruction Period* (Stanford, 1931) ; Suda L. Bane and Ralph H. Lutz, eds., *Organization of American Relief in Europe 1918–19* (Stanford, 1943) ; Herbert Hoover, *The Ordeal of Woodrow Wilson* (New York, 1958). On Hoover's foreign policy proposals, see Mayer, *Politics and Diplomacy of Peacemaking*, 24–27, 266–79, 479–83; George F. Kennan, *Russia and the West under Lenin and Stalin* (New York, 1962), 131–33.

and industry. Mark Requa, head of the FA's Oil Division, told a postwar reconstruction conference that cooperation must replace competition; Requa proposed a National Board of Trade, to consist of prominent business executives who would counsel and regulate industries. The bill for such an agency died in Congress. Meanwhile, the Fuel Administration also expired. After March, 1919, it looked after a few minor problems until finally on May 15 it gave up all powers. Wartime cooperation seemed at an end. The Wilson administration had "left the oil industry entirely to its own devices."[34]

The most powerful of all wartime agencies was the War Industries Board. The process by which it disappeared after the war indicates something of postwar thought and behavior over reconstruction—and what would soon be labeled "normalcy." Economist John Maurice Clark, who in the Twenties participated in the Carnegie Endowment's vast study of World War I, succinctly described the reconstruction process that allowed the WIB and other agencies to expire: "The general policy of the government," he wrote, "was to demobilize as rapidly as possible without obvious waste or injustice, and to leave to private enterprise the task of reabsorbing workers and re-forming the lines of industry." As Clark viewed the process from a pre–New Deal perspective, "the boom of 1919–20 proved that private industry had great powers of reabsorption and revival, while the depression of 1921 showed that such a great and rapid demobilization was attended by grave economic danger." To Clark, however, "it remain[ed] a doubtful question whether the retention of a larger amount of public supervision would have brought about a more desirable result."[35] Writing near the end of World War II, and obviously partisan to the kind of central regulatory power that the WIB had exercised during World War I, James Mock and Evangeline Thurber saw demobilization in a different light: "After the Armistice the government [took] the attitude that there would never be another war and that it would not be necessary again to call upon manufacturers for assistance." Officials in Washington were "so much interested in foreign affairs that they had no time for such domestic problems as the settlement of contracts and the returning of industry to a peacetime basis." The government adopted "principles of

[34] Nash, *U.S. Oil Policy*, 38–43. See also U.S. Fuel Administration, *Final Report, 1917–1919* (Washington, 1921). On petroleum regulation during the war, see Nash, *U.S. Oil Policy*, 29–38; Harold Williamson *et al.*, *The American Petroleum Industry*, II: *The Age of Energy, 1899–1959* (Evanston, 1963), 261–95.

[35] John Maurice Clark, *The Costs of the World War* (New Haven, 1931), 53.

laissez-faire" and made the transition from war to peace "by happenstance and by individual expedients."[36]

Somewhere between this evident support for federal regulation and Clark's implied distaste for it, Grosvenor Clarkson took a stand in 1923, as he described the recent demise of the War Industries Board. Clarkson seemed torn between the old received wisdom about free enterprise and individualism on the one hand, and the obvious wartime achievements of federal regulation on the other. Occasionally he pondered a synthesis of the two, as he envisioned "national intelligence" promoting American trade in the postwar world. The State Department, he said, should "work hand-in-glove with the Department of Commerce to open and hold the markets that our over-developed manufacturing industries need for full-time production." The ideas conceived and applied by the War Industries Board in war could be applied in peace by the Department of Commerce. Yet a problem remained: "How to maintain the price benefits of free competition [while obtaining] the benefits of the economies that can be effected only by association and united effort." Whatever the future of American commerce—and Clarkson was optimistic over its potential—it was clear to him that "the War Industries Board was the pioneer revealer of the immense wastes of production as generally conducted, and the greatest of demonstrators of the possibilities of economics."[37]

Yet the WIB died with the war, and with evident regret Clarkson recalled its passing: "The magnificent war formation of American industry was dissipated in a day; the mobilization that had taken many months was succeeded by an instantaneous demobilization." The WIB "might have elected to remain [intact] for a long time on the plea of its necessity in a disordered world, but it judged that . . . American business was competent to resume without coddling and nursing the stubborn independence it was loath to surrender." Clarkson wondered if the board or "some like controller of world economic force might not have dealt as well with reaction as the War Industries Board did with action."[38]

Clarkson was in a minority. Even Bernard Baruch himself, director of the WIB, proposed its dissolution, though Baruch recognized the

[36] Mock and Thurber, *Report on Demobilization*, 145–57.

[37] Grosvenor Clarkson, *Industrial America in the World War: The Strategy behind the Lines, 1917–1918* (Boston, 1923), 485–86.

[38] *Ibid.*, 487–88. For comparable views by a member of the WIB, see Cuff, "A 'Dollar-a-Year Man' in Government."

enormous jolt that could occur from the abrupt termination of federal controls and contracts. Between April 6, 1917, and June 1, 1919, the War Department alone had entered into approximately 300,000 contracts, disbursements on these exceeding $14,500,000,000.[39] The Armistice caught American industry in full production for war. Many firms were making additions to their factories in order to fulfill government contracts. Others had ordered huge stocks of raw material to turn into war goods. Still others had partly finished consignments for the government. The WIB, along with other selected federal agencies that also died, might have supervised and controlled settlement and cessation of these contracts and activities. About the only power the WIB did try to retain was price controls, and even this function Baruch would not abide.

Support for postwar price controls came from certain (but by no means all) American industrialists. As the war neared an end, they expressed hope for two developments: a continuation of price protection, and a modification of traditional antitrust policy. The fear of a price collapse after the war was widespread, and many industrialists pressured the WIB to sustain price controls after the Armistice. At the same time, the industrial cooperation that the board had encouraged during the war merely intensified the drive among American industrialists for a "genuine cartel system."[40]

WIB lawyers contended that the board needed only presidential approval to continue price controls after the war. But in the face of Wilson's obvious distaste for continued controls, the board made only a half-hearted attempt to arouse public support for controls; in November, when Wilson decreed complete dissolution of the WIB, the agency's personnel acquiesced without protest. One recent student of the board suggests that Baruch and other members were bothered by the disunity among businessmen over price controls. Determined to preserve the board's reputation as a great disinterested wartime agency, they felt that without complete support for price controls from the business community the board might find itself involved in partisan disputes after the war. Too, Baruch, for one, was not quite ready to abandon "the tradition of competition the nation had striven to maintain through the antitrust laws."[41]

The experience of another agency, the Industrial Board in the

[39] Mock and Thurber, *Report on Demobilization*, 147.
[40] Robert F. Himmelberg, "The War Industries Board and the Antitrust Question in November 1918," *Journal of American History*, LII (June, 1965), 59–74.
[41] *Ibid.*, 73.

Department of Commerce, further illustrates the ambivalence toward price controls within the business community after the war, and the difficulties of sustaining into peacetime the controls of war. The Industrial Board was actually a "reconversion" agency, not a war-born one. Secretary of Commerce William C. Redfield, supported by a group of businessmen concerned over currently soaring prices and wanting some mild federal supervision, established the IB in February, 1919. Redfield hoped it could bring about, through business agreements, an immediate reduction of prices to a level that would encourage purchases by government agencies and private citizens. In addition, and perhaps more important, much of the pressure behind Redfield's action came from the U.S. Chamber of Commerce and other organized business groups that wanted permanent changes in the existing antitrust laws and a move toward cartelization. Redfield was trying to "reorient the whole governmental attitude toward industrial cooperation." In fact, he pioneered the Commerce Department's promotion of trade associations and cooperative practices in industry —innovations more commonly attributed to Secretary of Commerce Hoover in the Twenties.[42]

The board hoped that any price agreements it could establish would be beneficial to industry, labor, the government, and the general public alike. To avoid conflict with antitrust laws, the board planned to rely on informal agreements. These it would achieve through conferences from time to time with the industries of the country, beginning with such basic ones as iron and steel. The board's original objective was to bring the tremendous buying power of the government itself into the market; they particularly hoped to encourage purchases by the railroads, at the time still under government control through the U.S. Railroad Administration. If the government would spend, the public would, too—or so ran the board's thinking originally. But it soon became clear that the board wanted not merely lower prices. Above all, it wanted power to make price-fixing agreements. The price level was less important than the privilege to control it.[43]

The board selected the iron and steel industry for the first agreement and quickly reached accord with the industry over a price schedule. But the Railroad Administration disagreed with the steel

[42] Robert F. Himmelberg, "Business, Antitrust Policy, and the Industrial Board of the Department of Commerce, 1919," *Business History Review*, XLII (Spring, 1968), 3–4.
[43] *Ibid.*, 10–12.

industry's (and the IB's) schedule. The conflict concerned more than prices. If Secretary Redfield and the members of the board "represented those segments of the business world which had been vigorously proposing the repeal of the anti-trust laws and the development of a business-controlled market under federal supervision,"[44] the Railroad Administration voiced support for the system of the free market. Director General of Railroads Walker Hines and Secretary of the Treasury Carter Glass believed that postwar prices must drop sharply, with wages and other costs falling in accordance with them, until a bottom had been reached. Once "bed rock" prices had been established, buying would resume on a large scale, production would increase, profit would reappear, and prices would begin to rise. Such a process, unfortunate but inevitable, seemed to be the view of not only Hines and Glass but of Wilson and Baruch as well. The Railroad Administration's "bed rock" level meant, in practice, a cost or near-cost level. In contrast, the Industrial Board wanted to establish a less drastic "fair and reasonable" price. The IB was unable to convince the RRD that its proposed prices for steel had set such a schedule. At issue were the very methods by which price schedules were determined, but the anti-trust tradition was also involved, and both Attorney General A. Mitchell Palmer and President Wilson declared their opposition to the IB's activities as violating the anti-trust laws. Meanwhile, criticism descended on the board from other directions. The American Federation of Labor, for example, objected to its action out of fear that price-fixing would lower living standards, though on the other hand some businessmen opposed the board out of fear that business would be expected to sacrifice profits but labor would not be asked to lower its wages proportionately. The board members, unable to control even one segment of the reconversion and reconstruction of the American economy, resigned in May.[45]

The Wilsonian dismantling went on. Already the War Industries Board had ceased to function. By early spring, 1919, only a few major wartime agencies remained in existence. Two of these, the U.S. Railroad Administration and the U.S. Employment Service, took more time to die. The process by which they did so demonstrated much about the state and outlook of American industry and American labor in 1919–20.

[44] E. Jay Howenstine, Jr., "The Industrial Board, Precursor of the NRA: The Price-Reduction Movement after World War I," *Journal of Political Economy*, LI (June, 1943), 238.

[45] *Ibid.*

V

Jobs and Rails

In December, 1918, ex-Senator Albert Beveridge of Indiana was living on a North Shore farm near Boston, working away with great energy on his magisterial biography of John Marshall. He still managed to retain an interest in current affairs and corresponded regularly with Senator William E. Borah of Idaho, fellow Republican and old Progressive. In mid-December, Beveridge wrote to him, "When are our men now in camp in this country to be discharged? Thousands of them have jobs waiting for them which they cannot get if they are held much longer. . . . I am holding open the place for the boy who was our chauffeur. . . . What is the point in keeping these men in service now that the war is over?"[1] Beveridge expressed a view common enough at war's end: get the troops out of uniform and into a job. But Borah knew far better than Beveridge that this was a goal easier stated than achieved.[2] The American economy in November, 1918, and the place of labor in it made a nettlesome complex. The war had been a great boon to much of organized labor. If Wobblies had been beaten, jailed, and killed, the bulk of American labor had flourished, gaining union recognition, shorter hours, higher wages, and federal mediation and conciliation services.[3] After the Armistice,

---

[1] Beveridge to Borah, December 16, 1918, Box 193, William E. Borah Papers, Division of Manuscripts, Library of Congress.

[2] See pp. 197–99 below on Borah.

[3] John S. Smith, "Organized Labor and Government in the Wilson Era, 1913–1921: Some Conclusions," *Labor History*, III (Fall, 1962), 265–86, stresses the cooperation and friendship between Wilson and labor. See also Robert L. Tyler, "The United States Government as Union Organizer: The Loyal Legion of Loggers and Lumbermen," *Mississippi Valley Historical Review*, XLVII (December, 1960), 434–51. Some hard figures are conveniently available in Daniel J. Ahearn, Jr., *The Wages of Farm and Factory Laborers, 1914–1944* (New York, 1945), 89–133, which shows that farm and factory wages increased approximately 150% between 1914 and 1920. For a connection between Wilson's wartime policy and his cooperation with labor, see Ronald Radosh, *American Labor and United States Foreign Policy* (New York, 1969). On the Wobblies during World War I, see Ch. 6, below.

labor talked about keeping these advantages. Management—much of it—talked about taking them away.[4]

On December 6–7 in the grand ballroom of Hotel Astor in New York, the American Academy of Political Science held a conference on "Labor Reconstruction." Frank A. Vanderlip of the National City Bank, dubbed "financial captain" by the president of the academy, played toastmaster before one thousand or so dinner guests. He mentioned restrictions on industry imposed during the war. These had been "necessary and wise," but now it was time to "return to our former individualism." Samuel Gompers, hoary AFL leader, spoke to the conference also. Gompers wanted "no rocking of the boat." He hoped for "industrial peace," but labor must not be asked to give up what it had won during the war. "There must be cooperation. We shall never go back to the old condition."[5]

As it turned out, Vanderlip was a better prophet than Gompers, though the two men were not entirely in disagreement to begin with. Gompers, every inch the conservative labor leader and by 1918 a vociferous anti-Bolshevik, would never challenge the likes of Frank Vanderlip. Yet labor—even the AFL—fell upon hard times almost immediately after the war.[6] The Wilson administration's reconstruction policy for labor (or rather its lack of one) contributed to this decline. Even such a fundamental matter as unemployment gained little attention from the administration (or from anyone else, for that matter) until it suddenly developed after the war. As the war neared an end, a few men in and out of the government expressed concern that the rapid demobilization of four million men might disrupt the labor market. For example, Felix Frankfurter, chairman of the U.S. Labor Policies Board, argued the case for sustaining, as a minimum, the wartime standards of wages and hours, as well as the restriction on work by women and children and the recognition of unions that had developed during the war. To prevent unemployment, Frank-

[4] The literature on this is voluminous, but a clear view of labor-management conflict in one major industry is in David Brody, *Labor in Crisis: The Steel Strike of 1919* (Philadelphia, 1965). For a general summary, see Philip Taft, *Organized Labor in American History* (New York, 1964), 341–71.

[5] "Labor Reconstruction," *Survey*, XLI (December 14, 1918), 331–36. See also AFL recommendations of January 15, made to the Senate Committee on Education and Labor, in which the AFL declared there "must be no reduction of rates." *New York Times*, January 16, 1919, 5:3.

[6] Radosh, *American Labor and U.S. Foreign Policy*, 275ff.; Irving Bernstein, *The Lean Years: A History of the American Worker, 1920–1933* (Boston, 1960), 334ff.

furter proposed an elaborate, controlled demobilization schedule.[7] Harold Moulton, an economist on the War Labor Policies Board, tried to focus public attention on the inability of the labor market to quickly absorb the AEF. The secretary of the Capital Issues Committee, Dudley Cates, showed a similar concern. But such talk about unemployment was negligible in 1918.[8] Then came the Armistice and abrupt cancellation of war contracts. When the war ended, the War Department had $6 billion outstanding in manufacturing contracts. Some $2.5 billion of the contracts were cancelled in four weeks. In Cleveland contract cancellations between November 11 and December 1 put 13,000 workers out of their jobs. During December adjustment in war contracts threw 22,000 more out of work. In the meantime 1,500 discharged soldiers had returned to Cleveland and joined the unemployed. By New Year's Day, 1919, the city showed a labor surplus of 60,000—approximately 48,000 above the normal unemployment figure for that season of the year. In Connecticut by January 15, 1919, some 40,000 war workers had been discharged in a three-week period. An AFL survey on January 14 showed 75,000 unemployed in Chicago, 20,000 in New Orleans and in Boston, 15,000 in St. Louis, and 17,000 in Toledo.[9]

By February the National City Bank of New York was calling for federal action. After surveying the economy, the NCB declared sup-

---

[7] Felix Frankfurter, "The Conservation of the New Federal Standards," *Survey*, XLI (December 7, 1918), 291–93; John Lombardi, *Labor's Voice in the Cabinet: A History of the Department of Labor from Its Origins to 1921* (New York, 1942), 302.

[8] Paul A. Samuelson and Everett E. Hagen, *After the War—1918–1920: Military and Economic Demobilization of the United States* (Washington, 1943), 5.

[9] *Ibid.*, 6–7; James R. Mock and Evangeline Thurber, *Report on Demobilization* (Norman, Okla., 1944), 170–80; *New York Times*, January 17, 1919, 14:2. *Monthly Labor Review*, IX (July, 1919), 132–33, contains figures for the period March 8 to June 21, 1919; see each issue thereafter for monthly figures in "selected industries."

U.S. Council of National Defense, *Readjustment and Reconstruction Activities in the States* (Washington, 1919), contains figures on employment in each state for the period January 1 to June 30, 1919, as reported by federal employment offices "maintained in cooperation with state and local organizations." Conditions varied from state to state, of course, and some states were more active in maintaining employment bureaus (and therefore in placing workers) than others. In Massachusetts, for example, the governor announced that the state had experienced little difficulty in placing returning servicemen. "Massachusetts," he said, "has plenty of work for those who want it." Perhaps in contradiction to this, the state legislature appropriated $10,000 for an investigation of "the reasons causing nonemployment of veterans." U.S. Employment Service figures indicate that between January 1 and June 30, 1919, some 68,000 persons registered seeking employment in Massachusetts, and just over 35,000 were placed by federal and state employment offices. *Ibid.*, 133–35.

port for "a large and enterprising public policy which would organize and coordinate the activities of national, state, and local governments, so as to create a large amount of work for the coming spring and summer." Only the "prestige and cooperation of the national government" could develop such a movement.[10]

The basis for a "large and enterprising policy" lay at hand in February, 1919. The U.S. Employment Service, for one, was a wartime agency still in existence and prepared to cope with unemployment as well as could any organization in the land. But by February the USES was in danger of extinction. The service had originated in 1907 as the Division of Information in the Bureau of Immigration. Designed primarily as an employment agency for immigrants, it began to expand its activities and in 1913 was transferred to the new Department of Labor; in that department in 1915 it became the USES. From 1914 to 1917 the service concentrated on farm labor, especially seasonal or migratory labor. In June, 1918, the War Labor Policies Board decided that "all recruiting of industrial labor for private and public work connected with the war shall be conducted through or in accordance with methods authorized by the USES."[11] In December, 1917, President Wilson allotted $825,000 from the National Security Defense fund to further the work of the USES. The service opened offices in each state and soon overshadowed the work of state employment agencies. Between July 1, 1917, and June 30, 1918, it found jobs for 1,890,593 persons. From January 1, 1918, to the end of the war, it placed over 3,000,000 workers, and at the close of the war it had established 850 offices throughout the nation.[12]

Suddenly with the Armistice the USES reversed its role from finding people for jobs to finding jobs for people, a task obviously at hand and one for which the service was obviously equipped. Through its 1,450 community labor boards, the service could learn where jobs were available as well as where there was a labor surplus. It could pass this information on to the WIB which, in theory, would try to avoid increasing the labor surplus by regulating cancellation of war contracts. Meanwhile, the War Department—again, in theory—would try to demobilize those troops who could find jobs, and for a time

[10] *New York Times,* February 3, 1919, 17:2.

[11] Department of Labor, *Annual Report, 1918* (Washington, 1918), 700.

[12] National Archives, *Handbook of Federal World War Agencies and Their Records, 1917–1921,* (Washington, 1943), 156; Daniel Hevenor Smith, *The United States Employment Service: Its History, Activities and Organization* (Baltimore, 1923), 1–34; Lombardi, *Labor's Voice,* 150–98.

retain those who could not. The Employment Service worked out a scheme whereby it stationed agents in army camps at home and abroad, and even on transports coming home from France, to take job applications from soldiers awaiting demobilization. The service then distributed this information throughout its nationwide network of offices.[13]

The service needed money to operate, and money was something Congress would not appropriate and something Wilson did not have. The service's funds for the fiscal year ending June 30, 1919, were about exhausted by February. Secretary of Labor William B. Wilson asked Congress for a deficiency appropriation of $1,800,000 to run the service until July. His request set off a debate in and out of Congress over the USES. The House Appropriations Committee slashed the service's budget for the upcoming fiscal year to one-third the amount the service wanted. On February 26, 1919, Secretary Wilson contacted the President in Paris, defended the work of the service, and begged the President to support it by pressuring Congress into making appropriations. The secretary cited the post-Armistice work of the service: some 1,500,000 people looking for work had registered with it; the service had referred some 1,300,000 of them to employers; approximately 1,000,000 of them had been hired. Employment offices, argued the secretary, were "universally recognized as a public function." Private agencies operating on a fee basis had merely stimulated unemployment and increased labor turnover, besides "taking millions of dollars out of the pockets of the wage earners of the country." The secretary believed that "a well organized, unified national system of labor exchanges" was "vitally necessary." He hoped there would be "no drifting back to pre-war methods of unemployment."[14]

The President, on board the U.S.S. *George Washington* returning to Paris after a hurried trip home in February, sent his regrets. He said that his own wartime emergency funds were "practically exhausted." He saw "no escape from disbandment" of the service but hoped it would be possible to keep a "skeleton organization."[15] But even a skeleton would be too much for some USES critics. Some of them claimed that the service was designed merely to furnish jobs

[13] *Ibid.*, 306; Mock and Thurber, *Report on Demobilization*, 90–94; Department of Labor, *Annual Report, 1919*, p. 286.

[14] Secretary Wilson to President Wilson, February 26, 1919, File 19G, Woodrow Wilson Papers, Division of Manuscripts, Library of Congress.

[15] President Wilson to Secretary Wilson, March 12, 1919, cited in Smith, *U.S. Employment Service*, 45.

for "organized labor's business agents or social welfare folks."[16] Secretary Wilson, in his February memorandum to the President, spoke of "systematic and underhanded propaganda" carried on against the USES by "the remnants of the Manufacturers' Association and a few other small organizations of reactionary employers." Their campaign, he thought, was responsible for the House Appropriations Committee's opposition to USES.[17] As early as February 3 the director general of the service, J. B. Densmore, told Senator William E. Borah that "a definite and calculated effort" was underway to "cripple" the service.[18] In June, Densmore complained to presidential secretary Joseph Tumulty that USES appropriations for the coming fiscal year had been denied "on a point of order" raised by Congressman Thomas L. Blanton (Democrat, Texas), who "seems for some reason to have bitter personal hatred toward me and a general unreasonable grievance against the Employment Service and the Department of Labor." Three times Blanton had managed to forestall appropriations by raising his "point of order."[19]

Yet the service had its supporters, too, and it did not die without a fight. A large number of newspapers, social welfare agencies, labor unions, and even manufacturers supported the service and wanted to see it stay alive.[20] J. B. Densmore sent Senator Borah a pamphlet by "a large employer of labor, who believes that a national employment system is the best safeguard against labor unrest." The pam-

[16] Resolution of Associated Manufacturers and Merchants of New York, in Lombardi, *Labor's Voice*, 309.

[17] Secretary Wilson to President Wilson, February 26, 1919, File 19G, Woodrow Wilson Papers.

[18] J. B. Densmore to Borah, February 3, 1919, Box 195, "Labor Matters," Borah Papers.

[19] Densmore to Tumulty, June 26, 1919, File 19G, Woodrow Wilson Papers. Blanton had objected that the USES, not being an agency authorized by law, could not receive funds from the House. For comment on Blanton's real motives—that he found the service extravagant, pro-union, and inefficient—see Lombardi, *Labor's Voice*, 313–14. For further opposition to the service, see *ibid.*, 120–21, 145–46, 310.

[20] *Ibid.*, 310. Secretary of Labor Wilson spoke of a "vast majority of employers" acknowledging the value of the service—see Wilson to Woodrow Wilson, February 26, 1919, File 19G, Woodrow Wilson Papers. From Pocatello, Idaho, the Brotherhood of Railway Carmen wrote to their senator asking him to do all in his power to retain the USES as "a permanent service." Joseph E. Brown, recording secretary, to William E. Borah, February 21, 1919, Box 195, "Labor Matters," Borah Papers. The attorney general of Montana wrote to Borah (who had earned a pro-labor label from the National Legislative and Information Service) asking the senator to support the service, which had been "a decided success in Montana." S. C. Ford to Borah, January, 1919?, Box 195, Borah Papers.

phleteer, in fact, raised the spectre of Bolshevism and thereby utilized an argument already rampant in other areas of American life by then. If returning servicemen did not receive jobs, he said, "we will open a fertile field to the Bolshevistic emissaries who now are seeking to win converts from the ranks of the involuntary jobless and discontented. . . . *Work, not words, is the antidote for Bolshevism.*"[21]

When Congress failed to grant emergency appropriations in early 1919, the service appealed to private organizations and to cities and states for funds. The response was generous. With its own funds the USES could have maintained fifty-six offices until the end of the fiscal year. With the donations it kept 490 of them open. Then on April 14, 1919, Secretary Wilson called an unemployment conference to meet in Washington later in the month. Delegates from twenty-eight states showed up, along with representatives of the Chamber of Commerce, the AFL, the Bureau of Labor Standards, and USES offices. The conference recommended a permanent USES as an independent bureau of the Department of Labor. A bill to this effect soon went to Congress.[22] In May, President Wilson cabled from Paris asking Congress to support the USES "upon an adequate scale." But the House seemed hung up on that point of order that Congressman Blanton chose to raise. When Congress finally granted an emergency appropriation of $272,000, it came too late to help much in the fiscal year ending on June 30. For the fiscal year 1920, the Service had requested $4,600,000. Congress granted it $400,000. Thereafter, the USES began a steady retrenchment.[23] In early July it closed 424 of its offices. In October it turned over all remaining branch offices to the states and cities where they were located; if the state or local government could not maintain them, they vanished. By March, 1920, the USES, reduced by now to a skeleton staff with paid offices in only three cities outside Washington, existed mostly as a clearinghouse of information on labor surpluses and deficits. Even this service depended on cooperation of state and city labor exchanges, and these were so mediocre or insufficient that even the service's clearinghouse

[21] Pamphleteer's italics. See Densmore to Joseph P. Tumulty, June 26, 1919, File 19G, Woodrow Wilson Papers, for copy of memo.

[22] HR 4305, by John I. Nolan (R-Calif.) and S 1442, by William S. Kenyon (R-Iowa). *Cong. Rec.*, 66 Cong., 1 sess. (May 31 and June 6, 1919), 490, 726.

[23] Albert Shaw, ed., *The Messages and Papers of Woodrow Wilson* (New York, 1924), II, 675; *Cong. Rec.*, 65 Cong., 3 sess. (February 28, 1919), 4651–67; 66 Cong., 1 sess. (May 29, 1919), 420–23; (July 1, 1919), 2154ff.

function failed.[24] American labor, at least the unemployed in its ranks, would wait until the Thirties to secure effective employment services from the federal government. Here was an area wherein World War I, so influential in many other respects, did not lay the foundation for New Deal policies to come.

The USES, however, was not the only agency in Washington that tried to reduce unemployment after the Armistice. Veterans especially gained attention from several federal offices, as well as from state and private agencies around the country. The War Department tried to launch a nationwide "Jobs for Soldiers" movement. The department itself set up no employment agencies but tried to work through the countless bureaus and committees that sprang up in practically every community after the war to help veterans locate jobs. Besides temporary agencies such as Bureaus for Returning Soldiers, Sailors, and Marines and the National Catholic War Council, hardy durables such as the Salvation Army and the Knights of Columbus all cooperated with the War Department to place returning servicemen. In May, 1919, the Civil Service Commission provided preferential rating in the District of Columbia for honorably discharged veterans or their widows and soon extended the rule to the rest of the country. In the winter of 1919–20, veterans received special consideration during the Census Bureau's recruitment of the 90,000 persons needed to take the 1920 census.[25]

One employment scheme that emerged from the Department of the Interior was more successful in revealing the endurance of agrarianism in American life than it was in finding jobs for veterans. Since the American Revolution veterans had received, or been offered, land as compensation for wartime service. In 1918–19 a number of enthusiasts both in and out of the government proposed schemes for settling veterans on the farm, partly because this would help forestall unemployment, but also because the family farm was, supposedly,

[24] Lombardi, *Labor's Voice*, 315; Smith, *U.S. Employment Service*, 47; *New York Times*, July 2, 1919, 22:3; "Present Scope and Activities of Federal Employment Service," *Monthly Labor Review* (May, 1920), 131; Department of Labor, *Annual Report, 1920* (Washington, 1921), 913–95.

[25] "Provisions for Employment of Ex-Service Men," *Monthly Labor Review* (February, 1920), 158–60; Benedict Crowell and Robert Forrest Wilson, *Demobilization: Our Industrial and Military Demobilization after the Armistice, 1918–1920* (New Haven, 1921), 107–9; *Readjustment and Reconstruction Activities in the States*; and Dixon Wecter, *When Johnny Comes Marching Home* (Cambridge, 1944), 374–75.

productive of ideal citizens and a virtuous life. The Labor Department, the Forest Service, the American Legion, the Catholic War Council, and several state legislatures all supported some kind of back-to-the-land scheme for veterans.[26] But the one proposal that captured the most attention germinated in the Interior Department. As early as March, 1918, eight months before the Armistice, several Interior officials began preparing a plan which they then tried to sell to the President. Interior Secretary Franklin K. Lane became the spokesman for the plan that he, Harry A. Slattery and Elwood Mead of Interior, William Kent of the Tariff Commission, and a few other officials drew up. Slattery perhaps conceived the plan, though Lane was easily persuaded to adopt it and continued to proselytize it long after Slattery himself had become disillusioned.[27]

Under the Interior plan the government would help ex-servicemen to settle on and develop some of the millions of acres of swamp, cut-over, arid, and abandoned lands available to those enterprising enough to reclaim them. Lane was disturbed over possible unemployment after the war, but he was bothered even more by the increase in farm tenancy and the consequent drift of Americans from the farm to the city. Lane, as well as Mead, Slattery, and other advocates of the Interior plan, wanted to increase the proportion of landowning citizens. Although the veterans might work in communities established to reclaim a swamp, or a cut-over region, and though the federal government in cooperation with state governments might even pay him a wage to help him establish a farm, the veteran was to gain simple title to his land. To Lane, landowning went hand in hand with patriotism.[28]

In his December, 1918, message to Congress, Wilson endorsed the Lane proposal. On May 19, 1919, Congressman Frank Mondell (Republican, Wyoming) introduced a bill, partially drafted by Elwood Mead, that contained most of what Lane wanted. Meanwhile, numerous other soldier settlement bills appeared in Congress, but none of them gained Lane's endorsement.[29] Even Lane's approval was not

---

[26] Bill G. Reid, "Franklin K. Lane's Idea for Veterans' Colonization, 1918–1921," *Pacific Historical Review*, XXXIII (November, 1964), 447–48; *New York Times*, April 7, 1919, 7:1; *Readjustment and Reconstruction Activities in the States*.

[27] Memo, Slattery to Lane, "Memoranda, 1918–20," V-A, B, C, D, Harry A. Slattery Papers, Duke University Library; Reid, "Lane's Idea," 452; William Kent to Woodrow Wilson, May 27, 1918, copy in "Letters, 1908–1920," Slattery Papers.

[28] Reid, "Lane's Idea," 543–56.

[29] *Ibid.*, 457–58; *Cong. Rec.*, 66 Cong., 1 sess. (May 19, 1919), 22 [HR 487 by

enough for the Mondell bill, which aroused far more opponents than backers. Veterans, probably less enamoured by the agrarian image than Lane was, gave it little support. As Dixon Wecter put it, "The city bred veteran, who could not tell clover from alfalfa, simply did not respond. . . ." Above all, opposition to the Lane-Mondell bill came from commercial farmers. Big landowners, business and labor groups, welfare workers, and women's clubs endorsed the bill, but farmers, officials in the Department of Agriculture, specialists in agricultural colleges, leaders of farm organizations, and editors of agricultural presses all set up a chorus of opposition. Said one farmer: "For God's sake, do not drive us to more complete serfdom by compelling us to compete with Uncle Sam in farming." Department of Agriculture spokesmen said the scheme would produce more farms, unwieldy surpluses, and agricultural depression. A National Grange spokesman redundantly called the plan "paternalistic, socialistic, communistic, and bolshevistic."[30]

President Wilson, preoccupied at Paris with the peace treaty, gave the bill only cursory attention, though perhaps he was right to do so. As the closest student of the bill has suggested, its critics were "probably correct in asserting that the chief victims of the scheme would have been the veterans settled under its provisions."[31] The Lane bill looked backward to a rural America already gone in 1919. American agriculture after the war suffered from a surplus of production. Had Lane been able to put them on the farm, World War I doughboys would simply have increased the surplus and swelled the ranks of depressed agriculture in the decade ahead.

Lane was unable to put veterans on the farm. The U.S. Employment Service lacked the funds to find many of them jobs. Civilian war workers, dismissed because of the sharp cutback in war contracts, joined veterans among the jobless in the winter of 1918–19. Still, unemployment did not become a conspicuous national problem in the year following the Armistice. During the first twelve months after the war, some four million members of the armed forces received discharges, as did two to three million workers in war plants. Unem-

---

Mondell]; (August 1, 1919), 3547 [HR 487 by Nicholas J. Sinnot]; (August 26, 1919), 4369ff.; 66 Cong., 2 sess. (December 10, 1919), 368; (January 17, 1920), 1676–77.

[30] Wecter, *Johnny*, 378; Bill G. Reid, "Agrarian Opposition to Franklin K. Lane's Proposal for Soldier Settlement, 1918–1921," *Agricultural History*, XLI (April, 1967), 167–80.

[31] Reid, "Lane's Idea," 460.

ployment compensation was all but nonexistent. Few workers received dismissal wages. There was virtually no work relief. Yet no immediate postwar depression set in—a matter of luck more than one of policy, say two economists who studied the demobilization and reconstruction process.[32] At least temporarily (for a downturn would come in 1920–21), the economy continued to boom after the Armistice. In spite of the hasty demobilization and cancellation of war contracts, it was impossible to end all governmental wartime activity at once. "Economically," say Samuelson and Hagen, "the first World War lasted until 1920." War expenditures continued after the war, to some degree. Demobilization itself required large outlays. Cancellation of war contracts often allowed industries to deliver an added output equal to one month's production, and some manufacturers spread this normal month's work over several by eliminating overtime. Many war contracts could not be cancelled even this quickly. After November 11 the United States extended $2 billion in loans to the Allies, and most of it was spent in the United States. Under these circumstances U.S. Treasury expenditures reached their World War I peak not during the war but in December, 1918; although monthly expenditures during 1919 declined, they remained high by prewar standards. Federal spending in 1915 amounted to $760 million. *"Monthly* expenditures exceeded this figure in every month of 1919 through August."[33]

Samuelson and Hagen, writing after the New Deal and after World War II, recognized the role of deficit spending in the economy and evidently regretted that it did not continue sufficiently to forestall the recession of 1920–21. But deficit spending by Washington in 1919 was like Washington's operation of the railroads—accepted for the emergency, in some cases even applauded, but for the most part deplored.

Eight months after the country entered the war, Wilson took control of the nation's railroads. Wartime mobilization had caused some insoluble operating problems for them. The huge volume of traffic moving eastward toward Atlantic ports had caused drastic freight car shortages and traffic congestion in the eastern terminals. Skilled

[32] Samuelson and Hagen, *After the War*, 8–12. But cf. Wilson F. Payne, "Business Behavior, 1919–1922: An Account of Post-war Inflation and Depression," *Journal of Business of the University of Chicago*, XV (July and October, 1942), vii–215.

[33] Samuelson and Hagen, *After the War*, 21–25 (authors' italics); see also George Soule, *Prosperity Decade: From War to Depression, 1917–1929* (New York, 1968), 96ff.; Payne, "Business Behavior, 1919–1922."

trainmen and craftsmen were lured away from the railroads to more lucrative jobs in war plants. Inflation and rising costs were potential causes for strikes by the railroad brotherhoods, as well as arguments for the railroad owners to ask for rate increases, which could set off a spiral of wage and cost increases. Railroad managers, trying to cope with the crisis, came up with operating innovations that antagonized shippers and labor interests. Thus practically all factions—shippers, labor, railroad executives, and much of the public—welcomed Wilson's declaration of federal control, though each hoped to see its own interests furthered by the action.[34]

Before the war, shippers generally had wanted regulation of rates —but only in order that the Interstate Commerce Commission might impose a ceiling on the railroads, which the commission generally had done. Regulatory commissions in the various states also supported rate controls as long as these rested in their own hands and favored local shipping interests. Railroad executives constantly had pleaded for higher rates, and when the ICC failed to grant them, they began arguing the concept of "efficiency"—namely, that a national system of railway transportation required social harmony (no strikes), constant improvement in service and equipment and consequently rate increases, and an end to wasteful competition and thus more federal supervision.[35]

Federal operation of the railroads during the war was, at its best, a model of the very efficiency that railroad interests had begun advocating. Yet at the end of the war federal operation found few supporters. Shippers often disliked the standardized rates that the government imposed. William G. McAdoo, director general of the railroads, paid little attention to politics in making administration appointments, naming instead the best men he could find. But when this policy led to a predominance of railroad executives in the Railroad Administration, shippers and state regulatory commissioners

[34] K. Austin Kerr, *American Railroad Politics, 1914–1920* (Pittsburgh, 1968), makes many of the points in the above paragraph—see especially pp. 39–71. An early and closely detailed account is William J. Cunningham, "The Railroads under Government Operation," *Quarterly Journal of Economics,* XXXV (February, 1921), 288–340; in a subsequent article, *ibid.,* XXXVI (November, 1921), 30–71, Cunningham covers the period from January 1, 1919, to March 1, 1920. See also "The Railroad Problem: A Discussion of Current Railway Issues," *Annals,* American Academy of Political and Social Science, LXXXVI (November, 1919), 17–90. On labor conditions and regulations during the war under government control, see H. D. Wolf, *The Railroad Labor Board* (Chicago, 1927).

[35] Kerr, *Railroad Politics,* 6–38.

cried foul. By the end of the war, shippers were completely alienated from federal operation and wanted to return to the good old days of the Progressive Era when regulation by the ICC had worked to their advantage.[36]

Walker Hines, principal aide during the war to McAdoo and eventually successor to McAdoo as director general in 1919, found little opposition to federal control as long as the war lasted. But with the Armistice, Hines later recalled, the "war spirit" evaporated and "almost every motive . . . pertaining to the subject underwent a complete and sudden change."[37] Hines may have overstated the contrast between pre-Armistice and post-Armistice talk about railroads, but he was right in one respect: with the end of the war, the question of federal control became immediately important. Wilson's December, 1917, proclamation taking over the railroads had placed no limit on the duration of control. The Federal Control Act of March 21, 1918, provided that control continue during the war and for a "reasonable time" thereafter, but not more than twenty-one months after the war. Wilson's policy toward the railroads during reconstruction matched his other domestic policy. He seemed unconcerned, confused, or both. In a message to Congress on December 2, 1918, he said that the railroads ought not return to the old conditions of unrestricted competition and multiform regulations but admitted that the government would soon relinquish control unless Congress came up with a policy.[38] He then sailed for Paris.

The central figure in the Wilson administration at war's end was McAdoo. As early as November, 1918, McAdoo, who was both secretary of the treasury and director general of the railroads, was thinking about resigning in order to do what countless other men were doing—get back to private life and, as he put it, "to recoup my fortune." "No one knows," he lamented to Colonel E. M. House, "how much I have had to sacrifice financially to stay in Washington these six years." He declared himself "wholly indifferent" to the "political effects" of resignation, but his actions in the next two years and even his November rationalizations over resigning demonstrated an intense preoccupation with politics. Wilson's departure for Paris would create embarrassment if McAdoo did not resign. In Wilson's absence, McAdoo would be the ranking Cabinet officer and would have to take

[36] *Ibid.*, 79–81, 101–2, 106, 112.
[37] Walker D. Hines, *War History of American Railroads* (New Haven, 1928), 42.
[38] *New York Times*, December 3, 1918, 1:7, 11:3.

charge of the general run of things. And since he was Wilson's son-in-law as well as his secretary of the treasury, he would evoke cries of "hereditary government" and "Crown Prince" from the Republican opposition. This association with Wilson bothered McAdoo the politician, and in 1920 it would help to prove his undoing as a contender for the Democratic presidential nomination. Here in 1918 he had more immediate political concern. The Republicans, he wrote, were certain to make a "political football" over the railroads in the next two years, trying to "harass and hamper . . . if not prevent, a successful demonstration of government control." [39]

Three months later McAdoo wrote to Wilson in Paris suggesting a strategy. Congress was, he noted, "going to do nothing about the railroads." But Republicans, "some reactionary Democrats," and certain railroad owners were taking advantage of federal control. The railroad owners and "their Republican allies" wanted federal control to continue for the twenty-one months after the war, as stipulated in the March, 1918, law. During this time, with their earnings guaranteed by the federal government, they would attack the administration and "render Federal control odious" by blaming the government for every inconvenience or detail of mismanagement. Wilson should return the railroads to private control at once. Congress would still be free to legislate, and the public could no longer blame the administration "for the faults and defects of private management which will again be brought glaringly to the public consciousness by the return to private control." [40]

Yet, without reference to political strategy, McAdoo favored retaining federal control for five years. In a long statement to the House and Senate Interstate Commerce Committee in December, McAdoo laid out three options: government operation for twenty-one months after the war, as provided in the March, 1918, Federal Control Act; prompt return of the railroads to private control; or extension of federal control for five years. The first option he disliked. The period was too short and allotted funds were insufficient for the government to effectively manage the railroads; the impending changeover to private control would grow nearer every month, and "a state of uncertainty and ferment" would set in. No business in the United States,

[39] McAdoo to House, November 29, 1918, Letterbook 66, Container 500, McAdoo Papers.

[40] McAdoo to Wilson, February 25, 1919, Container 218, William Gibbs McAdoo Papers, Division of Manuscripts, Library of Congress.

he said, "so imperatively requires disciplined organization and composed conditions of operations . . . as the railroad business." Immediate return to private control he flatly rejected, except as a political gambit, though even this option would be preferable to the "unsatisfactory, if not impotent," federal control exercised under wartime legislation. He saw only one wise alternative—to extend control for five years, thereby taking the railroads out of politics for a "reasonable period," during which the government would carry out improvements and "test the value of unified control" under proper conditions.[41]

McAdoo was pessimistic over gaining his five-year extension and talked about "conservative and reactionary interests" arrayed against him.[42] Yet as debate over the railroads developed in December, it was obvious that, except for certain shipping factions, hardly any bloc of railroad interest groups wanted a return to prewar conditions. Virtually no one argued for competition; all factions wanted federal regulation or some version of "scientific management." McAdoo's proposal for a five-year extension of federal control never gained serious support in Congress. On the other hand, Wilson rejected his proposed tactic to return the railroads to private control and thereby leave the problem to the Republicans. Wilson evidently agreed with Walker Hines, McAdoo's successor as director, that an immediate return to private control would leave the railroads in economic chaos.[43] Thus, as the new year began, Congress faced the option of allowing existing federal control to run its course and expire in September, 1920, or of coming up with new legislation to provide for some degree of federal regulation.

Beginning on June 2, 1919, when Congressman John J. Esch (Republican, Wisconsin) and Senator Atlee Pomerene (Democrat, Ohio) each introduced a bill, Congress received and considered a series of plans, bills, and committee reports designed to cope with what was now generally labeled "the railroad problem." One of the major proposals originated with Senator Albert Cummins (Republican, Iowa), who introduced a bill on September 2 and a modification of it on October 23. Cummins's proposal expressed "the clearest and most complete exposition of postwar efforts to impose scientific manage-

[41] McAdoo to T. W. Sims, chairman, Interstate and Foreign Commerce Committee, House of Representatives; and to Senator Ellison D. Smith, chairman, Senate Interstate Commerce Committee, December 11, 1918, Letterbook 64, Container 500, *ibid.*

[42] McAdoo to Albert Shaw, December 31, 1918, *ibid.*; McAdoo to Paul M. Warburg, December 26, 1918, *ibid.*

[43] Hines, *War History of Railroads*, 42–45.

ment conceptions on a privately controlled industry."[44] He would allow the government to consolidate lines, set rates scientifically upon a fixed and fair return, guarantee minimum earnings, provide improvements in the system, and arbitrate labor disputes in the name of social harmony.

Shippers disliked the Cummins plan, if only because it would take regulation away from the ICC and give it to a new Transportation Board. Railroad executives disliked the mandatory consolidation and redistribution of railroad income that Cummins proposed. Railroad labor naturally objected to the anti-strike provisions in the bill. In fact, labor—along with a few farm organizations and a scattering of intellectuals—supported the Plumb plan, a scheme of railroad nationalization devised by Glenn Plumb, general counsel for the Organized Railway Employees of America. Plumb proposed that the federal government sell bonds and buy the railroads, operating them under control of a board of directors representing the public, operators, and labor.[45]

As shippers, railroad executives, railroad labor, and congressional spokesmen haggled and maneuvered over the railroad problem, Wilson, from Paris, called Congress into special session in May. Acting on Walker Hines's recommendation, Wilson stated that the railroads would be returned to private control at the end of the calendar year. What kind of regulation would then be imposed was, he indicated, up to Congress. By November it was obvious that Congress would not pass a bill before the end of the year. Again in response to Hines's appeal, as well as to advice from Louis Brandeis, Wilson finally agreed

[44] Kerr, *Railroad Politics*, 143–44. For the text of these bills, see Rogers Mac-Veagh, *The Transportation Act 1920* (New York, 1923).

[45] Kerr, *Railroad Politics*, 149ff., offers a good, succinct account of the objections to the Cummins plan. Literature on the Plumb plan is extensive, but Frank Haigh Dixon, *Railroads and Government* (New York, 1922), 222–24, gives a brief summary. The Amos Pinchot Papers, Division of Manuscripts, Library of Congress, are full of material revealing support for the plan by Pinchot and other intellectuals and patrician reformers. "The A.B.C. of the Plumb Plan," Box 39, is typical. The William E. Borah Papers contain some interesting items of relevance, among them an invitation to Borah to attend a dinner conference at Plumb's home in Chevy Chase, Maryland, on July 4, 1919, where Plumb was to "explain in detail . . . labor's plan for the reorganization of the railways." The dinner list was heavy with liberal or Progressive Republicans and other individuals at varying degrees left of center. See Glenn Plumb to Borah, May 27, 1919, Box 196, Borah Papers. Borah's correspondence, if at all representative of other senators' mail, suggests the enormous pressures upon Congress to enact a bill but shows, as well, the divided sentiment over the question.

to postpone until March 1, 1920, his relinquishment of federal control.[46]

Wilson showed little interest in railroad legislation. In the absence of executive direction and amidst powerful cross-currents of lobbying and maneuvering, the railroad problem finally reached solution. The Esch-Cummins Act (the Transportation Act of 1920), providing for private operation under public regulation, was a compromise between current proposals and a synthesis of prewar and wartime experience with railroad regulation. Under the new law the ICC regained its prewar function as "supreme arbiter of railroad politics."[47] The commission was to initiate rates that would yield a fair return upon railroad property. Any company earning more than 6 percent on the value of its property was to pay half the excess to the government. Federal control of the railroads terminated at 12:01 A.M., March 1, 1920. To give the ICC time to investigate, prescribe, and make new rates for private operation under postwar conditions, the new law guaranteed an income for six months (March to September) to the carriers which had been under federal control.[48]

In such ways the Transportation Act of 1920 restored the Progressive Era regulatory system. But in other ways it altered that system and sustained some of the wartime changes. Labor disputes were now placed within the province of a Railway Labor Board, though the railroad brotherhoods opposed the entire railroad bill and asked Wilson to veto it.[49] The act also reflected a change in thinking about anti-

[46] *New York Times*, May 21, 1919, 1:1; Walker Hines, *War History*, 42–45; Kerr, *Railroad Politics*, 212–13.

[47] Kerr, *Railroad Politics*, 212–13.

[48] Walker Hines, who supervised the liquidation until he resigned as director general in May, 1920, reported that "operations of the carriers during these six months were extremely unsatisfactory," and the government had to make large payments to them in compensation for losses. See Hines, *War History*, 221–23. On the total costs of railroad operations, see John Maurice Clark, *The Costs of the World War* (New Haven, 1931), 236–44.

[49] It is difficult to apportion the opposition to and support for the Esch-Cummins Act. Institutionally, however—or perhaps occupationally—the lines were sometimes clear. The AFL, for example, denounced the law unequivocally. The railroad brotherhoods also protested against it, backing the Plumb plan instead. The U.S. Chamber of Commerce, on the other hand, predictably opposed the Plumb plan. Gompers himself did not like the Plumb plan, though he was unable to prevent the AFL convention from declaring support for it. *American Federationist*, XXVII (January, 1920), 73, and (March, 1929), 262–63; *New York Times*, August 6, 1919, 2:6; August 13, 1919, 3:3; October 31, 1919, 3:4; November 13, 1919, 1:6; May 2, 1920, 7:2; June 11, 1920, 18:1; June 20, 1920, 1:6; and Robert Zieger, *Republicans and Labor, 1919–1929* (Lexington, Ky., 1969), 24–25.

trust laws. The ICC now had power to promote consolidation of railroads into a limited number of systems and to approve combinations through leasing or any method short of complete consolidation.

Walker Hines, writing in 1927, thought the new railroad law of 1920 "expressed a revolution in the attitudes of the public toward railroad regulation." A recent study of the subject emphasizes the continuity of prewar and postwar railroad policy, with the Transportation Act producing "no fundamental changes in the regulatory system."[50] Yet, in the context of the postwar hysteria over Reds and other forms of radicalism, and given Wilson's essential disinterest, it is remarkable how much control remained in federal hands under the 1920 act. The World War experience may have antagonized shipping interests toward centralization and inconvenienced much of the public. But federal control had shown to other interests, such as railroad executives, the advantages of rationalization—which was the drift of their prewar thinking in the first place. The Transportation Act gave them the advantage of federal control, yet it left operations, along with substantial profits, in their corporate hands. National railroad policy was far from settled, however, and the question of regulation, rates, and railroad labor policy would plague the administrations of the Twenties.[51]

[50] Hines, *War History*, 225; Kerr, *Railroad Politics*, 231.

[51] Robert Zeiger, "From Hostility to Moderation: Railroad Labor Policy in the 1920's," *Labor History*, IX (Winter, 1968), 23–38; Robert K. Murray, *The Harding Era: Warren G. Harding and His Administration* (Minneapolis, 1969), 221–25, 238–64; Donald R. McCoy, *Calvin Coolidge: The Quiet President* (New York, 1967), 199.

VI

"Many Did Not Know the Difference
between Bolshevism and Rheumatism"

Americans and Un-Americans

The Armistice on the western front in November, 1918, did not pacify the American home front. The war against Germany ended, but an ideological war at home continued. If the Armistice caused one stratum of Americans to rejoice, not only over the peace but also over the new society they envisioned opening out ahead, to another stratum the defeat of enemies abroad cleared the way to concentrate on enemies at home. The latter of these gained ascendancy in the months between the Armistice and the election of 1920. Decimation of radical organizations, creation of patriotic clubs and programs, continuing imprisonment for political cause, eruption of violence between blacks and whites, hysteria over so-called subversives, arrest and deportation of aliens—this frenetic behavior and psychic trembling that scarred American life in 1919 arose from the impact of war. In turn, this particular panic, subsumed partially under the label "Red Scare," left a residue of mood and institutional power that sustained into the Twenties the Americanization drives of wartime, drove the Communist party underground (where it thrived on its martyrdom), produced nativist thrusts such as the Johnson Act of 1921 and the National Origins Act of 1924, and first and last shaped the society over which Warren G. Harding and Calvin Coolidge, after their fashion, presided.

When he led the country into war in 1917, Wilson, according to an old and perhaps apocryphal story, dolefully told a friend that war "required illiberalism at home to reinforce the man at the front," and that a "spirit of ruthless brutality" would enter American life.[1] Required or not, illiberalism and the brutality came, and the Wilson

---

[1] John L. Heaton, *Cobb of THE WORLD* (New York, 1924), 268–70. On the authenticity of this comment, see Jerold S. Auerbach, "Woodrow Wilson's 'Prediction' to Frank Cobb: Words Historians Should Doubt Ever Got Spoken," *Journal of American History*, LIV (December, 1967), 608–17; and letters from Arthur S. Link and Auerbach, *ibid.*, LV (June, 1968), 231–38.

administration did little to hinder their coming. The story of wartime censorship and conformity, and of vigilantes on the prowl, is familiar enough to require little characterization here,[2] but among the victims of this wartime xenophobia two groups in particular continued to suffer abuse or eradication even after the Armistice: conscientious objectors and political radicals of varying persuasions, especially Wobblies, Communists, and Socialists.

The conscription law of May 18, 1917, whereby the nation began to raise the AEF for war in France, offered little comfort or leeway to a conscientious objector. The act allowed exemption from military duty only for those who were members of "well recognized" religious organizations whose creeds forbade participation in war. The exemption extended only to combat service. A man with scruples against military service even in noncombat units or areas had no recourse, and the law contained no provision for political or philosophical objectors—or even for religious objectors unless they were affiliated with a "recognized" peace church.[3]

Whether because of the law's stringency or not, only a few men in the United States in 1917–18 claimed conscientious objector status. Just over 20,000 CO's underwent actual induction, but some 16,000 of them changed their minds, or were persuaded to do so, after reaching camps. Four thousand absolutists refused to change their views. Some 1,300 of these finally went into noncombat units, about 1,200 more gained furloughs to do farm work, and 100 or so undertook Quaker war relief work in Europe. About 500 suffered courts-martial; 450 of these finally went to prison, most of them to the Disciplinary Barracks at Fort Leavenworth, Kansas. Conscientious objectors were a tiny minority, when compared to some 170,000 draft evaders and to the 2,810,296 men inducted into the armed forces.[4] Even so, the CO's became objects of inflamed controversy, ostracism, and punishment. Just after the war Congressman Walter H. Newton of Minnesota lamented that it was "disgusting coddling to permit a soldier to fix his status in the Army by an unsworn statement that 'I object,' "

2 See bibliographical essay, pp. 218–20.

3 Act to Authorize the President to Increase Temporarily the Military Establishment of the United States, *Stat. at Large*, XL, 76–83 (1917); Walter Guest Kellogg, *The Conscientious Objector* (New York, 1919); Norman Thomas, *Is Conscience a Crime?* (New York, 1927); Secretary of War, *Statement Concerning Treatment of Conscientious Objectors in the Army* (Washington, 1919).

4 War Department, *Annual Report, 1919* (Washington, 1920), 36; Secretary of War, *Statement Concerning Conscientious Objectors*.

especially since most CO's—whom Newton labeled "consciousless objectors"—had been "pro-German, I.W.W., political Socialists, and cowardly slackers," who sought to "spread insidious and treasonable propaganda throughout this country. . . ." In 1919 the army inspector general offered an official judgment that CO's were "the most difficult and annoying [personnel] with which the War Department had to deal." While a "small minority" of them were real conscientious objectors, the "great majority were undoubtedly slackers, who were disloyal and who availed themselves of this pretext to evade service." One CO's response to such charges was blunt. Sentenced to Leavenworth and there quickly placed in solitary confinement, Roderick Seidenberg wrote later of his experience: "To steal, rape or murder, to slap an officer's face and call him a son of a bitch—these are the standard peace-time entrance requirements to the Disciplinary Barracks. But in time of war too firm a belief in the words of Christ, too ardent a faith in the brotherhood of man, is even more acceptable."[5]

The fate of the 4,000 CO's, and especially the ones in military prison, had by war's end become an issue of great moment to the National Civil Liberties Bureau and to a scattered few members of Congress. The NCLB (it became the American Civil Liberties Union in 1920) had come into existence during the war, first as an organization resisting American participation, and then, once American entry and conscription did come, trying to uphold the right of the CO's. Passage of the Espionage and Sedition Acts of 1917 and 1918 brought on still more violations of traditional freedoms, and the NCLB extended its work to help victims of this legislation. In defending civil liberties and conscientious objectors the NCLB found itself supporting labor groups and other leftist causes, though ideology had little to do with it. The Right simply needed no help at the time; the power of the federal government was not oppressive in that direction. The men and women who dominated the NCLB were themselves moderates who believed the government was benefiting the wealthy and privileged few and was persecuting radical minorities; hence it was the latter that the NCLB-ACLU supported.[6]

As the country entered the post-Armistice period, conscientious

---

[5] *Cong. Rec.*, 66 Cong., 1 sess. (July 23, 1919), 3063–66; War Department, Annual *Report*, 1919, 657; Roderick Seidenberg, "I Refuse to Serve," *American Mercury*, XXV (January, 1932), 91–99.

[6] Donald Johnson, *Challenge to American Freedoms: World War I and the Rise of the American Civil Liberties Union* (Lexington, 1963).

objectors and radical minorities needed all the aid and comfort that the NCLB could give them. After the war the crusade against Germany gradually but unmistakably turned toward a peculiar brand of conformity labeled "100% Americanism"—a brand with little tolerance for conscientious objectors or for other groups who had opposed the war, such as Wobblies and certain Socialists who were now, in common parlance, labeled radicals and subversives. As several studies have made abundantly clear, the war all but destroyed the IWW.[7] What the war did to American Socialists is less clear, though with the Wobblies they felt the searing impact of the postwar hysteria.[8]

The IWW had, perhaps inevitably, faced repression and condemnation since the day of its founding in Chicago in 1905. In dramatic and vivid terms the Wobblies spoke of overthrowing the existing capitalistic system. Much of this may have been rhetoric, born of the violent conflicts and oppressive conditions in the Rocky Mountains and far western mining and lumbering camps where much of the IWW operated.[9] But Wobbly talk of revolt and Wobbly scorn for church and flag as symbols of an unjust status quo stirred state and federal governments to frantic action. From 1905 until its virtual destruction as an effective force in the early Twenties, the IWW was a focal point for a drive to rid the nation of radicals. And come 1919, laws origi-

[7] William Preston, Jr., *Aliens and Dissenters: Federal Suppression of Radicals, 1903–1933* (Cambridge, 1966) ; Melvyn Dubofsky, *We Shall Be All: A History of the Industrial Workers of the World* (Chicago, 1969) ; Robert L. Tyler, *Rebels of the Woods: The IWW in the Pacific Northwest* (Eugene, 1967) ; and a personal recollection, Harvey O'Connor, *Revolution in Seattle* (New York, 1964), 81–124; but also cf. Fred Thompson, *The IWW: Its First Fifty Years, 1905–1955* (Chicago, 1955), for the views of a Wobbly whose enduring warmth for the cause is reflected in the title of his succinct history.

[8] There were important differences between Wobblies and Socialists, differences appreciated at the time by both groups, but during and after the war critics of the two tended to lump them together, along with an indiscriminate number of other radicals and subversives. For a comparison of Socialists and the IWW, see James Weinstein, "The IWW and American Socialism," *Socialist Revolution*, I (September–October, 1970), 3–42; Dubofsky, *We Shall Be All*, 168–70; Joseph R. Conlin, "The I.W.W. and the Socialist Party," *Science and Society*, XXXI (Winter, 1967), 22–36.

[9] William Preston has recently called attention to the experience of Wobblies in eastern states, a subject neglected by students of American radicalism. See "Shall This Be All? U.S. Historians Versus William D. Haywood *et al.*," *Labor History*, 12 (Summer, 1971), 435–53. And Robert Tyler, "The I.W.W. and the West," *American Quarterly*, XII (Summer, 1960), 175–87, may be right in his suggestion that American intellectuals romanticized the prewar Wobblies as "buckskin bolsheviks" coming out of a virile West to rejuvenate a jaded East. But as the growing literature on the IWW indicates, much of the hysteria and violence over the Wobblies did, in fact, occur in the West, especially around Seattle.

nally devised to destroy the Wobbly served further purposes as well: they were turned on an indiscriminate variety of Socialists, Communists, and other citizens and aliens. In 1912–13 in the Pacific Northwest, federal naturalization examiners defined the IWW as a group teaching opposition to organized government, and all its alien members (that is, men not yet American citizens) were barred from naturalization, even if they had dropped membership in the IWW.[10]

Government policy toward the IWW was not monolithic. At least one federal agency showed remarkable understanding and even sympathy for the Wobblies. In 1917, following a wave of strikes in the lumber camps of the Pacific Northwest, the President's mediation commission visited the area, investigated conditions, and issued a report of eminent objectivity (if also of futility). The commission noted that 90 percent of the men in the lumber camps were "womanless, voteless, and jobless," and that they had been made into disintegrating forces in society by the circumstances of their wretched lives. Men who joined the IWW saw it as a "bond of groping fellowship." But their "assertion of human dignity" was met head on by operators who, more out of pride than reasoned judgment, would not grant them such demands as an eight-hour day.[11] Other federal agencies were less understanding, and, as even the mediation commission acknowledged, the exigencies of war required stability and output in the lumber industry. One result was federal sponsorship of the Loyal Legion of Loggers and Lumbermen, an organization of workers recruited by the War Department, which at one time supplemented it with 10,000 men from the Signal Corps. The Legion produced lumber as well as some overdue reforms, but it aroused bitter resentment from the Wobblies because of its anti-strike provisions and its use of troops.[12] Meanwhile, other voices in the government were continuing to stress the "alien" nature of the Wobbly movement. In 1917 Congress approved a law that gave the Secretary of Labor authority to arrest and to deport any alien "advocating or teaching" the "un-

[10] Preston, *Aliens and Dissenters*, 68–69.

[11] *Report of the President's Mediation Commission* (Washington, 1918). See also *Report of Secretary of Labor*, 1918, pp. 21–23; and John R. Fitch, "A Report on Industrial Unrest: Summary of the Findings of the President's Commission," *Survey*, XXXIX (February 16, 1919).

[12] Robert L. Tyler, "The U.S. Government as Union Organizer: The Loyal Legion of Loggers and Lumbermen," *Mississippi Valley Historical Review*, XLVII (December, 1960), 434–51. Harold L. Hyman, *Soldiers and Spruce: Origins of the Loyal Legion of Loggers and Lumbermen* (Los Angeles, 1963).

lawful" destruction of property or the "overthrow by force or violence of the government" or opposition to "all forms of law" or advocating the assassination of public officials.[13] Such concern over would-be assassins is understandable, but what was "advocacy"? Were newsboys selling IWW papers on the streets advocating unlawful destruction of property? As William Preston points out, the very looseness and ambiguity of the law was precisely what the Immigration Bureau in the Department of Labor wanted. Deportation could become the cure for radicalism.[14]

In 1919–20 Attorney General A. Mitchell Palmer would use the 1917 law in an attempt to deport members of the IWW. He would use it even more as a weapon against American Communists—or reputed ones. On the eve of the Palmer raids there were two Communist parties in the United States; one was called the Communist party, and the other, the Communist Labor party. Each had emerged from what Theodore Draper simply labels the Left Wing of the American labor movement before World War I,[15] a wing made up—at least organizationally—of the IWW, the Socialist Labor party, and the Socialist Party of America. Socialist organizations first formed in the United States in the 1870's. From the beginning, bitter tactical and ideological strife characterized the movement. The Socialist Party of America, organized in 1901 and containing the majority of American socialists, was the more moderate wing, led by Eugene Debs. But in 1917, when the United States entered the war, the SPA split.[16]

In Europe, when the war came in 1914, the majority of Socialists renounced their former position, reaffirmed their nationalism, and supported their countries at war. Unlike the Europeans, the "vast majority of American Socialists opposed the war both before and after the United States became a belligerent."[17] But a number of notable Socialist intellectuals, such as William English Walling, W. J. Ghent, John Spargo, and Upton Sinclair, did opt for war and American nationalism, though each of these strong-willed figures found his

[13] Sec. 19, Immigration Act of February 5, 1917, *Stat. at Large*, XXXIX, 889; see also Sidney Kansas, *U.S. Immigration: Exclusion and Deportation* (New York, 1928), 109–10; Roy Garis, *Immigration Restriction* (New York, 1927).

[14] Preston, *Aliens and Dissenters*, 83–84.

[15] Theodore Draper, *The Roots of American Communism* (New York, 1957), 17.

[16] The literature on American socialism, and on the events mentioned above, is voluminous. See bibliographical essay for basic titles.

[17] James Weinstein, *The Decline of American Socialism, 1912–1925* (New York, 1967), 119.

own route to war—no sense of ideological comradeship or simple patriotism explaining their rejection of old Socialist doctrine.[18]

The schism in the party seriously wounded it. Yet the antiwar stand and the loss of influential figures did not by themselves ostracize or destroy the party. Hostility to the war—or at least to the draft—was amazingly widespread, extending to more than CO's, Wobblies, and Socialists.[19] Still, the Socialist party was "the only major national organization officially to condemn American participation in the war," and it became a favorite target for attack by the federal government and local vigilantes.[20] Many of its publications destroyed, many of its leaders indicted or even lynched, the party nevertheless gained votes after April, 1917, and at the end of the war Socialist leaders such as Eugene Debs and Victor Berger—even though they were currently under indictment for opposing the war—felt optimistic about the future, as, for different reasons, did countless American liberals and capitalists.[21]

In the meantime, an American Communist movement had begun to appear, made up predominantly of the foreign-language federations in the Socialist party. The war had destroyed Socialist strongholds

[18] Walling had years earlier gained contempt of prominent SPA leaders, including some figures such as Spargo who with him supported the war in 1917. Spargo in 1909 wrote of Walling as "mentally unbalanced, erratic in his movements . . . one of the most pathetic figures I have ever encountered." Robert Hunter warned of Walling's "mental and moral irresponsibility." Victor Berger, who opposed the war, labeled Walling an "impossiblist." See Spargo to J. G. Phelps Stokes, December 3, 1909; Hunter to A. Simons, December 3, 1909; Berger to Simons, December 6, 1909, Box 2, Socialist Party Papers, Duke University.

Spargo in 1917 issued a minority report on the party's antiwar stand, saying, "Internationalism presupposes nationalism. It is the interrelation of nations. The maintenance of national integrity and independence is an essential condition of internationalism. . . . Now that the war is an accomplished fact . . . it is our Socialist duty to make whatever sacrifices may be necessary to enable our nation and its allies to win the war. . . ." In time, Spargo's nationalism came to dominate him more and more. See Document no. 15, "Committee on War and Militarism, Minority Report," Socialist Party Papers; and Irwin Granich, "Mr. Spargo," *One Big Union Monthly*, II (February, 1920), 36.

On Ghent, see Ch. 9 below.

[19] H. C. Peterson and Gilbert C. Fite, *Opponents of War, 1917–1918* (Madison, 1957), 21–42.

[20] Weinstein, *Decline of Socialism*, 140.

[21] As Weinstein's detailed figures show, the SPA vote grew and shifted heavily eastward during the war. On the other hand, party membership steadily declined from 1916 to 1918, although membership began to climb again following the Bolshevik Revolution, and by 1919 reached 109,000. See membership figures, Socialist Party Papers; Weinstein, *Decline of Socialism*, 173–76, 232.

everywhere but in the industrial slums of the eastern seaboard. There, newly arrived immigrants (especially from Russia and Eastern Europe), unable to vote, excluded from most trade unions, and living in considerable poverty, easily identified with the Bolshevik Revolution of 1917. Often absolutist and doctrinaire, they talked of immediate and total overthrow of capitalism, rejecting the tactics of gradualism—for example, organization of trade unions to work for gradual improvement of the workers' status within the existing economic order. The Bolshevik Revolution had a magnetic effect upon these men. For years they had talked of revolution. Now suddenly one had come, if in a most unexpected time and place. Russian Bolshevism now became the model for American Communism, despite the fact, quickly made evident, that the latter understood the Russian revolution no better than the Russians understood American conditions. Old American leftists, now Communists, visited Moscow, accepted directions from Lenin, and began working to produce their own indigenous American Bolshevik revolution.[22]

They were a minute element in American life. In 1919 no more than .001 percent of adult Americans belonged to the two Communist parties; each of these, the Communist party and the Communist Labor party, was riddled with dissension, cross-purposes, and ineffectuality. Meanwhile, if old Socialists in the foreign-language federations tried to imitate Russian Bolsheviks and to look for revolution in the United States, veteran Socialists such as Morris Hillquit and Victor Berger scorned these notions as romantic—and dangerous—nonsense. As Berger pointed out, Russia on the eve of the revolution was a beaten country; in contrast, the United States emerged from the war stronger than before. "We cannot," said Berger, "transfer Russia to America."[23]

But unwittingly Berger had voiced a thought that by 1919 was coming to possess the United States: fear that the country was indeed on the brink of revolution, Russian style. As 1918 drew to a close, the Armistice only weeks past, all the wartime dissenters—CO's, Wobblies, Socialists, and now the new Communists as well—became by their very existence a threat to the peace just achieved. Men who had refused to fight Mr. Wilson's war, or men who now sought to obstruct or overturn the society that war had preserved, came under fire. The conformity of war became the conformity of peace. The enemy simply

[22] Draper, *Roots of American Communism.*
[23] *Ibid.*; Weinstein, *Decline of American Socialism*, 207.

changed names. He was no longer Hun; he was Red. Whatever his name, he was un-American.

Perhaps because they were already in jail, the several hundred CO's convicted by military courts during the war aroused less hysteria than other "subversives" did. In fact, the only major concern over conscientious objectors arose among a small element seeking the CO's release from prison, now that the war had ended. One of the busiest defenders of the CO's was Norman Thomas, vice-chairman of the NCLB. A religious objector himself, Thomas had worked fervently during the war to defend both religious and nonreligious CO's. In December, 1918, he and the NCLB set out to gain amnesty for "political, industrial, and military prisoners, including the few score conscientious objectors still in prison." They appealed for help in many directions, for example to Amos Pinchot, an articulate, well-to-do liberal lawyer in New York and brother of conservationist Gifford Pinchot. Thomas wrote to Senator Borah of Idaho, lamenting the "ferocious sentences" and the "barbarous punishments" meted out to political prisoners and asking Borah to support a general amnesty bill.[24]

Thomas was right. Punishment of CO's was barbarous. Solitary confinement in oppressive surroundings was mild discomfort compared to that suffered by men pricked with bayonets, given the water cure, or immersed in the filth of the camp latrines, head downward.[25] Reports coming to Senator George W. Norris provoked him to the judgment that, if the reports were "anywhere near the truth . . . we are more barbarous in the treatment of these unfortunate men, than were the men of the Dark Ages in the treatment of their prisoners."[26] Here and there small pressure groups appeared, such as the Friends of Conscientious Objectors in Brooklyn, calling on citizens to "write a letter to your newspaper telling it what you think of Americans imprisoning other Americans because they happen to think differently."[27] Members of the Socialist party in Chicago or-

[24] L. Hollingsworth Wood, chairman; Norman Thomas, vice-chairman; and others to Amos Pinchot, December, 1918, Box 39, Amos Pinchot Papers, Division of Manuscripts, Library of Congress; Thomas to William E. Borah, December 20, 1918, "Army Matters," Box 193, William E. Borah Papers, Division of Manuscripts, Library of Congress.

[25] Norman Thomas, *Is Conscience a Crime?* 143ff.

[26] Norris to G. W. Timm, January 14, 1919, Tray 10, Box 2, George W. Norris Papers, Division of Manuscripts, Library of Congress.

[27] Broadside, Labor File, Socialist Party Papers.

ganized a Prison Comfort Club and wrote to federal wardens in an effort to compile a list of "political prisoners."[28] Numerous labor organizations, including railroad brotherhoods, machinists' locals, and cigar-makers, endorsed a National League for the Release of Political Prisoners.[29]

General amnesty never came for the conscientious objectors. Wilson at first seemed to favor an amnesty, but in November, 1918, when he asked Attorney General Thomas Gregory for an opinion, Gregory was vehement in opposing the idea. "These people," he said, "are in no sense political prisoners, but are criminals who sided against their country." Wilson agreed, and evidently so did most of the country.[30] Wilson was already preoccupied with the peace settlement, and the National Security League and other professional patriots were concerned with bigger game than a small group of CO's who one by one began to gain release in the months after the war. For some, their sentences expired; some were released on parole; others the War Department let go without explanation. Some of them remained in prison until 1933, when in a Christmas amnesty they finally received a full and free parole from President Franklin D. Roosevelt.[31]

Writing in the Twenties, Norman Thomas judged that "active opposition to the objectors ebbed earlier than to other political prisoners."[32] Thomas might have been thinking about Big Bill Haywood or Eugene Debs and the political groups that each man represented. For even more than the tiny cluster of conscientious objectors, it was Wobblies and Socialists who, in their criticism or obstruction of wartime mobilization, had provoked opposition from the government and often went to jail during the war. Although most Wobblies and Socialists were American citizens, they as much as unnaturalized leftists became the target of Americans aroused over the presumed threat from aliens in the land.

Nine weeks after it declared war in April, 1917, Congress passed the Espionage Act. Two of its provisions called for fines (of $10,000) or prison (up to twenty years) or both for anyone who obstructed operation of the armed forces, tried to cause insubordination or

[28] "N.E.S., 1919," *ibid.*

[29] Labor File, *ibid.*

[30] Donald Johnson, *Challenge to American Freedoms*, 110.

[31] Mulford Q. Silby and Philip E. Jacob, *Conscription of Conscience* (Ithaca, N.Y., 1952), 16; Samuel Rosenman, ed., *The Public Papers and Addresses of Franklin D. Roosevelt* (New York, 1938–50), II, 540–42.

[32] Thomas, *Is Conscience a Crime?* 247.

disloyalty, or obstructed recruitment or enlistment in the armed services.[33] Under the act and later amendments, the Department of Justice prosecuted over 2,000 cases and gained over 1,000 convictions, including those of hundreds of Wobblies and Socialists. The Socialists who were indicted (and in many cases convicted) included some colorful and controversial personalities. The beautiful Rose Pastor Stokes, a onetime cigar-maker who married a millionaire Socialist in New York and became a celebrated figure in the city and the party, reportedly said that American soldiers "were not fighting for democracy but for the protection and safeguarding of Morgan's millions." Scott Nearing, fired from his teaching post at the University of Pennsylvania and then from Toledo University, was indicted, along with the American Socialist Society, for publishing a pamphlet, *The Great Madness*, which the government claimed tended to cause insubordination and disloyalty in the armed forces. Kate Richards O'Hare, national secretary of the Socialist party and prominent in the anti-war wing of the party, supposedly had declared that women in the United States were "nothing more nor less than brood sows, to raise children to get into the army and be made into fertilizer." Mrs. Stokes was convicted, but then the appeals court reversed the judgment because the trial judge's charge to the jury had been inflammatory and prejudicial to her rights. Nearing was acquitted, though the American Socialist Society was fined $3,000. Kate O'Hare spent a year in Missouri State Penitentiary, where she suffered discomfort but came out fighting.[34]

In the two most celebrated cases Bill Haywood and Eugene Debs were tried and convicted, though each man's subsequent fate differed notably. On September 5, 1917, the government launched a spectacular nationwide roundup of IWW leaders. Three weeks later, in a dramatic Chicago trial, Haywood and 165 other Wobblies were indicted for conspiring to obstruct the war. Thereafter for many months federal agents and local police raided IWW halls, destroyed IWW literature, and arrested thousands of Wobblies. In August, 1918, Haywood received a sentence of twenty years and a $30,000 fine. The sentences for Haywood and ninety-two other Wobblies totaled 788

[33] *Stat. at Large*, XL (1917), 217–19.

[34] *Annual Report of the Attorney General of the United States, 1918* (Washington, 1918), 47–53; Peterson and Fite, *Opponents of War*, 35–36, 184–86, 275–76, 280; Kate O'Hare to Otto Branstetter, February 24, 1920, Socialist Party Papers; Stanley Mallach, "Red Kate O'Hare Comes to Madison: The Politics of Free Speech," *Wisconsin Magazine of History*, LIII (Spring, 1970), 204–22.

years; their fines, $2,788,000. Roger Baldwin of the NCLB wrote to Wilson charging that the trial had been unfair and that the Justice Department had continuously prosecuted the IWW and hampered its efforts to raise a defense fund. Wilson did not reply to Baldwin's communication.[35]

The President—and the courts—would prove even more obdurate over Eugene Debs. The magnetic Debs had deliberately set out to get himself arrested. To arouse opposition to the war and to bait the government into trying him under the wartime laws, which he considered unconstitutional, Debs struck out on a lecture tour across the Midwest. With many of his Socialist friends in jail, he wanted "either to open the prison gates or to swing them shut behind himself."[36] The first goal he never achieved; the latter he finally attained. In a long, impassioned speech in Canton, Ohio, on June 16, 1918, he flayed war profiteers and other members of the "master class" and defended Wobblies and Russian Bolsheviks. Thirteen days later a federal grand jury in Cleveland indicted Debs for violation of the Espionage Act. On June 30 he was arrested, and on September 9 he went on trial. He received a sentence of ten years in prison. His lawyers appealed the decision to the Supreme Court on the grounds that the Espionage Act was unconstitutional. Debs was awaiting the court decision when the Armistice came. On March 10, 1919, the Court upheld his conviction, and a month later he entered prison at Moundsville, West Virginia; in June, 1919, he was transferred to the federal prison in Atlanta, Georgia. From Atlanta he would run for the presidency in 1920 on the Socialist ticket.[37]

The Espionage Act had brought Haywood and Debs to trial. In October, 1918, Congress passed another law that served in other ways to combat critics of the war. Designed to "exclude and expel from the United States aliens who are members of the anarchistic and similar classes," the Alien Act empowered the government, upon warrant of the Secretary of Labor, to deport "any alien who, at any

---

[35] "An Open Letter to President Wilson," from "I.W.W. Prisoners at Fort Leavenworth," *One Big Union Monthly*, I (May 1, 1919), 27–28; Philip Taft, "The Federal Trials of the IWW," *Labor History*, III (Winter, 1962), 57–91; Rand School of Social Science, Department of Labor Research, *The American Labor Year Book, 1919–1920* (New York, 1920), 92ff.; *Annual Report of the Attorney General of the United States, 1919* (Washington, 1919), 53–54; Dubofsky, *We Shall Be All*, 423–37; Joseph R. Conlin, *Big Bill Haywood and the Radical Union Movement* (Syracuse, 1969), 177ff.

[36] Ray Ginger, *Eugene V. Debs: A Biography* (New York, 1962), 372.

[37] *Ibid.*, 372–409.

time after entering the United States, is found to have been at the time of entry, or to have become thereafter a member of any anarchist organization."[38] One historian finds this act to have been "drafted and backed by the Department of Justice and the Bureau of Immigration" and "frankly prepared to remove any existing special immunities that favored radical aliens." Now guilt by association, even guilt by underlying thought, had become deportable offenses.[39] Whatever its origin, the Alien Act of 1918 supplied the legal underpinnings for the Palmer raids and the "deportations delirium" of 1919–20. Legislation designed for wartime would, after the Armistice, become a weapon for war upon citizens and aliens who, through belief or even association with suspect organizations, earned the wrath of hysterical government officials.

Either because they anticipated such action or because, on principle, they had always opposed the laws, critics of this wartime legislation began to work for its repeal immediately after the Armistice; in the meantime, they also tried to gain release for political prisoners already convicted under the laws. Along with Haywood and Debs, several figures on trial for their political views became celebrated symbols in 1919–20, as their supporters tried to keep them out of jail and their detractors sought to put them or keep them there: Socialist Victor Berger of Wisconsin, who at the time of his election to Congress in November, 1918, was under indictment for alleged violation of the Espionage Act; John Reed, radical young man of letters whose brilliant account of the Russian Revolution, *Ten Days That Shook the World*, brought him fame but whose activities on the Greenwich Village radical magazine, *The Masses*, brought him indictment under the Espionage Act; and Tom Mooney and Warren Billings, reputed anarchists charged with exploding a bomb in a preparedness parade in San Francisco on July 22, 1916, whose trial dragged on for many months amidst hysteria, perjury, and class animosities, with the two men finally spending twenty years in prison until they were pardoned in 1938.[40] The opposition and support that

[38] *Stat. at Large*, XL (1917–18), 1012; Kansas, *U.S. Immigration*, 58–59.

[39] Preston, *Aliens and Dissenters*, 182–83. Cf. discussion of the law by Anthony Caminetti, commissioner of immigration, in *Annual Report of the Secretary of Labor, 1918* (Washington, 1919), 278–80.

[40] On Berger, an informative essay is Edward J. Muzik, "Victor L. Berger: Congress and the Red Scare," *Wisconsin Magazine of History*, XLVII (Summer, 1964), 309–18; see also Roderick Nash, "Victor L. Berger: Making Marx Respectable," *ibid.*, 301–8. The standard biography of Reed is Granville Hicks, *John Reed: The*

these men raised demonstrate the deep conflict in American thought after the war between those who would sustain the conformity and chauvinism of wartime and those who would not. Rather than dying out after the Armistice, that conflict grew more and more impassioned through the postwar months and climaxed with the Palmer raids of January, 1920.

Even in November, 1918, in the midst of Armistice rejoicing, dissension and fear were manifest. Late in the month the NCLB registered a complaint with the War Department against treatment of conscientious objectors at Fort Leavenworth. Veteran muckraker Upton Sinclair launched a petition to Wilson calling for pardon of all men convicted on charges of opposing the war. Socialists in San Francisco and New York began raising funds to help finance Tom Mooney's defense.[41] The Supreme Court refused to review the Mooney-Billings case, but the court that had earlier sentenced Mooney to die commuted his sentence to life imprisonment.

The pleas for clemency were lost in the clamour for loyalty and security. The AFL was typical. At a Pan American Labor Conference in Laredo, Texas, several delegates offered a resolution asking for "justice and protection" for workers still in jail in the United States. When it became evident that Bill Haywood was one such worker, a storm of dissent broke out, and American labor leaders took turns denouncing Haywood. Said AFL President Gompers in reference to the IWW: "We could not tolerate any agency to interfere with our work for this holy war." Charles H. Moyer, who years earlier had stood trial along with Haywood in Boise, Idaho, on the charge of murdering Governor Frank Steunenberg, told the labor delegates: "Haywood is alive—in prison, a fate he richly merits. I warn you against him and his propaganda."[42]

On November 22 a Senate committee voted 9–2 to dismiss disloyalty charges against Senator La Follette, who had voted against the war declaration in 1917 and had spoken against the war while it was on; despite the vote, La Follette thought the "barbed wire fence"

Making of a Revolutionary (New York, 1936), but see also John Reed, *The Education of John Reed: Selected Writings*, with an introductory essay by John Stuart (New York, 1955). A major piece of research on Mooney and Billings is Richard H. Frost, *The Mooney Case* (Stanford, 1968).

[41] *New York Times*, November 13, 1918, 5:2; November 19, 1918, 22:3; November 20, 1918, 24:6; and November 25, 1918, 13:5.

[42] *New York Times*, November 16, 1918, 22:1–2; *Monthly Labor Review*, VIII (January, 1919), 302–4.

of suspicion had still not been cleared away.[43] He was right, though the suspicion extended beyond his personal case. Immediately after the Armistice, one of the largest patriotic organizations in the country, the American Defense Society, declared its opposition to the use of red flags in parades and at the same time warned its members against any sympathy for Germans.[44] The Society lumped Reds and Germans together. Other Americans, however, had begun to make a finer distinction and wanted to focus on Reds alone. Germany had surrendered; a new enemy now threatened.

Thanksgiving Day sermons across the land echoed warnings against Bolshevism. The United Spanish War Veterans denounced it. Ex-president William Howard Taft said it must be stamped out. The National Security League, an organization created before the war to promote military preparedness and which survived the war as a nationwide and well-financed agency promoting its particular version of patriotism, began an anti-Bolshevik campaign in December. An old Socialist, John Spargo, publicly denounced Bolshevism, as did more predictable figures such as Nicholas Murray Butler of Columbia University. As the new year began, Samuel Gompers pledged the AFL to fight against the spread of Bolshevism, while the Massachusetts Chamber of Commerce sought funds to fight the menace, and Secretary of Commerce William Redfield assailed it in an address to the National Foreign Trade Council.[45]

Amidst this growing alarm—and it would grow more shrill and more pervasive—a few signs of protest and even moderation appeared. Congressman James L. Frear of Wisconsin proposed that Congress investigate the National Security League, which, according to Frear, had smeared numerous congressmen, impugned their loyalty, and prostituted the name "Americanism" through proselytizing an "insolent" self-styled standard of behavior. A House committee did hold a few hearings, though these did little more than reveal the

[43] *New York Times*, November 16, 1918, 9:3; Belle C. and Fola La Follette, *Robert M. La Follette* (New York, 1953), II, 910–13.

[44] *New York Times*, November 14, 1918, 12:8; November 17, 1918, 11:2; and Joan M. Jensen, *The Price of Vigilance* (Chicago, 1968), 96.

[45] *New York Times*, November 29, 1918, 4:2; December 8, 1919, II, 1:1; December 10, 1918, 15:2; December 16, 1918, 3:6 and 5:5; January 8, 1919, 3:5; January 11, 1919, 12:8; January 15, 1919, 2:7; January 28, 1919, 2:7. On the National Security League's wartime activities and its affluent membership, see National Security League folder, Box 136, Elihu Root Papers, Division of Manuscripts, Library of Congress. Root was honorary president of the League in 1917–18.

League's wealthy patrons.[46] Several members of the Senate began to urge repeal of the Espionage Act, and in March Wilson commuted the sentences of fifty individuals convicted under the act.[47] In February the court dismissed an indictment brought against John Reed for making seditious speeches.[48] In Butte, Montana, W. F. Dunne, a Socialist leader of the town's electrical workers, won the Democratic nomination for mayor, though he had recently been convicted of sedition under wartime laws—evidence of Butte's Socialist and Wobbly heritage more than of the nation's tolerance.[49]

More revealing of the national mood was the fact that Victor Berger, elected to Congress in November, 1918, while under indictment for alleged violations of the Espionage Act, found himself barred from taking his seat. In December he went on trial, and in February he was sentenced to twenty years in prison.[50] Meanwhile, in January, forty-six Wobblies were sentenced in Sacramento for wartime "sabotage." About the same time twenty-seven more Wobblies received prison terms at a trial in Kansas.[51] In March the Supreme Court upheld the conviction of Eugene Debs. At the same time it handed down a decision that gave expression to Oliver Wendell Holmes's classic "clear and present danger" test of free speech. Speaking for a unanimous court, Holmes upheld the Espionage Act as not violating the First Amendment and found that Charles Schenck, who in 1917 had circulated pamphlets in Philadelphia comparing a conscript to a convict and urging readers to strike down this militarism, had violated the wartime law. Eight months later, evidently due to the influence upon him of Harvard law professor Zechariah Chafee, Jr., Holmes adopted a stricter definition of the word "intent" and in *Abrams et al.* v. *United States* entered a dissenting (and minority) view. This time Holmes defended the right of Jacob Abrams and associates to publish leaflets denouncing American intervention in the Bolshevik Revolution. Again, Holmes coined a classic phrase.

[46] *Cong. Rec.*, 65 Cong., 2 sess. (September 23, 1918), 10664–68; (March 3, 1919), 4921–25; Norman Hapgood, ed., *Professional Patriots* (New York, 1927).

[47] *Cong. Rec.*, 65 Cong., 3 sess. (January 9, 1919), 1171–73; (February 8, 1919), 2936, 2968; (February 12, 1919), 3230; *Annual Report of the Attorney General of the United States for 1919* (Washington, 1919), 506–9.

[48] Hicks, *John Reed*, 339–40.

[49] *New York Times*, March 26, 1919, 24:6; Weinstein, *Decline of Socialism*, 205–6.

[50] Muzik, "Victor L. Berger."

[51] Dubofsky, *We Shall Be All*, 438–43.

Truth, he argued in his *Abrams* dissent, was the only grounds upon which public policy could safely rest: "The best test of truth is the power of the thought to get itself accepted in the competition of the market."[52]

Holmes and the American public appeared to be moving in opposite directions, however. While the Justice had, along with his associate Louis D. Brandeis, moved toward defense of free speech, the uproar over Bolshevism and other presumed enemies within the republic became tumultuous. This mass hysteria (which it clearly seemed to be) has been subjected to considerable analysis, both by contemporaries and by later appraisers. In 1923 former Assistant Secretary of Labor Louis F. Post published *The Deportations Delirium of Ninteen-Twenty*, the story of "that delirious outburst in the United States against resident aliens which closely followed the World War and was generally known as 'the Red Crusade.' "[53] Post was no professional psychologist; he evidently used the term that came naturally to mind—delirium seemed to be the only word for the behavior he described.

Historians have, by and large, agreed with Post. In his brilliant study, *Strangers in the Land*, John Higham in 1955 wrote: "It is hard to explain the tug of wartime passions on the postwar mind except in terms at least partly psychological. The clamour for absolute loyalty, continuing relentlessly into peacetime, spoke, perhaps, an unwillingness to surrender the psychic gratifications the war had offered." The war had stimulated the warmth of nationalism; the sense of identity with a powerful nation and its cause evoked a feeling of security not easily put aside. Men who felt it "had little difficulty supposing that the war had not ended, that the adversary had merely assumed another guise and still presented a deadly challenge to loyalty and a summons to hatred."[54] A decade after Higham offered such an analysis, Stanley Coben published a learned essay that incorporated evidence on human behavior collected by anthropologists and social psychologists. Coben's study of the Red Scare suggests that millions of Americans are permanently ready to launch a purge. Hostile toward certain minorities, fanatically patriotic, certain that

[52] Fred D. Ragan, "Justice Oliver Wendell Holmes, Jr., Zechariah Chafee, Jr., and the Clear and Present Danger Test for Free Speech: The First Year, 1919," *Journal of American History*, LVIII (June, 1971), 24–25.

[53] Louis F. Post, *Deportations Delirium* (Chicago, 1923).

[54] John Higham, *Strangers in the Land* (New York, 1963), 222.

internal enemies threaten national welfare, they are ready to seek security from the intruder they see threatening their psychic equilibrium. In 1919 the rapid changes in American life brought on first by industrialization and urbanization and then by World War I may have left many Americans in such disequilibrium that they could not relieve their anxieties and regain their sense of security without drastic action. The postwar drive for "100% Americanism" and the anti-Red hysteria may well have been an attempt to reaffirm traditional beliefs and customs and to enforce conformity by eradicating the alien who appeared to be wrecking the traditional society. Deportation was, literally, a purge.[55]

Yet there may have been more rationality, more conscious and deliberate motivation, behind the Scare than this retrospective psychoanalysis indicates. When the wartime crusade against things German surged into the postwar period as a crusade against things "un-American," it was not entirely fortuitous—or irrational—that the enemy was now labeled Red. For if Americans in 1919 were hungering for the security that nationalism brings, if they feared the intrusion of alien ideas and values, nothing at war's end seemed a greater threat to the established American economic and social order than the Bolshevism currently exploding out of Russia. It is now a common if not the unanimous view among students of World War I that Woodrow Wilson himself feared revolution and was determined to carry American-style liberal capitalism out into the world as an alternative to the equally proselytizing ideas represented by Lenin and the Russian Bolsheviks.[56] Surrounding Wilson were men such as Robert Lansing and Herbert Hoover, equally and sometimes more determined in their reasoned opposition to the Bolshevik Revolution. And a considerable body of Americans agreed with them.[57] The irrational behavior, the psychic trembling, arose over the presumed appearance within the United States of a movement inspired and led

[55] Stanley Coben, "A Study in Nativism: The American Red Scare of 1910–20," *Political Science Quarterly*, LXXIX (March, 1964), 52–75.

[56] Two recent studies that offer this thesis are Arno J. Mayer, *Politics and Diplomacy of Peacemaking: Containment and Counterrevolution at Versailles, 1918–1919* (New York, 1967); and N. Gordon Levin, Jr., *Woodrow Wilson and World Politics: America's Response to War and Revolution* (New York, 1968). But see the older, and influential, studies by William Appleman Williams, *The Tragedy of American Diplomacy* (Cleveland, 1959), and "American Intervention in Russia, 1917–1920," *Studies on the Left*, III (Fall, 1963), 24–48; IV (Winter, 1964), 39–57.

[57] Peter G. Filene, *Americans and the Soviet Experiment, 1917–1933* (Cambridge, 1967), 39–63.

by Bolsheviks and their American cohorts intent upon taking over the country. For those prone to find it, the evidence for such a program lay all around them in 1919. For those not yet persuaded of the threat, countless agencies and individuals appeared ready to convince them.

In March, Governor John H. Bartlett of New Hampshire signed an "anti-revolution" bill and announced plans to rid New Hampshire of Bolsheviks. In the U.S. Senate a judiciary subcommittee which had been investigating pro-German propaganda in the United States veered left in early February and began studying Bolshevik propaganda instead. On March 10 the committee received evidence supplied by Postmaster General Albert Burleson that the IWW, among other organizations, was in its main essentials a Bolshevik agency. Burleson, who described the evidence as "matter which has been found in the mails since the signing of the Armistice," had been a real watchdog in his office from the day Wilson appointed him. Censorship, interception, and scrutiny of other peoples' mail was nothing new to him.[58] The committee's hearings enjoyed wide publicity all through the spring, and by summer, 1919, enthusiasm for action was rampant. The Allied Loyalty League was formed to fight Reds. Governor J. J. Cornwall of West Virginia told a national paint, oil, and varnish association that radicals planned to overthrow the government. The Benevolent Order of the Elks pledged to fight the menace, as did the Knights of Columbus and the Lithuanian Catholic Society of America.[59]

Much of this uproar evidently was in response to a series of events in 1919 that did, in the context of the times, seem perilous to those Americans prone to feel imperiled. In February "the first major general strike in American history" began in Seattle, when some 60,000 organized workmen failed to report for work, schools closed, and the downtown city became all but deserted. By the time the strike ended in failure for the workers, Mayor Ole Hanson had become, at least by his own grandiose conception, an anti-Bolshevik hero who spent

[58] *New York Times,* March 30, 1919, 18:3; Burleson to Lee S. Overman, February 18, 1919, in Senate Judiciary Subcommittee, *Bolshevik Propaganda* (65 Cong., 3 sess.), 1110ff. A fuller report, covering the original object of German propaganda as well as the later Bolshevik material, is in Senate Subcommittee of the Judiciary Committee, *Brewing and Liquor Interests and German and Bolshevik Propaganda* (66 Cong., 1 sess., 1919), Serial 7597–99.

[59] *New York Times,* July 10, 1919, 15:4; July 27, 1919, 14:1; August 17, 1919, IV, 7:4; August 19, 1919, 32:2; September 23, 1919, 19:8.

much of the next twelve months proclaiming the danger of revolution and himself as savior from the menace.[60] In September, 1919, after months of tension and bargaining, a harrowing and bitter strike in the steel industry broke out, during which U.S. Steel played upon existing anxiety and charged labor with Bolshevik affiliation. Some notable American Communists were, in fact, actively backing the strike, though most labor leaders, especially those in the AFL, were desperately trying to affirm their own Americanism, and many American Communists actually opposed the strike as a futile trade-union tactic.[61] Also in September police in Boston went on strike, and newspapers promptly labeled their action Bolshevik. Governor Calvin Coolidge of Massachusetts for a moment became a national celebrity when he turned out the entire State Guard and called upon loyal policemen as well to aid him in restoring "law and order" and, in a judgment on the strike, declared: "There is no right to strike against the public safety by anybody, anywhere, any time."[62] Paralleling these strikes on the West Coast and the eastern seaboard, strikes and violence erupted in the South and in the Rocky Mountains in 1919.[63] Then in November the United Mine Workers struck the coal industry, and immediately American Legion posts, the National Security League, and other patriotic societies cried for action to prevent a Bolshevik revolution in the coal industry. The mine companies emulated their steel compatriots and declared the strike a Bolshevik plot.[64]

In this context of postwar economic readjustments, of wartime nationalism seeking new outlets of expression, and in a world where Bolshevik Revolution was—at least in Russia—a hard reality, the

[60] Robert L. Friedheim, *The Seattle General Strike* (Seattle, 1964). The Hanson rhetoric may be sampled in his *Americanism versus Bolshevism* (Garden City, N.Y., 1920) and his "Fighting the Reds in Their Home Town," *World's Work*, XXXIX (December, 1919–March, 1920), 123–26, 302–7, 401–8, 484–87.

[61] David Brody, *Labor in Crisis: The Steel Strike of 1919* (Philadelphia, 1965); Irving Bernstein, *The Lean Years: A History of the American Worker, 1920–1933* (Boston, 1960), 93; Draper, *Roots of American Communism*, 197–201.

[62] Donald R. McCoy, *Calvin Coolidge: The Quiet President* (New York, 1967), 83–94.

[63] Wayne Flynt, "Florida Labor and Political Radicalism, 1919–1920," *Labor History*, IX (Winter, 1968), 73–90; Philip L. Cook, "Red Scare in Denver," *The Colorado Magazine*, XLIII (Fall, 1966), 309–26.

[64] *Reports of the Department of Labor, 1920* (Washington, 1921), 103–15; A. Ford Hinrichs, *The United Mine Workers of America and the Non-Union Coal Fields* (New York, 1923); Selig Perlman and Philip Taft, *History of Labor in the United States* (New York, 1935), IV, 469–88.

catalyst to panic came with a series of inexplicable bombings around the country. As Robert Murray has suggested, "the word 'radical' in 1919 automatically carried with it the implication of dynamite." The current stereotype portrayed the Red with "wild eyes, bushy, unkempt hair, and tattered clothes, holding a smoking bomb in his hands."[65] In the spring of 1919, when some bombs began to go off, American radicals instantly became suspect. In March the *Chicago Tribune* announced discovery of a radical plot to plant bombs in Chicago. In Franklin, Massachusetts, where four men died from a bomb explosion, IWW literature was found in the room where they died. Already the IWW had been linked to bombings when, in Sacramento in January, forty-six Wobblies had been found guilty of sabotage, some of it with bombs, though the reconstructed ingredients of the bombs that the government offered as evidence were labeled "ol' rags an' bottles" by *Nation* magazine.[66] On April 28 a homemade bomb arrived by mail at the office of Mayor Ole Hanson in Seattle. A leak in the package led to discovery of the bomb before it exploded. The next day, a similar package arrived at the home of former Georgia Senator Thomas W. Hardwick of Atlanta. The maid opened the package, the bomb exploded, and she lost both hands. Other people began to receive bomb packages. Sixteen of them turned up in a New York post office when a perceptive clerk discovered them in time. Post offices, now on the alert, finally intercepted eighteen more. The bombs, all Judge Kenesaw M. Landis, who had sentenced Victor Berger and Bill alike and in uniform wrappers, had been mailed to men with reputations for anti-radicalism, such as Anthony J. Caminetti, commissioner of immigration; Senator Lee S. Overman, chairman of the Senate committee investigating Bolshevism; Postmaster General Albert S. Burleson, notorious for his wartime bans on radical literature; and Haywood. Then on the evening of June 2, within the same hour, more bombs exploded in eight different cities. In at least six cases the evident target was a public official of some note, such as Attorney General Palmer. The Palmer family had just gone to bed that evening when the front of their Washington home was demolished by the explosive. The bomb-thrower had made a miscalculation. He evidently stumbled on the front step, set off the bomb prematurely, and

---

[65] Robert K. Murray, *Red Scare: A Study in National Hysteria, 1919–1920* (Minneapolis, 1955), 68–69.

[66] *New York Times*, January 17, 1919, 1:4; March 2, 1919, 6:2; Dubofsky, *We Shall Be All*, 440.

blew himself to bits. Enough of his body and clothing remained intact to indicate that he was an Italian alien from Philadelphia. An anarchist pamphlet found near the door read in part: "We will destroy. . . . We are ready to do anything and everything to suppress the capitalist class. [signed] THE ANARCHIST FIGHTERS." [67]

Newspapers publicized the bombings with glaring banners—and often with equally blaring emotion. Attorney General Palmer in June asked Congress for immediate funds to help protect the country from bombings. Senator Overman called a special session of his subcommittee on Bolshevik propaganda. Several bills designed to curb Bolshevism were introduced in a special session of Congress in May and June. And Ole Hanson gave voice to what soon became a widespread chorus: deport all radicals. At Fort Collins, Colorado, General Leonard Wood, a leading contender for the Democratic presidential nomination in 1920, asserted his motto, tactic, and rationale for dealing with Reds: "S.O.S.—ship or shoot. I believe we should place them all on ships of stone, with sails of lead and that their first stopping place should be hell. We must advocate radical laws to deal with radical people." [68]

Even while the drive for deportation of alien radicals was gaining speed, sporadic raids on homegrown radicals began. In June, New York state officials raided the Rand School of Social Science in New York, as well as the headquarters of the IWW and the left-wing Socialists. [69] The raids were the work of the Lusk Committee, created by the New York legislature in March "to investigate the scope, tendencies, and ramifications of . . . seditious activities and report the results of its investigations to the legislature." State Senator Clayton R. Lusk, committee chairman, declared that the purpose of the raids was "Names!—Names of all parlor bolsheviki, IWW, and socialists. They will be a real help to us later on." [70]

[67] Murray, *Red Scare*, 79; *Attorney General A. Mitchell Palmer on Charges Made against Department of Justice by Louis F. Post and Others*, Hearings before the Committee on Rules, House of Representatives (Washington, 1920), 165.

[68] *Cong. Rec.*, 66 Cong., 1 sess. (June 30, 1919), 2050; *New York Times*, May 26, 1919, 17:3; June 4, 1919, 2:5; June 19, 1919, 15:8; Cook, "Red Scare in Denver," 316.

[69] The Rand School was founded in 1906 to "offer to the public an opportunity for the systematic study of socialism." The school provided courses in history, economics, socialist theory, and other subjects, as well as special lectures and conferences. See "The Rand School of Social Science," Box 6, Socialist Party Papers.

[70] The published report of the Lusk Committee, *Revolutionary Radicalism: Its History, Purpose and Tactics*, 4 vols. (Albany, 1920), contains an outstanding set of

Later the tactics of the Lusk Committee grew in popularity else-where in the nation, as did still other means of defending the repub-lic.[71] In July, Attorney General Palmer complained about the lack of any law enabling him to deport aliens. Under existing legislation, only those guilty of advocating anarchist ideas could be expelled. Even so, the law (the Immigration Act of 1918) was so murky that it had already been used as the basis for deporting thirty-six Seattle Wobblies, who were put on board a "Red Special" and, amidst high publicity, rushed toward Ellis Island for deportation. There the Wob-blies became caught up in a conflict between the Immigration Bureau and the Department of Labor that presaged further conflict to come between the two agencies when, following the massive raids late in 1919 and early in 1920, the bureau would seek to deport virtually at will, while the Labor Department would act with much more re-straint.[72] But meanwhile, the Justice Department precipitated much of the federal government's anti-radical action of 1919. The key figure in that department was Attorney General Palmer.

Initially after the war Palmer was every inch the liberal.[73] He even argued for Debs's release from prison. But then, either out of growing presidential ambition or out of his own genuine mounting hysteria or both, he began to respond to the increasing public hostility toward radicals. That he himself had been the target of an anarchistic bomb-thrower could hardly have been irrelevant. In the summer of 1919 he began to move against radicalism. In August he established a general intelligence, or anti-radical, division in the Justice Depart-ment. At its head he placed young J. Edgar Hoover, who promptly began to assemble an elaborate card index file of radical organiza-tions, publications, and leaders.[74] On November 7, Justice Depart-

---

documents—though the conclusions of the committee itself are always dubious and often absurd. The comment by Lusk above is quoted in Murray, *Red Scare*, 100. Thomas E. Vadney, "The Politics of Repression, a Case Study of the Red Scare in New York," *New York History*, XLIX (January, 1968), 56–75, deals with the ouster in 1920 of five Socialists from the New York state assembly.

[71] Cf. the reactions of the press and city governments in Colorado and Florida. Cook, "Red Scare in Denver," and Flynt, "Florida Labor and Political Radicalism."

[72] Preston, *Aliens and Dissenters*, 198ff.; Zechariah Chafee, Jr., *Freedom of Speech* (New York, 1920), 240.

[73] Stanley Coben, *A. Mitchell Palmer: Politician* (New York, 1963), 198, 201.

[74] Robert K. Murray, "The Outer World and the Inner Light: A Case Study," *Pennsylvania History*, XXXVI (July, 1969), 265–89; *Report of Attorney General, 1919*, 15; Chafee, *Freedom of Speech*, 269–72; Max Lowenthal, *The Federal Bureau of Investigation* (New York, 1950), 83ff.

ment agents raided the headquarters and branches of a New York labor society, the Union of Russian Workers. State and local officials carried out smaller raids on suspected radicals throughout the country, and state legislatures passed a mass of "criminal syndicalism" laws, "red flag" laws, and other measures designed to stifle the IWW and other revolutionary movements.[75]

Congress, in response to a barrage of petitions and appeals to "drive from these shores all disloyal aliens," began to formulate deportation bills. Senator Kenneth McKellar of Tennessee even proposed that radical native-born Americans be expelled to a special penal colony on Guam.[76] As one contemporary critic observed, some of the proposed bills were "evidently struck off in the characteristically American reaction to unpleasant events—to pass a law to stop them, without much thought as to [the law's consequences and implementation]."[77] For example, Congressman James B. Aswell of Louisiana prepared a bill to punish by death any aliens found guilty of throwing a bomb or committing "any act with the object to destroy life or property." Senator Harry S. New of Indiana introduced an anti–red flag bill, endorsed by the National Security League, to penalize by fine (up to $5,000) or imprisonment (five years) or both anyone displaying a red or black flag or emblem at a meeting or parade. The Kansas legislature carried this notion a step further and forbade use of any emblem of any hue if it was "distinctive of bolshevism, anarchism, or radical socialism." A number of bills appeared in Congress to check immigration, forecasts of the 1921 and 1924 exclusion acts. Other bills, drawn to implement Americanization of aliens, were in fashion with the drive already begun to achieve "100% Americanism." During the 66th Congress fourteen bills dealing with naturalization or immigration were introduced. In December, Congressman Albert Johnson of Washington offered all of them as a single package. Another Johnson bill defined "anarchistic and similar classes" to include those who distributed handbills or displayed cartoons—and made such actions a deportable offense.[78]

[75] *New York Times*, November 8, 1919, 1; Murray, *Red Scare*, 196–97; Elbridge F. Dowell, *A History of Criminal Syndicalist Legislation in the United States* (Baltimore, 1939), 89ff.; Chafee, *Freedom of Speech*, 187–94.

[76] *Cong. Rec.*, 66 Cong., 2 sess. (December 20, 1919; January 10, 1920), 990ff., 1334.

[77] Kate H. Claghorn, "Alien and Sedition Bills Up-to-Date," *Survey*, XLII (July 19, 1919), 590–92.

[78] *Cong. Rec.*, 66 Cong., 1 sess. (May 29, 1919), 391, 428; (June 12, 1919), 1064;

Not all of these bills met with unanimous approval. Senator Borah, who in February, 1919, had allowed his name to appear on the letterhead of an anti-Bolshevik newspaper association, was by 1920 alarmed over the course of events. He praised *New York World* editor Frank Cobb for his "splendid editorial upon the strange lunacy which is now prevalent . . . —this idea that you must destroy all guarantees of the Constitution in order to preserve the rights of the American people." To a correspondent who had evidently provoked him, Borah declared, "We cannot deal with the situation which now confronts us by deporting a few people. Besides, why should we deport people into Russia and then go to the great expense of sending troops over there to shoot them?"[79] Opinion from a number of liberal journals was equally caustic. "What," asked a *Survey* editorialist, "is going to be the outcome of all this legislation? Will it stop unrest? Yes! Just as shaving the dog will keep his hair from growing. In fact, shaving is said to promote growth."[80]

But Palmer had begun shaving. On December 21 some 250 deportees set sail for Russia from New York aboard the U.S.S. *Buford*, promptly labeled the "Soviet Ark." Then late in the afternoon on Friday, January 2, 1920, Justice Department agents, in a concerted raid on Communist (and reputedly Communist) headquarters, began arresting thousands of persons in major American cities. They poured into private homes and clubs, pool halls and cafes, and seized citizens and aliens, Communists and non-Communists, and tore apart meeting halls and damaged and destroyed property. In two days close to 5,000 persons were arrested, and possibly another 1,000 were jailed in the mopping up that followed during the next few weeks. The arrests were carried out with total disregard for due process, and the treatment of the masses under arrest was sometimes barbarous. Agents jailed their prizes, held them incommunicado and without

(November 3, 1919), 7881; (November 19, 1919), 8823. For the mood of congressional debate by the end of the year, see *ibid.*, 66 Cong., 2 sess. (December 20, 1919), 983–1002; for list of immigration bills, see *ibid.*, 66 Cong., 1 sess., 9405; for list of alien bills, *ibid.*, 9421; also *Survey*, XL (January 10, 1920), 387–88; and Kate H. Claghorn, "Aliens and Sedition in the New Year," *Survey*, XLIII (January 17, 1920), 422–23. For discussion of various federal sedition bills, see Chafee, *Freedom of Speech*, 194ff.

[79] Clyde P. Steen, president, National Association of City Editors, to Borah, February 20, 1919; Borah to Cobb, January 13, 1920; Borah to Warren E. Dennis, January 5, 1920, Box 197, Borah Papers.

[80] *Survey*, XLIII (January 17, 1920), 423.

counsel, and interrogated them. Those who could demonstrate American citizenship gained release, though often into the custody of state officials who hoped to try them under state syndicalist laws. Aliens were released a few days later unless they were members of the Communist party or the Communist Labor party. These the Justice Department hoped to deport.[81]

Under existing immigration law, only the Department of Labor and its subordinate agencies, such as the Bureau of Immigration, had authority to arrest and deport aliens. For some time during and since the war the Immigration Bureau had cooperated with the Justice Department by launching deportation proceedings against aliens, once the Justice agents had arrested them. This was cooperation, but it was illegal, and J. Edgar Hoover admitted as much. There was, he said, "no authority under the law permitting this Department to take any action in deportation proceedings relative to radical activities."[82] But Anthony Caminetti, commissioner general of the Immigration Bureau, was seemingly as committed to an anti-radical drive as were Palmer and Hoover, and by January, 1920, the Justice Department and the Immigration Bureau had evolved a technique: raid swiftly, seize evidence, and, while holding them in isolation, cross-examine aliens before they could gain legal counsel, and then deport. As William Preston suggests, "Like a pig in a Chicago packing plant, the immigrant would be caught in a moving assembly line, stripped of all his rights, and packaged for shipment overseas—all in one efficient and uninterrupted operation."[83] Yet, as Preston then shows, Hoover's and Caminetti's efficiency was their undoing. They were administrators, not policy-makers or judges, and the very excesses of the raids, their blatant disregard for fundamental rights, aroused opposition from individuals and organizations that, until now, had not been vocal in opposition to the Red hysteria. Suddenly a renewed appreciation for toleration and freedom of expression arose. The Interchurch World Movement denounced the lawlessness of the raids. A committee of twelve prestigious lawyers and law professors issued

---

[81] Coben, *Palmer*, 223–30; Murray, *Red Scare*, 212–17; Draper, *Roots of American Communism*, 202–4; Preston, *Aliens and Dissenters*, 220–21; Kate H. Claghorn, *The Immigrant's Day in Court* (New York, 1923), 444ff.; Post, *Deportations Delirium*, 1–148.

[82] On laws and procedures for deporting aliens, see Claghorn, *Immigrant's Day in Court*; Hoover quoted in Preston, *Aliens and Dissenters*, 210.

[83] Preston, *Aliens and Dissenters*, 220.

a *Report* which censured the department for its infractions of the Bill of Rights.[84]

Perhaps most crucial was the response within the Department of Labor. Secretary William B. Wilson had never condoned the anti-radicals in his department, but he was unaware of their machinations until the raids occurred. He promptly repudiated them, restored due process in deportations, and improved control over hearings for aliens. Assistant Secretary of Labor Louis F. Post, who carefully and personally reviewed case after case, refused to adopt the sweeping definition of the law that Palmer, Hoover, and Caminetti had wanted to apply. Secretary Wilson ruled that mere membership in the Communist party was not sufficient justification for deportation. Post, who had final authority to sign deportation orders, refused to deport the hundreds of aliens who, though arrested, were obviously unfamiliar with illegal doctrines. Post estimated that the Department of Labor, on behalf of the Justice Department's detectives, had issued about 6,000 warrants of arrest for alien "Reds." Palmer's agents had carried out some 4,000 arrests, but after hearings Post cancelled the warrants for about 3,000 of these. Less than 1,000 deportations resulted from the Palmer raids.[85] The earlier cooperation between the Justice and Labor departments turned to bitter enmity, and Palmer finally forced an investigation of Post and Secretary Wilson. The inquiry aborted, and Post, if anything, emerged with an enhanced reputation. Palmer continued to aspire for higher office.[86]

[84] Murray, *Red Scare*, 239ff.; National Popular Government League, *Report upon the Illegal Activities of the United States Department of Justice* (Washington, 1920).

[85] Preston, *Aliens and Dissenters*, 222–25; Post, *Deportations Delirium*, 167; cf. figures by Caminetti in *Reports of the Department of Labor, 1920* (Washington, 1921), 312–13.

Probably the most notable figure deported was Emma Goldman, anarchist, lecturer, publicist, feminist, agitator for free speech, advocate of birth control, and critic of Soviet Communism. Along with her notorious friend Alexander Berkman, "Red Emma" had been arrested and imprisoned during the war. In 1919 J. Edgar Hoover set out to deport both her and Berkman. In November, 1920, her old friend Louis Post reluctantly signed the deportation order. In his view she had to be deported, given the law as it stood, though it troubled him to enforce it. Emma Goldman never forgave him. See *Letter from the Attorney General: Investigation Activities of the Department of Justice*, 66 Cong., 1 sess., Sen. Doc. 153 (Washington, 1919); Post, *Deportations Delirium*, 12–21; Emma Goldman, *Living My Life* (New York, 1931), II, 708ff.; Richard Drinnon, *Rebel in Paradise* (Chicago, 1961).

[86] House Committee on Rules, *Investigation of Administration of Louis F. Post, Assistant Secretary of Labor, in the Matter of Deportation of Aliens* (Washington, 1920), Hearing, 66 Cong., 2 sess.; Post, *Deportations Delirium*, 223–74.

Meanwhile, the Red Scare abated. The great labor conflicts of 1919 had eased off, leaving American workers discouraged and defeated. If the strikes of 1919 had fed the fear of social revolution, labor's retreat into quiescence now created a reassuring calm, as American labor entered the "lean years" of the Twenties.[87] The final withdrawal of American troops from Russia in 1920 and the failure of Communist revolutions in Germany and Central Europe brought at best a certain reassurance, though one student of American attitudes toward Soviet Russia sees the violence of the Red Scare settling into "an apolitical complacency" soon after the raids. The stereotyped Russian, "though still bearded," became "simply a plaintive old man, vulnerable to intoxicating theories."[88] Palmer himself kept on raising the spectre of Bolshevism, and in the weeks before May Day, 1920, he issued elaborate warnings against violence, terror, and plots that might erupt on that historic day. When nothing of the sort occurred, Palmer promptly claimed credit—his timely warnings had staved off revolution.[89] By now even Congress (at least some of it) was irritated with the attorney general.[90] Just as it wound up its investigations of Louis Post, it invited Palmer to appear before the House Rules Committee and defend his actions. Palmer read a long speech, one that required two sessions of the committee. The committee decided to drop its inquiry, and the attorney general went on working for the presidential nomination.[91]

Palmer's failure at the convention did not necessarily mark a return

[87] Bernstein, *Lean Years.*

[88] Filene, *Americans and Soviet Experiment,* 63–64.

[89] Coben, *Palmer,* 234–36; Murray, *Red Scare,* 252–53.

[90] Cf. remarks by Congressman Albert Johnson of Washington and Congressman George Huddleston of Alabama on Louis Post's actions. In April, Johnson (who would sponsor the 1921 act restricting immigration) complained that "the radicals, both native and alien, are organized as never before. They defend each other. It makes no difference to what particular organization they belong, or what they call themselves. Anarchist, communist, syndicalist—they are all the same. They connive day and night for the same thing. They know what they want—revolution by force." Huddleston deplored the raids and commented that "a great many of those arrested did not know the difference between Bolshevism and rheumatism. They were illiterate, they were poor, they were friendless, aliens many of them, and far from home. They were not voters, and they had no money; they had no voice, and so they had no champion." *Cong. Rec.,* 66 Cong., 2 sess. (April 12, 1920), 5551; (April 23, 1920), 6086.

[91] Coben, *Palmer,* 241–42; House Committee on Rules, *Attorney General A. Mitchell Palmer on Charges Made against Department of Justice by Louis F. Post and Others,* Hearings, 66 Cong., 2 sess. (Washington, 1920); Post, *Deportations Delirium,* 269–71.

to moderation in American politics, though clearly the hysterical phase of the Red Scare had passed by late 1920. Events in New York helped break the spell. The absurd excesses of the Lusk inquiry there, along with the state legislature's attempt to expel five Socialist members, finally provoked some imposing and influential figures in the state to demand, and gain, a halt to such inanities. An aroused professor of law at Harvard University in 1920 described the course of events that led up to the expulsion attempt:

Since the 15th day of June, 1917 [with passage of the Espionage Act], the nation had been led on by its panic-stricken fear of adverse opinion to abandon one national tradition after another. . . . One by one, the right of freedom of speech, the right of assembly, the right to petition, the right to protection against unreasonable searches and seizures, the right against arbitrary arrest, the right to a fair trial, the hatred of spies, the principle that guilt is personal, the principle that punishment should bear some proportion to the offense, had been sacrificed and ignored. . . . At last the leaders of thought were awakened to the realization that a government cannot be saved, is not worth saving, at the cost of its own principles.[92]

The "leaders of thought" included not only the Bar Association of the City of New York and the New York Board of Aldermen but even conservative groups such as the National Security League. "The American people," wrote Zechariah Chafee, "long bedrugged by propaganda, were shaken out of their nightmare of revolution. . . . A legislature trembling before five men—the long-lost American sense of humor revived and people began to laugh. That broke the spell."[93]

But the laughter registered tension as much as relaxation. An enduring residue of xenophobia remained, and it would surface from time to time in the Twenties. In John Higham's phrase, the United States in 1920 had not recovered from "the distempers" of 1915–19. The fever of war and the panic over revolution had passed, but "a hardy virus was still at work." Names and objects and tactics changed, but "nothing occurred in 1920 to destroy the ongoing force of 100 percent Americanism."[94] William Preston, noting one distinction between the anti-radicalism of 1919 and later manifestations of Americanism, points out that nativism was not dead in 1920. It had "simply separated from antiradicalism and would thereafter reveal its spirit in crusades for racial purity and restriction." Robert Murray

[92] Chafee, *Freedom of Speech*, 335–36.
[93] *Ibid.*, 338.
[94] Higham, *Strangers in the Land*, 233.

has suggested an even wider influence: "In the broader view, the whole pattern of thought and action common to the 1920's was in part traceable to the Red Scare."[95]

The evidence for this is persuasive. It was characteristic of each president's personality that amnesty for CO's and other political prisoners came a little easier under Harding than under Wilson. In response to a proposal to pardon Debs, Wilson, as his friend and secretary remembered it, said: "While the flower of American youth was pouring out its blood to vindicate the cause of civilization, this man, Debs, stood behind the lines sniping, attacking, and denouncing them. . . . This man was a traitor to his country and he will never be pardoned during my administration." Harding, in the face of considerable opposition, finally commuted the sentence of Debs and twenty-three other political prisoners in mid-December, 1921 (Harding wanted Debs to "eat his Christmas dinner with his wife"), and in June, 1923, commuted the sentences of twenty-seven Wobblies.[96] But in the meantime other Wobblies continued to suffer physical and judicial assault. On Armistice Day, 1919, in the lumber town of Centralia, Washington, the local American Legion post planned to celebrate the occasion with a parade and destruction of the local IWW hall. When the outnumbered Wobblies defended their headquarters, a bloody gunfight broke out, the Legionnaires stormed the place, pursued the fleeing Wobblies, caught one of them, Wesley Everest, and castrated and then lynched him. In Butte, Montana, on April 21, 1920, fourteen Wobblies were shot in a riot.[97] In October the Supreme

[95] Preston, *Aliens and Dissenters*, 230; Murray, *Red Scare*, 233. Cf. Paul L. Murphy, "Sources and Nature of Intolerance in the 1920's," *Journal of American History*, LI (June, 1964), 60–76, which, among other things, traces the course of "antiradicalism" through the Twenties and shows its connection with the Red Scare but also its relationship to the opportunistic individuals and the social tensions at work in the decade itself.

[96] Joseph P. Tumulty, *Woodrow Wilson as I Know Him* (New York, 1921), 504–5; Robert K. Murray, *The Harding Era: Warren G. Harding and His Administration* (Minneapolis, 1969), 168–69. *One Big Union Monthly*, II (March, 1920), 6–21; II (April, 1920), 12–14; (June, 1920), 39, contains a "Partial List of IWW Prisoners," with a brief biographical entry on each Wobbly.

[97] Federal Council of Churches of Christ in America, *The Centralia Case—A Joint Report on the Armistice Day Tragedy at Centralia, Washington, November 11, 1919* (New York, 1920); Ralph Chapin, "The Background of Centralia," *One Big Union Monthly*, II (May, 1920), 17–19; Chapin, "The Picket Line of Blood," *ibid.* (June, 1920), 9–13; *New York Times*, April 22, 1920, 2:4; Robert L. Tyler, "Violence at Centralia, 1919," *Pacific Northwest Quarterly*, 65 (October, 1954), 116–24; Robert K. Murray, "Centralia: An Unfinished American Tragedy," *Northwest Review*, VI (Spring, 1963), 7–18.

Court upheld the wartime conviction of Bill Haywood and a hundred other Wobblies. Shortly thereafter Haywood jumped bail, dropped out of sight, and soon reappeared in Russia. His actions hardly endeared him to American patriots, and Wobblies themselves rationalized his actions—as he himself did—or tried to forget him.[98]

For those Wobblies and other wartime prisoners still in jail, the ACLU and other organizations carried on into the Twenties the campaign for amnesty that they had launched just after the war. Finally, on December 15, 1923, Coolidge commuted the sentences of all Wobblies still in prison for wartime conviction.[99] After a struggle Victor Berger gained release of a sort from his wartime conviction. When Congress excluded him from his seat in 1919, Milwaukee Socialists unanimously renominated him. He won handily, with 40 percent more votes than in 1918, but demonstrations and protests against him broke out around the country, and for a second time Congress denied him a seat. "Lynched again," said Berger. "Twelve men . . . convicted me of disloyalty, but 25,000 voters vindicated me, and it was the duty of the House to seat me." The Milwaukee Socialists immediately renominated him. This time he lost, presumably due to the Harding landslide, but he ran again in 1922 and won. In 1921 the Supreme Court, on a technicality, overthrew his wartime conviction. When he appeared in Congress in December, 1923, his colleagues welcomed him.[100] By then the Socialist party Berger had served was all but moribund. Debs died in 1926, and, as James Weinstein expresses it, "the fate of Debs was the fate of the Party." Despite wartime persecutions, the party had held on and even gained in votes. But the Red Scare, as well as the growing fragmentation of the party over the Russian Revolution and over issues at home, left the Socialists "stranded and isolated" by the mid-Twenties.[101]

[98] Conlin, *Big Bill Haywood,* 197ff. Haywood, homesick, restless, and obscure, died in Russia in 1928. He was buried in the Kremlin, though not for any Communist leanings. His most recent biographer writes that Haywood was never a Communist, never understood its ideology or its concern for theory. "The trouble with us old Wobblies," he told an American reporter in Russia, "is that we all know how to sock scabs and mine guards and policemen or make tough fighting speeches to a crowd of strikers but we aren't so long on this *ideological* stuff as the Russians." *Ibid.,* 206.

[99] *Amnesty for Political Prisoners,* Hearings before the Committee on the Judiciary, House of Representatives, 67 Cong., 2 sess., March 16, 1922 (Washington, 1922) ; *Amnesty to Prisoners since the Armistice,* Sen. Doc. 241, 66 Cong., 2 sess., 1920 (Washington, 1920) ; McCoy, *Coolidge,* 197.

[100] Muzik, "Berger and the Red Scare."

[101] Weinstein, *Decline of Socialism,* 326ff.

As for the American Communists, the Palmer raids drove them underground and reduced their membership. In 1920 there were 8,000 to 15,000 members in the party, most of them foreign-speaking; after 1920 the membership rolls dwindled still more. Yet, in Theodore Draper's view, the Red Scare served the Communist movement, at least one faction of it. The more doctrinaire American Communists, prone to theoretical systems, had never favored any compromise with capitalism or support for moderate tactics, such as voting in elections or organizing into trade unions. Instead, they insisted upon direct action, violence, overthrow, and seizure of power. The Palmer Raids simply confirmed these Communists in their belief that they were the American counterpart of the pre-1917 Bolsheviks in Russia. Just as the latter had worked against czardom, so now Communists in America must plot in underground isolation against the system in America. And the underground was, notes Draper, "the breeding ground for future leaders." An ordeal by fire, it "created martyrs and heroes." Revolutionary movements "have survived so many different kinds of persecution in so many different places that it is a particularly ignorant illusion to imagine that that is the way to get rid of them."[102]

Despite the obvious decimation of American radicalism by the early Twenties, fears of the Left still abounded. The U.S. Army during the decade carried on anti-radical training and seminars. Washington, having broken relations with Russia after the 1917 Bolshevik Revolution, refused to recognize the USSR until 1933. Restrictions on immigration grew tighter during the Twenties as first the Johnson Act of 1921 and then the 1924 National Origins Act imposed a quota system that drastically checked the migrant tide. Loyalty oaths, textbook censorship, and an "American plan" for labor unions—essentially an anti-union drive—were characteristics of American society in the decade.[103] The common denominator behind all of these policies, programs, and attitudes was the ideology that by 1919 had acquired a label: "100% Americanism."

[102] Draper, *Roots of American Communism*, 205–9, 223, 272, 390–93.

[103] Preston, *Aliens and Dissenters*, 244–45; Robert Paul Browder, *The Origins of Soviet-American Diplomacy* (Princeton, 1953); Robert A. Divine, *American Immigration Policy, 1924–1952* (New Haven, 1957), 1–25; Paul L. Murphy, "Normalcy, Intolerance, and the American Character," *Virginia Quarterly Review*, XL (Summer, 1964), 445–59, and "Sources and Nature of Intolerance in the 1920's"; Bessie L. Pierce, *Public Opinion and the Teaching of History in the United States* (New York, 1926); Howard K. Beale, *Are American Teachers Free?* (New York, 1936); Allen M. Wakstein, "The Origins of the Open Shop Movement, 1919–20," *Journal of American History*, LI (December, 1964), 460.

Americanism and its antithesis (the fall from grace usually labeled "un-Americanism") are peculiar phenomena. As David Shannon has observed, there is no such thing as "un-Norwegianism," and the "idea that something is un-French would seem as strange to the ear of a Parisian as the idea of un-Americanism." The concept of Americanism arose in part out of an anxiety over national identity. The ethnic and religious diversity of American society and brevity of its history have long made Americans uneasy over who and what they are.[104] In 1919 the uncertainty—which of course in expression often sounded like dogmatic assurance—focused sharply on recent immigrants. In the minds of professional patriots, every one should be Americanized; but it was immigrants, including the yet unnaturalized as well as those still to come, if any, who were the major problem. The Red Scare and the deportations delirium had produced one tactic: rid the country of unassimilated and supposedly unassimilable elements. For those who remained, another method was in order: melt them into a monolithic mold labeled "100% American."[105]

This concern over immigrants and their degree of Americanism was hardly new to American thought in 1919. Ever since the 1880's much of the country had been worrying about immigration, especially that new tide flowing in from Southern and Eastern Europe. Basically, three viewpoints developed toward immigration: close the gates to any more, absorb all newcomers by uplifting and Americanizing them, or recognize and even encourage the diversity and heterogeneity of cultures that Italian-Americans and Polish-Americans and other hyphenated newcomers could contribute to American life. The latter, under the label "cultural pluralism," had the fewest advocates in the years before World War I. The other two viewpoints were widespread.[106] Beginning with the 1882 Oriental Exclusion Act, the drive to shut off immigration gained momentum until it peaked in 1924 with the National Origins Act. The tactic of accepting and then absorbing the immigrant arose essentially from two impulses—be-

[104] David A. Shannon, "Socialism and Labor," in C. Vann Woodward, ed., *The Comparative Approach to American History* (New York, 1968), 246–47; Eric Larrabee, *The Self-Conscious Society* (Garden City, N.Y., 1960).

[105] Higham, *Strangers in the Land*, 254ff.; Edward George Hartmann, *The Movement to Americanize the Immigrant* (New York, 1948), 216ff.; Francis A. Kellor, "What Is Americanization?" *Yale Review*, VIII, n.s. (January, 1919).

[106] Milton M. Gordon, "Assimilation in America: Theory and Reality," *Daedalus* (Spring, 1961), 263–85; Merle E. Curti, *The Roots of American Loyalty* (New York, 1946).

nevolence and fear. Settlement workers, coming in contact with immigrants in the industrial slums, tried to help them adjust to their new and bewildering world. On the other hand, there were militant nationalists who wanted most of all to make good citizens out of these uprooted people. Beginning in the 1890's various patriotic societies, out of fear and distaste for the immigrants' ideas, appearance, and behavior, tried to reshape them in an American image. Before the war this Americanization was restricted to scattered individuals, organizations, and agencies. The war turned this impetus for Americanization into a national crusade. Assimilation became a paramount goal. In 1915, July 4 became "Americanization Day." About the same time "America First" appeared as a slogan.[107]

As it did for so many other realms of thought and action in the war, the federal government produced an agency (in fact, several of them) that reflected this surging enthusiasm for conformity. In 1914 the Committee for Immigrants in America, the leading Americanization body in the country, originated, staffed, and even financed a Division of Immigrant Education in the U.S. Bureau of Education. For the next four years the DIE issued bulletins, circulars, and press releases and served as "a focal point and general clearing house for all matters concerning Americanization and the immigrant problem."[108] In 1918 the bureau established an Americanization Division to educate immigrants in the nation's "industrial requirements," its history, its "manners and customs," and its "ideals" and to win the immigrants' "loyalty . . . and hearty cooperation in the war for freedom and democracy."[109]

Meanwhile, American industrialists had begun to discover that Americanization of the immigrant could not only disabuse him of any alien and radical notions he might have, such as Socialism; he could also become a happier, and therefore more efficient, worker if

[107] Divine, *Immigration Policy*, 2–25; Higham, *Strangers in the Land*, 237, 243; Hartmann, *Movement to Americanize*, 105–215; "Americanization Day, a New Idea for July 4," *Survey*, XXXIV (May 25, 1915), 189; "Americanization Day in 150 Communities," *ibid.*, XXXIV (July 31, 1915), 390.

[108] Hartmann, *Movement to Americanize*, 98, 101–2; Darrell Hevenor Smith, *The Bureau of Education* (Baltimore, 1923), 39.

[109] *Department of Interior, Annual Report, 1918* (Washington, 1919), 393. For the work of this and other government agencies, see Hartmann, *Movement to Americanize*, 88–215; and Report of Commissioner of Education, June 30, 1919, in *Department of Interior Annual Report, 1919* (Washington, 1920). See also Lewis Paul Todd, *Wartime Relations of the Federal Government and the Public Schools, 1917–1918* (New York, 1945), 40–70.

he was taught English. If he could read the American language, he could read safety bulletins in the plant and civic manuals that taught him reverence for the Constitution, and thereby become a better citizen. In 1918 U.S. Steel's Bureau of Safety, Sanitation, and Welfare declared that education and Americanization of foreign-born workers was a "national problem of vital importance," and the bureau felt it vital to work for "a hundred percent America." In August, 1918, the superintendent of International Harvester's plant in Milwaukee launched a war bond drive with the declared hope that Milwaukee's employees—many of whom were German-Americans—would prove to be "absolutely 100 per cent loyal."[110]

By war's end the term that Theodore Roosevelt used in 1915 while campaigning for American preparedness had become a national slogan.[111] In 1919–20 "100% Americanism" was the alternative to deportation. Talk about Americanization and programs and organizations to implement it abounded, carrying such names as the National Civic Federation, the American Defense Society, the National Association for Constitutional Government, and the Better America Federation. Each of these had appeared by 1920. During the Twenties others arose alongside them, such as the American Citizenship Foundation (1923), the United States Flag Association (1924), the National Patriotic Council (1924), and Sentinels of the Republic (1926).[112] Publishers rushed into print varied manuals and series designed for use by citizens and schools carrying on Americanization work.[113] Public schools and universities rearranged their curricula to

[110] Gerd Korman, *Industrialization, Immigrants, and Americanizers: The View from Milwaukee, 1866–1921* (Madison, 1967), 136–64.

[111] Robert B. Pitkin, "What Is 100 Per Cent Americanism?" *The American Legion Magazine*, LVII (May, 1954), 24–26; Herman Hagadorn, *The Works of Theodore Roosevelt* (New York, 1925), XXI, 333. Again and again during his public career Roosevelt orated on Americanism. A good representative statement is Roosevelt to S. Stanwood Menken, president of the National Security League, January 10, 1917, in Elting E. Morison, ed., *The Letters of Theodore Roosevelt*, VIII (Cambridge, 1954), 1143–48.

[112] Hapgood, ed., *Professional Patriots*, 153–90; Bessie Louise Pierce, *Citizens' Organizations and the Civic Training of Youth* (New York, 1933), 3–14; Edwin Layton, "The Better America Federation: A Case Study of Superpatriotism," *Pacific Historical Review*, XXX (May, 1961), 137–47; Howard C. Hill, "The Americanization Movement," *American Journal of Sociology*, XXIV (May, 1919), 609–42.

[113] See, for example, *Americanization: Principals* [sic] *of Americanism, Essentials of Americanization, Technic of Race-Assimilation, Annotated Bibliography*, comp. and ed. Winthrop Talbot (New York, 1920), which opens with a fifty-three-page bibliography. The Carnegie Corporation of New York sponsored publication of a series, "Americanization Studies," among them Frank V. Thompson, *Schooling of*

emphasize more than ever their instruction in Americanization.[114] Social workers launched Americanization plans.[115] Americanization bills, mostly in support of education, appeared in Congress, where they generated loquacious debate.[116] Some kind of Americanization campaign got underway in virtually every state after the war. In Pennsylvania, after learning that Italians "greatly predominated" in the work force in its system, the Pennsylvania Railroad inaugurated English language courses for them. The "original purpose" was to make them "more efficient workmen by teaching them English so that they might better understand the orders of their foremen."[117] In New York a reconstruction commission distinguished "between the mere learning of the English and the education of the mind, the feelings, and the will to the ideals of American citizenship."[118] In Nebraska the legislature prohibited the teaching of any subject in any language other than English in any denominational, parochial, or public school. Languages other than English could be taught, as languages, in grades above the eighth.[119] Cotton manufacturers of New Bedford, Massachusetts, organized a movement to teach all operatives in their mills to speak English and to respect "American

---

the Immigrant (New York, 1920) ; Robert E. Park, *The Immigrant Press and Its Control* (New York, 1922) ; P. A. Speek, *A Stake in the Land* (New York, 1922). For all titles, see Robert M. Lester and James E. Gourley, *The Diffusion of Knowledge: A List of Books Made Possible Wholly or in Part by Grants from Carnegie Corporation of New York and Published by Various Agencies during the Years 1911–1935* (Philadelphia, 1935).

[114] Hartmann, *Movement to Americanize*, 235–61; Pierce, *Public Opinion and Teaching of History*, 70ff.; and see items in *Addresses and Proceedings of the National Education Association of the United States . . . 1920*, LVIII (Washington, 1920).

[115] "The Uniting of Native and Foreign Born in America," *Proceedings of the National Conference of Social Work . . . 1919* (Chicago, 1920), 729–60; and *Proceedings . . . 1920* (Chicago, 1920), 479–502.

[116] *Cong. Rec.*, 66 Cong., 1 sess. (November 19, 1919), 8823; 66 Cong., 2 sess. (January 20, 1920), 1777–80; (January 21, 1920), 1824–34; (January 24, 1920), 1983–95; (January 26, 1920), 2050–59; (February 4, 1920), 2438; *New York Times*, October 17, 1919, 4:2; October 29, 1919, 12:2; January 17, 1920, 10:7; January 27, 1920, 7:1.

[117] U.S. Council of National Defense, *Readjustment and Reconstruction Activities in the States*, 279–80.

[118] *Ibid.*, 210–11.

[119] *Ibid.*, 184; and Jack W. Rodgers, "The Foreign Language Issue in Nebraska, 1918–1923," *Nebraska History*, XXXIX (March, 1958), 1–22. Colorado, Indiana, Iowa, Kansas, Oklahoma, Oregon, and South Dakota also forbade teaching of a foreign language below the high school level. See "Recent Legislation Forbidding the Teaching of Foreign Languages," *Minnesota Law Review*, IV (May, 1920), 449.

ideals . . . American standards of conduct, and American ideas of liberty." Boy Scout troops would "reach the younger generation who need instruction and training in American citizenship."[120] Amidst all this enthusiasm for the American language, the Cleveland school board seemed out of step in offering jobs to people who could speak Lithuanian, Crotian, Italian, and other languages heard in Cleveland. The board, needing help in taking the new school census, offered to pay the workers five cents a name.[121]

The most potent and enduring expression of Americanism to appear after the war was the American Legion. The Legion symbolized the contribution of World War I to the burgeoning Americanization drive. An organization with the same name had flickered into existence briefly in 1915, sponsored by General Leonard Wood. It quickly disappeared but contributed its name and many of its members to the American Legion that GHQ coaxed into being in France in 1919. Organized at a Paris caucus in March, the Legion gained a charter from Congress in September and held its first convention in November. Its preamble, written by ex-Major Hamilton Fish, Jr., of New York, declared that among other things the Legion was "to foster and perpetuate one hundred percent Americanism." Among all the veterans' organizations founded since 1898, the Legion was the first to use this phrase officially, though Legionnaires always had difficulty defining it. Ivy Lee, a public relations expert hired to analyze the term, was unable to do much with it. In practice, however, the first major un-American objects that the Legion sought out to attack were the aliens who had refused to serve in the American armed forces during the war. Legionnaires called them "alien slackers" and wanted to deport them. But quickly political radicals, alien or not, slackers or not, became the Legion's favorite symbol of un-Americanism.[122] Ex-doughboy Wesley Everest, castrated and lynched in the Legion raid on Wobbly headquarters in Centralia, Washington, on Armistice Day, 1919, bore witness to this.

Such violence was not confined to the Legion. The race riots of

120 *Christian Science Monitor*, December 24, 1918, cited in U.S. Council of National Defense, *Readjustment and Reconstruction in the States*, 129.

121 *Cleveland Press*, March 11, 1919; cited *ibid.*, 256.

122 Rodney G. Minott, *Peerless Patriots: Organized Veterans and the Spirit of Americanism* (Washington, 1962); Richard Seelye Jones, *A History of the American Legion* (Indianapolis, 1946); Cromwell Tidwell, "Luke Lea and the American Legion," *Tennessee Historical Quarterly*, XXVIII (Spring, 1969), 70–83.

1919,[123] Klan lynchings of the Twenties, and gang warfare in Chicago showed that Americans of varied persuasions could assault their fellow man with ferocity and often with glee. Violence in America, as old as the nation itself, obviously increased during and because of the war, which sanctioned killing and vigilante repression. These did not end suddenly with the Armistice. Still, John Higham appears correct in saying that the Americanization movement after the war resorted to persuasion more than it did to coercion[124]—though the persuasion often turned into intimidation. And the intolerance and conformity born of that intimidation endured as the Americanization drive surged on into the Twenties. There, like other ideas and instruments nourished by World War I, it permeated American society.

[123] See pp. 157–58 below.

[124] Higham, *Strangers in the Land,* 259. One observer has suggested a metaphorical, if not a literal, explanation of the country's disposition to violence after the war: "We had indulged in wild and lascivious dreams. We had imagined ourselves in the act of intercourse with the Whore of the World. Then suddenly the war was over and the Whore vanished for a time and we were in a condition of coitus interruptus." Charles W. Ferguson, *The Confusion of Tongues* (Garden City, N.Y., 1928). As Ferguson might have concluded, it remained to find release upon other objects, such as Communists, blacks, or hyphenated Americans.

VII

*"It Is Wonderful to Hear the
Fate of Nations Discussed"*

Wilson and the World

Months before the war ended, Woodrow Wilson began to concentrate on the postwar peace settlement that he hoped to formulate.* After November, 1918, the task came more and more to possess him, until finally he all but abdicated leadership at home in desperate pursuit of his diplomatic goals. Between December, 1918, and July, 1919, Wilson spent ten days in the United States, so preoccupied was he with the peace conference in Paris. He came home for good in July, but then in September he suffered a stroke that left him partly paralyzed, and for the next seven months he was bed-ridden and out of touch with the nation as it stumbled through 1919 toward normalcy. In December, 1919, a veteran newspaperman summarized the current state of national politics: "I have been in Washington a good bit and the situation there is bad as it can be—no government—no policies —almost every Cabinet officer a candidate for President and making his decisions and framing his actions on his own personal and candidatorial and political exigencies rather [than] on what the people need. The Congress is chaotic. There is no leadership worthy of the name."[1]

It is far from certain that a more healthy and active president could have prevented the national spiral downward from Armistice exhilaration and reform talk to the brutal repression policies of 1919–20. But clearly Wilson's administration did nothing to halt the country's drift rightward. Otis Graham has put the thought sharply: "Harding

---

* In view of the extensive historical literature available on the subject of this chapter, I have chosen to focus special attention here on historiography. On this subject I can hardly ignore, much less try to overcome or go beyond, two generations of scholarship. Also, I find the diplomatic historians in this case to be as interesting—and their work as revealing—as the diplomacy they studied.

[1] Samuel G. Blythe to Albert Beveridge, December 1, 1919, Box 214, Albert Beveridge Papers, Division of Manuscripts, Library of Congress.

might as well have been in the White House from 1918 onward."[2] But if Wilson defaulted on leadership at home after the war, he became in international politics a figure of renown. Having led the nation into and through World War I, Wilson now proposed to re-shape the world more nearly in the American image. This grandiose design has suffered varying fates at the hands of scholars ever since Wilson first began to formulate his postwar plans. Few, if any, sub-jects in twentieth-century American history have received more in-tensive analysis than Wilson and the peace. A survey of this rich historiography is instructive. It reveals as much about historians and the climate in which they worked as it does about the peace confer-ence, and demonstrates—if such demonstration is still necessary— the relativism of historical analysis. The questions historians have asked, the very paradigms by which they have operated, have changed over the decades since Wilson and his colleagues assembled at Versailles.[3]

In 1929, summarizing ten years of historiography on the Paris peace conference of 1919, Robert Binkley found that at first journal-ists, not historians, displayed the greatest zeal in offering a synthesis on the conference. Their work was of dubious validity, written more to demonstrate "colossal plots and treasons" than to delineate the day-to-day routine of the peace talks. Among all the leaders at Versailles, Wilson had been discredited most of all. "He was held responsible for all disappointments . . . denounced as a man of absurd vanities,

---

[2] Otis L. Graham, Jr., *The Great Campaigns* (Englewood Cliffs, N.J., 1971), 113.

[3] Bruce Kuklick, "History as a Way of Learning," *American Quarterly*, XXII (Fall, 1970), 609–28, applies to U.S. foreign policy makers, if not to historians, the notion of paradigms described in Thomas Kuhn's seminal book, *The Structure of Scientific Revolutions* (Chicago, 1962). Kuklick finds that after 1941, but not before then, "the set of premises defining Wilsonian policies became dominant not only among policy-makers but also with the Congress and the public." In Kuklick's view, "knowledge of the experience of World War I" has been "so essential to post–World War II diplomats" that one may speak of a "Wilsonian paradigm" operating among U.S. foreign policy makers, who since 1941 or so have looked at the world the way Wilson did in the World War I period. Recently, in connection with Vietnam espe-cially, that paradigm appears to be crumbling. Most of the people Kuklick discusses were men prominent in national politics, not historians. But one may suggest that historians have contributed to that paradigm, that in a rough and general fashion the historical consensus on Wilson has tended to develop in the same fashion as this historical paradigm, though it took shape earlier than 1941, and historians were criticizing American presence in Vietnam (and the Wilsonian rationalization for that presence) well before American political leaders began to voice such criticism.

ignorant of European affairs, yet refusing to take advice . . . too stubborn, too pliant, too hypocritical, too naively sincere."[4] In the face of such calumnies, Ray Stannard Baker had stepped forth as Wilson's champion. Baker, who was Wilson's press representative at Paris and later his official biographer, began publishing a defense of Wilson as early as 1919. In Baker's account the peace conference was a conflict between new and old forces: the League vs. territorial guarantees and economic concessions; investigation by experts vs. tactics of barter and bluff; publicity vs. secrecy. And, as Baker portrayed him, the leader of the new forces was Woodrow Wilson. He overcame his enemies at Paris, who without him would have achieved a vindictive treaty, but then the U.S. Senate betrayed him by refusing to ratify his noble dream. Or so said Ray Stannard Baker.[5]

According to Binkley, this interpretation by Baker "dominated the history of the Peace Conference for four years," after which rebuttals began to appear. Charles Seymour published *The Intimate Papers of Colonel House* in 1928 to demonstrate that Wilson "ruined the peace with fruitless intransigence."[6] Robert Lansing, secretary of state from mid-1915 to February, 1920, published his reminiscences in order, as Binkley put it, "to prove that if his advice had been followed Wilson would have kept out of trouble."[7] Meanwhile, the fundamental chore of researching and appraising the Paris conference step by step barely got started. During the Twenties, brilliance of style, fantasies of interpretation, and a search for conspiracies and blame predominated the historiography of the 229 days from the Armistice to the signing of the peace on June 28, 1919.

The decade of the Thirties produced "two broad tendencies in peace conference publications"—factual surveys and controversial memoirs.[8] Surveying this material in 1939, Paul Birdsall, who him-

[4] Robert C. Binkley, "Ten Years of Peace Conference History," *Journal of Modern History*, I (December, 1929), 607–29.

[5] Ray Stannard Baker, *What Wilson Did at Paris* (Garden City, N.Y., 1919); Binkley, "Ten Years of Peace Conference History." On his press role, see Baker's "Notebook," Box 124 and 125, Ray Stannard Baker Papers, Division of Manuscripts, Library of Congress; Baker, *American Chronicle: The Autobiography of Ray Stannard Baker* (New York, 1945), 368ff.; Robert C. Bannister, *Ray Stannard Baker: The Mind and Thought of a Progressive* (New Haven, 1966), 183–87.

[6] Binkley, "Ten Years," 619.

[7] *Ibid.*, 613.

[8] Paul Birdsall, "The Second Decade of Peace Conference History," *Journal of Modern History*, XI (September, 1939), 362–78.

self published an influential study of Versailles,[9] judged that "every-thing that has appeared in the category of memoirs and letters, as well as much purely historical writing, has tended to increase the stature of Wilson." In contrast, Colonel House was increasingly discredited for his disposition to compromise Wilsonian principles. Nevertheless, as reflected in Birdsall's essay, the chief interest of peace conference historians in the 1930's lay with such matters as boundary disputes, reparations, and France's preoccupation with her own security. In fact, to Birdsall, this "traditional French pro-gram provided Woodrow Wilson and Mr. Lloyd George with their chief problem at Paris."[10]

The most striking thing about the Binkley and Birdsall surveys is the absolute omission of Russia from their discussion—a fact which evidently reflects the virtual neglect of this subject by the historians and memoirists each man was appraising. Historiography of the period 1919–39 appears to have been written from a view that focused sharply on Western Europe. Russia, Communism, revolutions of the left or the right, the absence of Lenin from the Big Four deliberations —such matters were peripheral if raised at all. Even in the mid-Fifties, in a survey of Wilsonian literature, Richard L. Watson, Jr., found little material that related to Wilson's policies or views toward Russia and Communism.[11] But about 1950 an important shift began in American historiography. New books on American and Allied inter-vention in Russia in 1918 raised the question of Wilson's anti-Bolshe-vism. George Kennan's weighty history of Soviet-American relations, 1917–20, called attention, among other things, to the relationship between events at Versailles and American-Allied policy toward Russia.[12] And in a series of publications beginning in 1952, William Appleman Williams and others who followed his lead have all but

[9] Paul Birdsall, *Versailles Twenty Years After* (New York. 1941).

[10] Birdsall, "Second Decade."

[11] Watson, "Woodrow Wilson and His Interpreters, 1947–1957," *Mississippi Valley Historical Review*, XLIV (September, 1957), 207–36.

[12] George F. Kennan, *Soviet-American Relations, 1917–1920*, I: *Russia Leaves the War* (Princeton, 1956); II: *The Decision to Intervene* (Princeton, 1956). See also Kennan's *Russia and the West under Lenin and Stalin* (Boston, 1960); Pauline F. Tompkins, *American-Russian Relations in the Far East* (New York, 1949); Betty Miller Unterberger, *America's Siberian Expedition, 1918–1920: A Study of National Policy* (Durham, 1956); John A. White, *The Siberian Intervention* (Princeton, 1950); Richard Ullman, *Anglo-Soviet Relations, 1917–1921* (Princeton, 1961–68).

turned upside down the traditional view of Wilson at Versailles. From Williams's 1952 study, *American-Russian Relations, 1781–1947*,[13] to Arno Mayer's 1967 publication, *Politics and Diplomacy of Peacemaking: Containment and Counterrevolution at Versailles, 1918–1919*,[14] American historians have spelled out in ever more elaborate detail the anti-Bolshevism that supposedly animated Wilson and his fellow peace conference delegates in 1919. Mayer's book, surely the largest if not the last of these studies, surveys affairs in all the major European countries as well as in the United States in 1918–19, and tries to show how Wilson and the other peacemakers worked to stabilize governments throughout Europe somewhere between a left and a right extreme, and at the same time to contain, if not to destroy, the Russian Revolution. Thus, in Mayer's analysis (and his is representative of a growing body of literature), Russia replaces Germany as the chief preoccupation of Wilson and the Allied governments. If the newer historiography is correct, this fear of revolution—especially the Bolshevik version—was a primary obsession not only for Wilson but also for policy-makers of the Twenties.[15]

Granted that the Cold War may have conditioned some of this post-1945 emphasis on Wilson's anti-Bolshevism, the evidence for American opposition to the Russian Revolution in 1918–19 is, in fact, abundantly clear—even though it was less clear to historians writing between World War I and II than to those writing since 1945.[16] One may, for instance, cite the vehement opposition to Bolshevism that Robert Lansing expressed in 1918. On October 26, Lansing wrote:

[13] William Appleman Williams, *American-Russian Relations, 1781–1947* (New York, 1952).

[14] Arno J. Mayer, *Politics and Diplomacy of Peacemaking: Containment and Counterrevolution at Versailles, 1918–1919* (New York, 1967).

[15] See bibliographical essay for recent titles.

[16] Obviously the historian's familiar frame of reference is at issue in these changing views of Versailles. But without developing the argument any further, perhaps it is enough to note that the anti-Bolshevism of the Versailles peacemakers was evident in the documents all the time after 1919; events of the post-1945 period, when U.S.-Russian relations reached nadir, simply called attention to material earlier overlooked or minimized. The facts emphasized in the Thirties are no more or no less true than those emphasized by historians of the Cold War era. The emphasis, the questions asked of the facts, the framework provided for the facts—these have changed with changing historians in changing times. If this is so, it is simply another example of E. H. Carr's definition of history: "a continuous process of interaction between the historian and his facts, an unending dialogue between the past and the present." *What Is History?* (New York, 1964). The dialogue at the moment is neither more nor less true than that of the Thirties or Forties. It is, however, the dialogue most relevant to those historians looking for perspective on the Cold War.

"There are at work in Europe two implacable enemies of the Individual and its guardian, Political Equality and Justice. These enemies are absolutism and Bolshevism. The former is waning; the latter is increasing." As Lansing viewed it, Bolshevism was "a great international movement of ignorant masses to overthrow government everywhere and destroy the present social order. Its appeal is to the unintelligent and brutish elements of mankind to take from the intellectual and successful their rights and possessions and to reduce them to a state of slavery." Lansing judged Bolshevism to be "the most hideous and monstrous thing that the human mind has ever conceived." A "Bolshevik Germany or Austria" was "too horrible to contemplate," and would be "far worse than a Prussianized Germany." His conclusion: "We must not go too far in making Germany and Austria impotent or we may give life to a being more atrocious than the malignant thing created by the science of Frankenstein."[17]

Lansing's strategy expressed in the last sentence of his memorandum has lately been explored in great detail by Arno Mayer, who sees it as Wilson's strategy as well.[18] Yet for every view such as Lansing's, one can find contemporaries of his who seemed all but oblivious to things Russian. In 1917 Wilson created The Inquiry, a board of experts made up of economists, historians, geographers, and other professionals knowledgeable about Europe, who were to draw up data and proposals for Wilson's use at the Paris peace talks.[19] Yet prior to the conference, the Inquiry compiled not one report on the "possible menace of Bolshevism to European society." Instead, as Lawrence Gelfand's study of them shows, these experts concerned themselves with such matters as territorial boundaries, ethnic self-determination, and natural resources. Russian Bolshevism was, to them, a "temporary, abnormal condition," and all of their plans "assumed the imminent establishment of a democratic constitutional government in Russia."[20]

The Inquiry was not alone in assuming—or at least in hoping—that the Bolsheviks would not last in Russia. In fact, by January, 1919, when the peace conference opened, the Wilson administration had spent over a year groping for a policy that would help to establish a

[17] Lansing memo on absolutism and Bolshevism, October 26, 1918, quoted in Lawrence Gelfand, *The Inquiry: American Preparation for Peace, 1917–1918* (New Haven, 1963), 212–13.

[18] Mayer, *Politics and Diplomacy of Peacemaking.*

[19] Gelfand, *The Inquiry.*

[20] *Ibid.*, 211–14.

more or less representative government in Russia. When the February, 1917, revolution overthrew the czarist government, Wilson promptly recognized the new provisional regime and even dispatched a good will fact-finding mission to Russia in the spring of 1917. Headed by elder statesman and veteran diplomat Elihu Root, this group of Americans, some of them claiming to be experts in Russian affairs, totally misread the country and the conditions they encountered there.[21] Whether or not more insight on their part might have prepared the way for another American policy, when the Bolsheviks seized control of Russia in October, 1917, the Wilson administration chose not to extend diplomatic recognition. Instead, U.S.-Russian relations began to deteriorate, so much so that some analysts have located the beginnings of the Cold War in this period following the Bolshevik Revolution of 1917.[22] In the summer of 1918 Wilson ordered American forces into Russia. Some 5,000 U.S. troops landed at Archangel alongside 2,400 British and 900 French troops dispatched there. Nine thousand more Americans moved into Vladivostok on the Pacific coast of Russia, as did 72,000 Japanese troops.[23] Speculation over these landings has been abundant ever since they occurred. Historical analysis has concentrated on five or six basic interpretations: Wilson intervened in order to help the anti-Bolshevik forces in Russia regain power and crush the Bolshevik Revolution; he intervened to resume the eastern front war against Germany, since the Brest-Litovsk treaty of March, 1918, between the Germans and the Bolsheviks had ended the war in the east; he intervened in the name of self-determination of peoples, hoping that American troops in Vladivostok, for example, would help rescue several thousand Czech prisoners of war who had escaped and were trying to get back home and fight the Germans; he intervened in Siberia to keep an eye on the Japanese and to guarantee a continued open door policy in Asia at the end of the war; he intervened in Archangel because the British and the French—admittedly anti-Bolshevik—wanted him to, and Wilson was anxious to maintain good relations with these Allies as the war neared a close and the peace talks drew nearer; he inter-

[21] See Box 192, Elihu Root Papers, Division of Manuscripts, Library of Congress; Case File 64, Woodrow Wilson Papers, Division of Manuscripts, Library of Congress.

[22] Charles S. Maier, "Revisionism and the Interpretation of Cold War Origins," *Perspectives in American History*, IV (Cambridge, 1970), 313–47.

[23] By September there were 7,400 British troops in North Russia, as well as 1,000 French and over 1,300 Italians. Ullman, *Anglo-Soviet Relations*, I, 243, 252, 261.

vened to strike at the Bolsheviks because he believed that they were actually German agents.[24]

Some of these views are in conflict; others supplement or qualify one another. This medley of voices by historians matches that sounded by Wilson and his contemporaries, a fact which suggests that there may never have been a "policy"—deliberate and articulated—behind the intervention. Instead, Wilson and his advisers may have been confused and uncertain of just what they were doing, much less why they were doing it. Rather than a reasoned scheme, American diplomacy may have been a day-to-day matter, often turning on the contingent and the unforeseen, though perhaps in retrospect moving in one direction more than in others.[25]

Certainly Wilson received a barrage of conflicting advice. Lincoln Colcord, a native of Maine who was in 1918 the Washington correspondent of the *Philadelphia Public Ledger*, wrote to Wilson in July, begging him not to intervene. "The world," said Colcord, "is on the brink of committing one of its terrible historic crimes. If the Allies intervene in Russia in support of any counter-revolution whatsoever, there will be a wrong peace compacted with the imperial German government this fall, and Russia will be the spoils of the world." Russia, said Colcord, was "striving towards the same new world for which the peoples everywhere are fighting [though] doing it with shocking directness, according to her own lights." The West had refused to recognize Russia's unique problems and her need to develop revolution in her particular way. If Wilson would establish "outright sup-

[24] I would hesitate to assign any or all of these interpretations exclusively and directly to a particular historian. But generally Kennan's books have denigrated any Wilsonian plot or purpose, and instead he finds the Archangel troops being "sent against the better judgment of their own government, in deference to the pressure of the Allies." Wilson, in fact, "never fully understood or approved" American intervention. See Kennan, *Decision to Intervene*, 379–80. William Appleman Williams constructs an elaborate Wilsonian *Weltanschauung* that guided Wilson to intervene in order to contain Bolshevism and to expand American capitalism. See especially his essays in *Studies on the Left*, III (Fall, 1963), 24–48; IV (Winter, 1964), 39–57. Gordon Levin, in *Woodrow Wilson and World Politics* (New York, 1968), tries to relate several themes and concludes that Wilson's Siberian intervention "was based primarily on the . . . desire to use American influence in support of Russian liberal-nationalism against the interrelated threats posed both by German imperialism and by Russian Bolshevism to Russia's March Revolution." Ullman, *Anglo-Soviet Relations*, emphasizes Britain's political role in the intervention.

[25] Cf. Christopher Lasch, "American Intervention in Siberia: A Reinterpretation," *Political Science Quarterly*, LXXVII (June, 1962), 205–23.

port of the Soviets," then an "active Red army could be put into the field against Germany . . . the Bolshevik program towards confiscation could be modified, and [the Bolsheviks] could be brought into a workable state of co-operation with the western democracies."[26]

Simeon Strunsky, a Russian by birth and a self-styled student of Russian affairs who in 1918 was on the staff of the *New York Evening Post*, advised Wilson that Russia must be "saved for freedom," a condition which Strunsky evidently defined as lying somewhere between the Bolsheviks and the old czarist regime. This might mean "forcible intervention in Russia's internal affairs," but Wilson had earlier displayed a comparable and "magnificently courageous" policy in Mexico, and Strunsky thought the world would not cavil at the action. Wilson, who had sent troops and agents into Mexico from 1913 to 1917 to alter the course of that revolution, and who in July, 1918, would order troops into Russia, found Strunsky's suggestion repugnant. Strunsky "entirely misrepresented the spirit and principles of this government if he [was proposing that it] interfere with the form of government in any other government."[27]

War Industries Board Director Bernard Baruch, who concluded that "Russia's greatest enemy" was going to be "hunger and privation," suggested to Wilson that Herbert Hoover should head a mission to Russia. "If anything at all has trickled into their minds from the outside world," said Baruch, "the Russians will realize in sending him you are sending someone to help, not to conquer."[28] Baruch may have believed just what he said—as perhaps did Wilson, who agreed that Hoover would be ideal except for his greater value at home just then as Food Administrator.[29] But the real Hoover was a stark contrast to the man Baruch described to Wilson. For by March, 1919, Herbert Hoover would be declaring to Wilson the "utter foolishness" of "Bolshevik economic conceptions" and suggesting to the President how to deal with the "murderous tyranny" that the Bolsheviks had imposed upon Russia. First, Wilson should refuse to recognize the Bolshevik regime. Second, he should offer to send food relief to Russia if the Bolsheviks would promise to stop fighting in Russia and stop fomenting revolution abroad; thereby, Hoover hoped, the

[26] Lincoln Colcord to Woodrow Wilson, July 7, 1918, Case File 64, Wilson Papers.

[27] Simeon Strunsky to Joseph Tumulty, "Memorandum on Russia," and Wilson to Tumulty, February 23, 1918, *ibid.*

[28] Baruch to Wilson, July 13, 1918, *ibid.*

[29] Wilson to Baruch, July 15, 1918, *ibid.*

Russian people might be persuaded to "themselves swing back to moderation and themselves bankrupt these [Bolshevik] ideas."[30]

By the time Hoover dispatched this lengthy memorandum to Wilson, American troops had been in Russia for over six months, the war had ended, and Wilson had been in Paris for some two months working on the peace treaty. Whatever the motive or design that had driven Wilson to order troops to Russia, his policy toward the Bolsheviks—and the continued presence of American troops on Russian soil—was inseparable from his goals and strategies at the peace conference. Wilson's aims and methods at Paris ran head-on into conflict with those of Lenin, who, though uninvited to Paris and scornful of its deliberations, was as vital a figure in those deliberations as any member of the historic Big Four. Wilson, according to Gordon Levin, went to Paris with a particular vision: "The Wilsonian goal was to create an international civil society . . . making orderly and responsible world citizens out of the hitherto aggressive European nations." Wilson proposed to change Europe, if not the entire world, into an American image (at least Wilson's American image), to the advantage of liberal capitalism everywhere. In the process the burgeoning American economy would expand commercially, politically, and morally throughout the world. "Wilsonian America was to be the historical agent of the world's transformation from chaos and imperialism to orderly liberal rationality."[31] But, again according to Levin's analysis, at every turn and on every level of tactic and goal Wilson's vision clashed with Lenin's. Wilson was trying to reform and hold onto an old, inherited system. Lenin was trying, by revolutionary violence, to bring about a new social and economic order that in theory held no place for capitalism, liberal democracy, or nation-states—the very things Wilson came to Paris to sustain.

This view of Wilson, pitting him in epic ideological conflict with Lenin, is one way of appraising the peace conference. From the Cold War perspective of mid-century, it is an appealing and plausible view. But there are other perspectives. In place of Levin's elaborate and often abstract design, one may use John M. Thompson's more succinct comparison of Wilson and Lenin: "Both men tended to be messianic; each was convinced that he and he alone had the proper prescription for saving the world. But Wilson wanted reform and Lenin revolu-

[30] Hoover to Wilson, March 28, 1919, cited in Mayer, *Politics and Diplomacy of Peacemaking,* 24–26.
[31] Levin, *Wilson and World Politics,* 4–5.

tion."[32] On a more mundane level, one may merely chronicle Wilson's days at Paris, trace the debate in the United States over continued American occupation of Russian soil, note the rising opposition to Wilson's treaty even before he brought it home for Senate signature, look at American policy toward Latin America and other parts of the world in 1919, and in the process realize that ambiguities and contradictions are just as manifest in American foreign policy after World War I as is single-minded anti-Bolshevism.

From any perspective Wilson is the crucial and central figure in American foreign policy during these months. Virtually his every action has been weighed, from the time late in 1918 when he decided to personally attend the peace conference, to March, 1921, when, defeated and shattered, he rode down Pennsylvania Avenue to the inauguration of Warren G. Harding. On November 18, 1918, Wilson announced that he was going to Paris. Debate immediately broke out over this decision, and historians have carried on the argument ever since.[33] Criticisms of Wilson's decision ranged from trivial to telling: his trip was unconstitutional, unprecedented, unseemly; Wilson would be a poor negotiator in Paris, where he would become enmeshed in personal quarrels, but an able one from Washington, where he could remain aloof and yet influential. On November 12 Secretary of State Lansing advised Wilson not to go: "I pointed out," Lansing recorded later, "that he held at present a dominant position in the world, which I was afraid he would lose if he went into conference with the foreign statesmen [and] that he would be criticized severely in this country for leaving at a time when Congress particularly needed his guidance. . . ." Lansing recalled that Wilson "did not like what I said. His face assumed that harsh, obstinate expression which indicates resentment at unacceptable advice. He said nothing, but looked volumes."[34] One might be cynical of the secretary's reasoning, since, if Wilson himself did not attend the conference, Lansing would be the most likely head of the American delegation. But Senator George W. Norris had objections in no way related to personal am-

[32] John M. Thompson, *Russia, Bolshevism, and the Versailles Peace* (Princeton, 1966), 17.

[33] An influential and readable survey of this issue is Thomas A. Bailey, *Woodrow Wilson and the Lost Peace* (New York, 1947), 71ff. A recent study is James C. Startt, "Wilson's Mission to Paris: The Making of a Decision," *Historian*, XXX (August, 1968), 599–616.

[34] Lansing Diary, November 12, 1918, Robert Lansing Papers, Division of Manuscripts, Library of Congress.

bition. "I regret a great many things connected with this trip," said Norris. "He is going to Europe surrounded by a luxury and a splendor that dazzles anything ever done in behalf of a monarch." And Norris was skeptical of Wilson's capacity to bring back an acceptable treaty. "One of the great objections that I have always had to President Wilson is his extreme partisanship. . . . He has made it impossible for well-meaning, conscientious men to work with him."[35]

In addition to his partisanship, many Republicans resented Wilson's presumption that he still spoke for the American people. Wilson had campaigned for a Democratic majority in the recent congressional election and had made the forthcoming peace conference a party issue, only to see his party lose heavily to the Republicans. Out of their own partisanship if not from conviction, Republicans now proclaimed Wilson repudiated and objected to his presence in Paris.[36] In January, 1919, when Republican party elder Elihu Root wrote to Henry Cabot Lodge, new chairman of the Senate Foreign Relations Committee, "I hope you . . . know something about what the President is trying to do in Europe," Lodge shot back: "I know nothing about what the President is trying to do. . . . I doubt if he knows himself."[37]

Lodge's personal distaste for Wilson (a reciprocal matter for Wilson) and his prominent and often vindictive role in later opposing Wilson's treaty raise doubts about his sarcastic judgment. It was not Wilson's mere presence at the conference that bothered Lodge and other critics. It was Wilson's program—both what he sought at Paris and what he actually gained in the treaty—that the critics deplored, though their deprecation varied from those who were shocked over the treaty's harshness to those who were chagrined over the treaty's apparent undermining of American interest and security.[38]

On the eve of the conference Ray Stannard Baker wrote from Paris: "We have a remarkable group of experts here in the Peace Commission; I am getting acquainted with them. . . . It is wonderful

[35] Norris to M. L. Phares, December 11, 1918, Tray 9, Box 1, George W. Norris Papers, Division of Manuscripts, Library of Congress.

[36] Beveridge to Ernest Bross, Managing Editor, *Indianapolis Star*, January 29, 1919, Box 214, Beveridge Papers. D. F. Fleming, *The United States and the League of Nations, 1918–1920* (New York, 1932), Ch. 2, is an extensive discussion of this point.

[37] Root to Lodge, January 2, 1919; Lodge to Root, January 3, 1919, Box 161, Root Papers.

[38] Fleming, *The U.S. and the League*; Thomas A. Bailey, *Woodrow Wilson and the Great Betrayal* (New York, 1947).

to hear the fate of nations, the boundaries of old empires, discussed as malleable elements. Never I think was the world in such plastic state, never such a sense of receiving life and new possibilities."[39] Yet Wilson's program, as spelled out in his Fourteen Points address of January, 1918, and subsequent speeches and papers, called for no such "new possibilities." Wilson had talked loftily of a "just and lasting peace" and of achieving a "peace without victory," all of which would, indeed, have been enough to satisfy the yearnings of most visionaries. But insofar as his personal vision was clear to himself at the time, or is now evident in retrospect, he sought to further American and world interests (the two being largely synonymous to him) by working for still more "national self-determination," after a war that had in part resulted from gross nationalistic rivalries; and for "free trade," which meant extending America's turn-of-the-century open door policy to the world and not merely to the Far East. The League of Nations, his fourteenth point in January, 1918, finally in 1919–20 became his sole hope of justifying the terrible war he had led the nation into in 1917 and the imperfect treaty he helped to write in 1919. But even from the beginning the League was, in his view, evidently intended to bolster and sustain an international system of nation-states, capitalistic in trade, and governments friendly to if not patterned after that of the United States. Richard Hofstadter's succinct judgment, delivered over twenty-five years ago, is still good: "Wilson's struggle with Clemenceau and Lloyd George was not a struggle between an Old Order and a New Order, but merely a quarrel as to how the Old Order should settle its affairs."[40]

As Wilson and the European delegates entered into their parleys, running from January to June, Americans at home demobilized, entered into their reconstruction period, moved toward the Red Scare, and from time to time talked about the peace conference and wondered and worried about what Wilson was doing in Paris. Even before the peace conference opened, the League became an acrimonious issue. William E. Borah, who in the 1919–20 Senate debate over the League would show himself to be one of sixteen irreconcilables opposed to the organization in any form, voiced pointed objections as early as December, 1918. To a correspondent who had written him

[39] Baker Notebook, December 27, 1918, Container 124, Baker Papers.
[40] Richard Hofstadter, *The American Political Tradition and the Men Who Made It* (New York, 1948), 272.

supporting the idea of a League, Borah replied: "Do you propose to give to a league of nations . . . the power to say when war shall be waged [or] not? Are you in favor of abandoning the Monroe Doctrine and permitting European nations to determine the affairs of the Western continent? Are you in favor of joining a league which . . . would have the power to conscript American boys and take them to Europe to settle difficulties?" To Borah, the idea of such a League was "Prussianism pure and simple," though he also found it to be "a combination of the doctrines of Lenin and Trotsky and Wilhelm and Ludendorff."[41]

Borah here voiced some of the standard arguments soon to be heard against the League. Other criticisms surfaced in early 1919. Albert Beveridge found Wilson "as wrong as wrong can be. . . . We have already burdened ourselves with a debt that our grand children will not see paid; if we now bind ourselves to support, maintain, foster, and otherwise manage the affairs of the ten or fifteen (or maybe twenty) new republics in the Balkans, Poland, Russia, etc. . . . we shall pile upon the backs of the people still further billions." By early spring Beveridge proposed a Republican battlecry: "Get Out of Europe and Stay Out."[42] But as Will Hays, Republican national chairman, would soon point out to Beveridge, it was hard to establish a party position on the peace talks or the League. "It is impossible to take a party position when the party is split this way and that way. It has been impossible as yet even to get the forty-nine [Republican] Senators to take a united position. There are not exactly forty-nine different positions, but almost. . . . I wonder if you appreciate the difficulties of the situation?"[43]

Hays was, of course, correct about the multifarious views in the party. Henry Cabot Lodge expressed objections to the League similar to Borah's, though for different reasons. Borah was close to the archetypical isolationist. Lodge was a fervent expansionist, objecting to the League not because it involved the United States in the world but because it would, in his view, restrain American freedom of action in the world.[44] Henry White, about the only Republican to accompany

[41] Borah to Rev. Charles W. Gilkey, December 30, 1918, Box 195, William E. Borah Papers, Division of Manuscripts, Library of Congress.

[42] Beveridge to Ernest Bross, January 29, 1919, Box 214, Beveridge Papers; Beveridge to Borah, April 27, 1919, Borah Papers.

[43] Hays to Beveridge, July 8, 1919, Box 215, Beveridge Papers.

[44] Robert James Maddox, *William E. Borah and American Foreign Policy* (Baton

Wilson to Paris, chided Lodge for his unduly chauvinistic view of the League: "I agree with you," White wrote to him, "that if we enter upon any League of Nations it will be more for the benefit of the world at large than for ourselves, and also that [as Lodge had said] 'it must be with a view to maintaining the peace of Europe.' But surely that is why we went into the war, and no one advocated more earnestly our doing so than you." White feared that, without the League, "we can only revert to the old and only final method of settling international disputes, namely war."[45]

In June, Senator Frank Brandegee, irreconcilable from Connecticut, offered further evidence of Republican disunity. Brandegee, who for some time had openly denounced the League, fulminated over dalliance and undue moderation by Elihu Root and his "friends in N.Y." Brandegee exploded: "If you fellows over in N.Y.—with what you represent and control . . . banks . . . trusts, *et al.* . . . are going to . . . truckle to Wilson . . . God help you! I will not. . . . Other people want to shield their carcasses behind a camouflage and let us take the bayonet thrusts, the poisonous gas, and the cold blue steel, while they count their profits. I am getting a trifle *weary* of being the *goat. Do you get me?*"[46]

Despite such disunity, by midsummer, 1919, with Wilson back from Paris and the Treaty of Versailles before the Senate Foreign Relations Committee for its consideration, Will Hays and Henry Cabot Lodge were counting votes and estimating their chances to modify Wilson's treaty.[47] Even Wilson's supporters were by now registering despair over the outcome at Versailles. William Allen White, the Republican newspaperman from Emporia, Kansas, who had been in Paris during the spring, ventured an appraisal of the treaty just after it was completed. "I am immensely torn about my duty. . . . I cannot feel that the President is to be blamed. . . . I have seen day by day his struggle. . . . He was bound to the rocks with the vulture forever at his entrails. But they have—those damned vultures—taken

---

Rouge, 1969); William Appleman Williams, "The Legend of Isolationism in the 1920's," *Science and Society*, XVIII (Winter, 1954), 1–20; cf. David Mervin, "Henry Cabot Lodge and the League of Nations," *Journal of American Studies*, 4 (February, 1971), 201–14, which pictures Lodge as a party tactician more concerned with political advantage than with any particular fixed attitude on foreign policy.

[45] Henry White to Henry Cabot Lodge, March 7, 1919, copy, Box 161, Root Papers.
[46] Brandegee to Root, June 9, 1919 (his italics), Box 137, *ibid.*
[47] Will H. Hays to Elihu Root, July 1, 1919, *ibid.*

the heart out of the peace, taken the joy out of great enterprise of the war, and have made it a sordid malicious miserable thing like all the other wars in the world." White's metaphors referred to the terms of the treaty, such as reparations from Germany, territorial annexations by France, assumption of control by Britain and France over former Turkish and German territories in Africa and the Near East, and the treaty's failure to spell out a "peace without victory" or to establish the basis for a "just and lasting peace."[48] White's disillusionment was all the greater because of his original exaltation of the war: "We had such high hopes of this adventure; we believed God called us, and now at the end we are put to doing hell's dirtiest work, starving people, grabbing territory—or helping to grab it for our friends; standing by while the grand gesture of revenge and humiliation links this war up with the interminable chain of wars that runs back to Cain. It was not for this that our Americans died—clean beautiful great visioned men who came seeking the Grail."[49]

Its lush prose notwithstanding, Ray Stannard Baker clipped White's statement to his notebook and remarked, "expressing what so many of us feel." Baker himself had experienced some of White's exaltation and despair. In July, 1919, he spoke to a gathering in Amherst, Massachusetts. Baker had been gone from the United States for some eighteen months, spending most of this time in Paris. "I left America," he said, "at what was undoubtedly one of the great moments of our history; one of the great spiritual moments. I shall never forget the exaltation which then moved the soul of America. . . . Here was a vast evil threatening the world. We wanted to give everything we had to beat it down." But now in July, 1919, what Baker saw and heard disturbed him. In an America "scarcely hurt at all by the war, [not even] frightened . . . stronger than ever before as a nation . . ." there were "voices raised in high places . . . asking this great, strong, unhurt nation . . . to withdraw from any further contact with the agony of Europe. . . . They want us to live to ourselves, increase our own prosperity . . . and refuse to take our part in the heavy task of reconstruction." To Baker, "the leadership of

---

[48] On the deliberations and results of the peace conference, see an early work by Birdsall, *Versailles Twenty Years After*, as well as the recent studies by Mayer, *Politics and Diplomacy of Peacemaking*, and Seth P. Tillman, *Anglo-American Relations at the Paris Peace Conference of 1919* (Princeton, 1961).

[49] William Allen White to Ray Stannard Baker, June 3, 1919, Box 125, Baker Papers.

the world" had now passed from Britain and France to the United States. The "need and call" now was "to begin the patient and painful reconstruction of the world." The first essential step toward such a grandiose goal was ratification of the Treaty of Versailles and entrance of the United States into the League.[50]

William Allen White despaired over the treaty. Baker, agreeing on its gross imperfections, saw no better alternative and thought it "a great mistake to regard the treaty, as some of our Liberals do, as a final settlement."[51] Wilson, however, soon came to insist on ratification of the treaty precisely as it stood when completed, including the automatic entry into the League that ratification of the treaty entailed. The fight between Wilson and opponents of the League is wearily familiar: Senate hearings and debates, Wilson on a desperate tour westward in the fall of 1919, trying to evoke support for the treaty only to collapse in Pueblo, Colorado, and for the next seven months to remain sick and all but shut off from the nation as it staggered on through reconstruction, Red Scare, and finally Senate rejection of the treaty. In 1945 Thomas A. Bailey labeled Wilson's refusal to accept compromise in the treaty's terms as "The Supreme Infanticide." Wrote Bailey: "With his own sickly hands Wilson slew his own brain child."[52]

Sick he may have been, and certainly he was stubborn. But Wilson's monomania over the League, if such it was, arose not entirely from some compulsive attachment to an expansionist, capitalistic, anti-Bolshevik stance. Wilson had suffered a blood clot in Paris in April and then a massive stroke in Pueblo in September. With his collapse in Colorado, Wilson became permanently incapacitated. His left side was paralyzed, he had difficulty reading, and he found speaking a chore. He also displayed anosognosia, or denial of his illness, which is evidently a common sequel to the type of brain injury he suffered. Edwin Weinstein, a professor of neurology who has closely studied Wilson's case, does not specifically relate Wilson's physical deterioration to his unyielding position on the treaty issue, but he does stress Wilson's determination to maintain the illusion of power and leadership—which obviously was threatened by the hated Henry Cabot Lodge and his fellow Republicans demanding compromise

[50] "Speech on the Peace Treaty," July 19, 1919, typed copy, Container 97, *ibid.*
[51] Baker to Elizabeth G. Evans, August 7, 1919, copy, *ibid.*
[52] Bailey, *Wilson and the Great Betrayal,* 277.

and even repudiation of the League as the price for their approval of the treaty.[53] But for Wilson the League was transcendently important. As Richard Hofstadter, no stranger to psychological interpretation, put it years ago, Wilson's efforts to save the League "became a matter of the most desperate psychological urgency for him. His plans had been hamstrung, his hopes abandoned one after another, until nothing but the League was left. . . . The League was now a question of moral salvation or annihilation, for everything he stood for hung in the balance." Precisely because of the Treaty's imperfections, Wilson needed the League to forestall the wars that the treaty's terms might engender. And without a lasting peace, "what justification could he find for having led the country into war? His sense of guilt hung over him like a cloud."[54]

Wilson's singlemindedness over the League, then, may have arisen more from psychological need than from some supposed metaphysical vision of America's mission and hegemony. His policy toward Mexico in 1919, for example, revealed far more flexibility and even restraint than he ever showed over the League issue. Several incidents and policies of the war period, added to some pivotal developments in 1919, built up tremendous pressure on Wilson to intervene again in Mexico as he had done in 1914 and 1916. Mexico had refused to break relations with the Central Powers during the war; in fact, evidence was strong that German agents found receptive ears among Mexican politicians both before and after America's entry into the war.[55] Early in 1918 Mexican President Venustiano Carranza issued a series of oil decrees that appeared to begin genuine enforcement of Article 27, that troublesome clause in the 1917 Mexican Constitution declaring Mexican ownership of all subsoil products. The clause, as everybody knew, threatened the vast holding of American and other foreign-owned oil installations in Mexico. With the end of the war American oilmen and various American diplomats began pressuring Wilson to at least assert the rights of American oil interests in Mexico, if not to intervene with military force and put down the

[53] Edwin A. Weinstein, "Woodrow Wilson's Neurological Illness," *Journal of American History*, LVII (September, 1970), 324–51.

[54] Hofstadter, *American Political Tradition*, 276.

[55] James A. Sandos, "German Involvement in Northern Mexico, 1915–1916: A New Look at the Columbus Raid," *Hispanic American Historical Review*, L (February, 1970), 70–88; Michael C. Meyer, "The Mexican-German Conspiracy of 1915," *The Americas*, XXIII (July, 1966), 76–89.

Mexican Revolution once and for all. Meanwhile, the War Department drew up plans for a possible war with Mexico, and in Congress spokesmen for several powerful American oil corporations began working for the downfall of Carranza and for turning Mexico into a protectorate of the United States.[56]

Senator Albert B. Fall of New Mexico was a central figure in this plot. In September, 1919, Fall became chairman of a special Senate subcommittee investigating Mexican affairs, and he promptly turned its hearings into a propaganda vehicle to bring about U.S. intervention in Mexico.[57] A potent agency supporting Fall's work was the National Association for the Protection of American Rights in Mexico (NAPARIM). Representing oil companies and other corporations with interests in Mexico, NAPARIM soon began spending some $20,000 a month publishing and distributing anti-Carrancista material which supposedly documented chaos in Mexico, abuses to Americans there, and the Bolshevistic nature of the Mexican government. In the midst of the rising Red Scare of 1919, the NAPARIM naturally made contacts with American Legion posts and local chambers of commerce, asking them to pressure Congress for action.[58] From El Paso, Zack Cobb, who during the war was in charge of Mexican affairs on the War Trade Board, voiced a common view: "The United States has got to see that Mexico is straightened out." Conditions there, reported Cobb, were "rotten [and] getting worse. Carranza is as smart as he is stubborn. If left alone he would disregard American life so as to make it easier to confiscate American property. He and his kind must go." Cobb proposed that Wilson "maneuver Mexico into asking for League intervention."[59] Ex-senator Beveridge tried to pressure a more sympathetic source. He wrote to Albert Fall declaring, "We ought to have straightened things out [in Mexico] years ago. The very least . . . that should be done is to . . . establish

[56] Clifford W. Trow, "Woodrow Wilson and the Mexican Interventionist Movement of 1919," *Journal of American History*, LVII (June, 1971), 46–72; Manuel A. Machado, Jr., and James T. Judge, "Tempest in a Teapot? The Mexican-United States Intervention Crisis of 1919," *Southwestern Historical Quarterly*, LXXIV (July, 1970), 1–23.

[57] U.S. Senate, *Investigation of Mexican Affairs*, Report and Hearing before a Subcommittee on Foreign Relations, 66 Cong., 2 sess., 2 vols. (Washington, 1919–20) ; Michael C. Meyer, "Albert Bacon Fall's Mexican Papers: A Preliminary Investigation," *New Mexico Historical Review*, XL (April, 1965), 165–74.

[58] Trow, "Wilson and the Mexican Interventionist Movement."

[59] Zack Lamar Cobb to W. G. McAdoo, August 4, 1919, Container 223, William Gibbs McAdoo Papers, Division of Manuscripts, Library of Congress.

the same sort of protectorate over it that we now have over Cuba," though even this would be "a weak and timid measure" going "about one-tenth of the distance we ought to go and the distance that, historically speaking, we surely will go."[60] In October, 1919, the Fall committee and interventionists in the State Department gained support when a Mexican revolutionary faction trying to discredit the Carranza government kidnapped U.S. Consul William O. Jenkins in Puebla and held him for $150,000 ransom. Jenkins quickly maneuvered his own release, only to be arrested by Mexican officials on charge of collusion with his kidnappers.[61]

Despite all these incidents and the mounting hysteria for American intervention, Lansing, running the State Department with little or no communication with Wilson, demanded and finally gained Jenkins's release. For his part Wilson refused to repeat his actions of 1914 and 1916, when he had sent the troops into Mexico. In September, 1919, during his tour across country to arouse support for the League, Wilson said he did not consider Mexico a threat to the security of the United States. He could hardly say otherwise. At the very time when he was campaigning for the League, it would have been impolitic to deny his principle of self-determination to Mexico while upholding it for Czechoslovakia, Poland, and other nations recognized by Versailles. But after Wilson's stroke and his withdrawal from active control over foreign affairs, Mexican policy became largely the work of Secretary Lansing, whose notes to Carranza in the winter of 1919 brought the United States and Mexico close to war. In December, Senator Fall proposed a resolution requesting Wilson to break relations with Mexico. Fall himself, along with Senator Gilbert M. Hitchcock of Nebraska, called on Wilson to plead the case of intervention. Wilson refused to budge and several days later wrote a letter reasserting his control over foreign affairs: "The initiative in directing the relations of our government with foreign governments is assigned by the Constitution to the Executive, and to the Executive only." Fall, along with Lodge, Lansing, and other eager interventionists, stood repudiated. Wilson would not attempt to thwart or influence the course of the Mexican Revolution.[62]

[60] Beveridge to Fall, September 1, 1919, Box 215, Beveridge Papers.

[61] Charles C. Cumberland, "The Jenkins Case and Mexican-American Relations," *Hispanic American Historical Review*, XXXI (November, 1951), 586–607; David Glaser, "1919: William Jenkins, Robert Lansing, and the Mexican Revolution," *Southwestern Historical Quarterly*, LXXIV (January, 1971), 337–56.

[62] Daniel M. Smith, "Lansing and the Wilson Interregnum," *Historian*, XXI (Feb-

But American troubles with Mexico over Article 27 were far from settled. Early in 1920 Senator Fall's close friend Edward Doheny, whose Pan-American Petroleum Company was a heavy investor in Mexico, expressed both optimism and concern over the future: "We are undertaking big work in Mexico for this year, from which . . . we expect big results. We are going ahead with supreme faith in the proper final adjustment of the Mexican situation." This euphemism Doheny then clarified: nothing other than "full recognition of the rights of the American owners of petroleum properties in Mexico, *as and when acquired*, will ever be satisfactory to us."[63] In April, 1920, Carranza was assassinated and a new government headed by General Alvaro Obregon came to power in Mexico. Bainbridge Colby, who had succeeded Robert Lansing as secretary of state, tried to establish relations with the new government by offering recognition in exchange for guarantees by Mexico not to apply Article 27 retroactively. But Wilson and Colby left office without gaining that guarantee and without extending recognition.[64] During his postwar months in office Wilson did not intervene in Mexico, even when he had pretext and support for doing so, but neither could he entirely abide the challenges that Article 27 and other features of the Mexican Revolution had raised for the United States. Somewhere between unqualified expansion of American capitalism and unqualified respect for Mexico's self-determination, Wilson groped for a policy toward the Mexican Revolution.

Meanwhile, in 1919–20, the Russian Revolution presented still another angle to Wilson's vision of the world and America's mission in it. Even before the Armistice of November, 1918, which undercut all pretext for American troops to occupy Russian soil (if indeed they were there to prosecute the war in the first place), Wilson was under pressure to withdraw his troops and to extend recognition to the Bolsheviks. In August a conference of state secretaries and party officials of the Socialist Party of America adopted a proclamation calling for recognition: "Since the French Revolution established a new high mark of political liberty in the world, there has been no

---

ruary, 1959), 135–61; David H. Stratton, "President Wilson's Smelling Committee," *Colorado Quarterly*, V (Autumn, 1956), 164–84.

[63] Doheny to William Gibbs McAdoo, February 2, 1920, Container 229, McAdoo Papers (Doheny's italics).

[64] Daniel M. Smith, *Aftermath of War: Bainbridge Colby and Wilsonian Diplomacy, 1920–1921* (Philadelphia, 1970), 102ff.

other advance in democratic progress and social justice comparable
to the Russian Revolution. . . . We denounce as utterly incompatible
with any principle of democracy or international decency any and
all plans of invasion [and] protest against the continued isolation of
the Soviet Government . . . which is being held incommunicado by
the governments of the world."[65] But the Socialist Party of America
was a pariah within its own country in 1918. More representative of
American opinion—and closer to Wilson's own view—was the November petition from a group of industrialists, financiers, and other
figures in New York. They cited the "bloodthirstiness of the leaders
of the Bolshevist party in Russia" and asked Wilson to appeal to "the
conscience of the world" and make "the instigators of this dreadful
conspiracy thoroughly understand that if they persist a day of reck-
oning is sure to come."[66] Robert Lansing, though equally horrified
at the Russian Revolution, advised Wilson that "any protest on our
part might even have the effect of inducing increased acts of violence,
and thus bring about the very thing . . . we seek to prevent."[67]

But as the weeks went by after the Armistice and Wilson gave little
sign of ordering American troops home from Russia, criticism
increased. A constituent wrote to Senator Borah asking about the
occupation and wondering, "Can it be possible that the American
people in collusion with Great Britain are indirectly taking over the
Kaiser's job of ruling the world?" Borah did not know why American
troops were "in Russia at all" or why they had ever gone there. "Certainly whatever the theory was, we have no occasion for an army at
this time unless we propose to do as ex-President Taft says, 'Kill them
off,' a policy which I am not in favor of and which no man who has
any human principles left in him ought to think of."[68] Borah, in fact,
already had a reputation for defending the Bolsheviks, though as he
wrote to one critic: "I have not defended the . . . Bolshevists unless
it be considered defending them to have objected to sending our

[65] "Proclamation on Russia," adopted August 10–12, 1918, Box "National Office,
1914–18," Folder "N.O., 1916–18," Socialist Party Papers, Duke University.

[66] Samuel Gompers, Oscar S. Straus, Herbert L. Carpenter, Cleveland H. Dodge,
Alton B. Parker, Louis Marshall, and president of Chamber of Commerce of New
York, editor of *Christian Work*, and president of the New York Board of Trade and
Transportation to Wilson, November, 1918, File 64, Wilson Papers. On American
opinion generally, see Peter G. Filene, *Americans and the Soviet Experiment, 1917–
1933* (Cambridge, 1967).

[67] Lansing to Wilson, November 8, 1918, File 64, Wilson Papers.

[68] McCord Shinkle to Borah; Borah to Shinkle, December 11, 1918, Box 194,
Borah Papers.

troops there to shoot them down. While I do not believe in their practices I do not consider it our business to go there and engage in bloody riots with them."[69] Borah also criticized the administration for not having a Russian policy or, if it had one, for keeping it secret. Other members of Congress also expressed concern over inability to get official information from the administration about the occupation forces. In May, Wilson's secretary Joseph Tumulty informed a Michigan congressman, perplexed over the matter, that the War Department would order an "expeditious withdrawal" of all American troops at Archangel "as soon as the ice would permit."[70] The weather did, in fact, shape American policy at Archangel, and when the harbor ice thawed in the spring, the Archangel troops left for home.[71] But 10,000 Americans remained at Vladivostok on the Russian Pacific, and no ice-bound harbors blocked their evacuation.

In June a Senate resolution asked Wilson to tell the Senate why U.S. soldiers were in Siberia.[72] Secretary Newton D. Baker drafted a reply for Wilson. According to Baker, American forces had originally been dispatched to Vladivostok to "save Czech-Slovak armies . . . threatened with destruction by hostile armies" and to "steady any efforts of the [anti-Bolshevik] Russians at self-defense." In February, 1919, the United States had agreed to a Japanese plan calling for "supervision of the Siberian railways by an international committee." The American troops in Siberia were furthering the work of this committee—they were, wrote Baker, "helping to keep open a necessary artery of trade" since the "population of western Siberia and the forces of Admiral Kolchak are entirely dependent upon these railways."[73] Baker evidently did not consider it necessary to add that Kolchak was a leader of the anti-Bolsheviks fighting a civil war for control of Russia. For those who had needed the clarification it was now finally evident that Wilson's Russian policy was designed to limit if not destroy Bolshevism.

In October, 1919, the President made a decision that unmistakably revealed his position, one that Herbert Hoover had recommended

[69] Borah to J. M. Russel, January 21, 1919, *ibid.*

[70] Gilbert A. Currie to Joseph Tumulty, May 22, 1919, File 64, Wilson Papers; Tumulty to Currie, *ibid.*

[71] George F. Kennan, *Russia and the West under Lenin and Stalin* (Boston, 1961), 87–88.

[72] *Cong. Rec.*, 66 Cong., 1 sess. (June 27, 1919), 1864.

[73] Baker to Tumulty, July 22, 1919, File 64, Wilson Papers ("Sent to President of Senate 7/25/19").

to him as early as March, 1919. Boris Bakimoteff, the Russian ambassador in Washington representing the provisional government overthrown by the Bolsheviks, had sought to purchase 29,000 tons of wheat on credit from the U.S. Grain Corporation. Bakimoteff planned to use 20,000 tons of it for relief of the civilian population of Petrograd "and such adjoining regions as may be freed from Bolshevik control." The remainder was allotted to Archangel for relief "under similar conditions, of the civilian population of Northern Russia." Wilson approved the transaction, since he considered it "of the utmost importance and urgency that food be made available for the civilian population [and since] economic relief of this character is the mosι effective means of limiting the spread of Bolshevism and of protecting, thereby, the . . . United States from the danger of subversive propaganda."[74]

Such gestures of opposition to Russian Bolsheviks and American Reds were hardly enough to satisfy Elihu Root. The veteran statesman, who had served Theodore Roosevelt as secretary of war and then secretary of state and had headed the Root Mission to Russia in 1917, wanted Russia free from either German or Japanese domination and felt that prevention of such control was "a matter of distinctively American policy." That policy could be furthered by supporting the anti-Bolshevik Kolchak government. "Everybody who is not flirting with the Bolsheviks," he wrote Henry Cabot Lodge, "recognizes the duty to help the Kolchak government," though the United States had been "helping them in a weak and petty way wholly incommensurate with the emergency,—a little dab of arms here, a little bunch of soldiers there, a few railroad engineers somewhere else—the kind of namby-pamby business that Theodore used to hate so vigorously. We ought to recognize the Kolchak government."[75]

Other Americans were concerned primarily with Russian trade, whether with Kolchak's government or another one. The president of a Trenton, New Jersey, bank wrote to Borah, expressing approval of Borah's plea that the United States recognize the Bolsheviks: "I don't," he said, "believe in the practicability of the Soviet government myself [but] I don't think we can tell any other nation what form of government they should have." Recognition should come, however, only on the assumption that the Bolsheviks "pay the nation's foreign

---

[74] Wilson to Julius H. Barnes, U.S. Wheat Director and President of U.S. Grain Corporation, October 22, 1919, File 64, Wilson Papers.
[75] Root to Lodge, November 1, 1919, Box 161, Root Papers.

debts. Our bank . . . bought some of the Russian . . . bonds."[76] In May the American Commercial Association to Promote Trade with Russia declared that "the present demoralized state of our European export market makes the opening of Russian trade . . . imperative." The association, claiming it represented "thousands of investors and . . . working people," had been trying for four months "to secure a concrete statement of Russian policy from the Administration." The association's members all had "a vital interest in trade with Russia and no interest whatever in Russian internal politics or propaganda." The association appealed to Borah for help: "We are . . . totally ignorant as to whether the Administration intends to permit trade with Russia tomorrow or whether it proposes to bar us from this greatest open market in the world until the very end of time or at least until March 4, 1921."[77]

These complaints about American policy—or the lack of it—were not the only expression of American opinion about Russian Bolshevism to be registered in 1919–20. In the Senate, for example, criticism of American military presence in Russia had been condemned since the Armistice by Senators Hiram Johnson (Republican, California), Robert M. La Follette (Republican, Wisconsin), and others.[78] But senatorial opposition to Bolshevism was louder than these critics. In January, 1920, a subcommittee chaired by Senator George Moses (Republican, New Hampshire) began inquiries into the activities of one Ludwig C. A. K. Martens, described by Moses as the "so-called Ambassador of the Russian Soviet government in this country."[79] Martens, a German born in Russia, had come to the United States in 1916. In April, 1919, in the World Tower Building in New York, Martens opened the Russian Soviet Government Information Bureau, staffed mostly by Americans. As Theodore Draper has noted, this was an unprecedented organization, "set up as a diplomatic mission, without diplomatic recognition." Martens himself tried to use the bureau to establish commercial relations with American capitalism, but the left wing of the American Communist movement was more interested in revolution and wanted to use the bureau to further it.[80]

---

[76] Edward C. Stokes, Mechanics National Bank, Trenton, to Borah, March 1, 1920, Box 198, Borah Papers.

[77] Harold Kellock, executive secretary of ACAPTR, to Borah, May 20, 1920, *ibid.*

[78] *New York Times*, December 13, 1918, 13:1; December 31, 1918, 5:1; January 3, 1919, 2:7; January 14, 1919, 3:2; February 18, 1919, 1:3.

[79] *Cong. Rec.*, 66 Cong., 2 sess. (December 20, 1919), 952–56.

[80] Theodore Draper, *The Roots of American Communism* (New York, 1957), 162;

Senator Moses's committee reported that Martens was a revolutionary who did not deserve ambassadorial status and should be deported.[81] This was an obvious, even redundant, judgment, since the State Department had never considered bestowing such a rank upon Martens in the first place, and the attorney general was already trying to deport him. But the hysterical tone of the Moses report harmonized with the panic over Reds reaching its peak in the winter of 1919–20.[82] Journalist William Hard found the report "an indictment of American intelligence." It was "scandalously crooked in its arguments . . . so fearful of the existence of communism in the world . . . so basely devoted to blowing bubbles of panic out of a dish of stale suds," that Hard feared the United States could become "the laughing stock of London."[83]

Whatever his character and his credentials, Martens, if only as a tactic designed to gain recognition, was trying to establish commercial ties between the United States and Russia. And so were numerous American citizens by the summer of 1920. But Woodrow Wilson, seemingly aloof from the furor over Reds at home and abroad, offered scant comment on his Russian policy. In June, Secretary of State Colby finally advised him that it might be time for a policy statement. "There is," said Colby, "a disposition in some quarters to criticize our policy as not enterprising or sagacious from a commercial point of view. The authors of such criticisms evidently have not in mind the fundamental reasons for our aloofness."[84] By August, Colby was declaring, however ambiguously, some of those "fundamental reasons." The Wilson administration favored neither a Bolshevik Russia nor dismemberment of the country. "We want a peaceful settlement of existing difficulties in Europe," he informed the American ambassador in London. Since "dismemberment of Russia would retard any general solution," the United States denied recognition to those Baltic states, Lithuania, Latvia, and Estonia, which had separated from Russia. As for establishing commercial relations with the Bol-

Lusk Committee, *Revolutionary Radicalism: Its History, Purpose and Tactics*, 4 vols. (Albany, 1920), I, 639ff.

[81] *Senate Reports*, B, no. 526 (Washington, 1920). In January, 1921, Martens voluntarily returned to Russia. See "Decision of the Secretary of Labor in the Case of Ludwig C. A. K. Martens," *Monthly Labor Review*, XII (January, 1921), 194.

[82] Cf. the opinion of the Lusk Committee in *Revolutionary Radicalism*, I, 644ff.

[83] Hard to Borah, April 18, 1920, Box 198, Borah Papers. On the report see also Moses to Borah and Borah to Moses, March 10, 1920, *ibid.*

[84] Colby to Wilson, June 11, 1920, Bainbridge Colby Papers, Division of Manuscripts, Library of Congress.

sheviks, Wilson feared that to do so would soon lead the United States to diplomatic recognition as well. And, as Colby informed American embassies abroad in July, any negotiations with the Bolsheviks would result in "a sacrifice of moral strength" in return for temporary material advantages. The United States, said Colby, "shares the revulsion of the civilized world against the tyranny which holds Russia in its power."[85] The Bolshevik regime, he told the Italian ambassador, was "based upon the negation of every principle of honor and good faith, and every usage and conviction . . . upon which it is possible to base harmonious and trustful relations."[86] The United States could not, said Colby, "recognize . . . a government which is determined and bound to conspire against our institutions."[87] Soon after Colby issued his statements, the general manager of the Scripps-Howard newspapers, William W. Hawkins, held a confidential interview with Woodrow Wilson. According to Hawkins, Wilson declared: "Bolshevism is a mistake. . . . If left alone, it will destroy itself. It cannot survive because it is wrong."[88]

Wilson deplored the ideology behind the Bolshevik Revolution, intervened with armed forces in 1918, and finally desisted from further armed intervention. The American army at Archangel had been far less effective than those troops which landed in Mexico in 1914, but its very presence on Russian soil had an immeasurable effect on future U.S.-Soviet relations. And the policy of moral condemnation voiced by Wilson in 1918–19 hardened into an unreasoning article of faith that, during most of the last half century, has characterized U.S. government policy as well—though Bolshevism has not, as Wilson supposed it would, destroyed itself.

Nor did American capitalism suffer the fate envisioned for it by Lenin in 1918. American troops remained in Vladivostok until April, 1920. Their presence indicated Wilson's concern over American commerce in the Far East—with expanding it and protecting it from Japanese as well as from Russian competitors.[89] In July, 1918, Lan-

[85] Colby to Ambassador in London, August 2, 1920, *ibid.*; see also Smith, *Aftermath of War*, 62ff.

[86] Colby to Baron Camillo Avezzano, August 10, 1920, U.S. Department of State, *Papers Relating to the Foreign Relations of the United States, 1920* (Washington, 1935–36), III, 463–68.

[87] Colby, quoted in Smith, *Aftermath of War*, 67.

[88] William W. Hawkins to B. Colby, August 11, 1933, Colby Papers.

[89] Jerry Israel, *Progressivism and the Open Door: America and China, 1905–*

sing proposed that the United States, Britain, France, and Japan create a new international bankers' consortium to advance funds to China.[90] At the time China was in the grip of revolution, one that had begun in 1911 and that would eventually spawn the Nationalist government of Chiang Kai-shek as well as the movement that finally overthrew him, the Chinese Communist forces of Mao Tse-tung. Already in 1919 the revolution was generating internal warfare and factional struggle as tumultuous as those in Russia after 1917 and in Mexico after 1910. Wilson sought to check the Mexican Revolution and refused to recognize the legitimacy of the Russian Bolsheviks. Toward China, on the other hand, he displayed much concern, sought to counter Japanese penetration there, and supported the bankers' consortium in China, ostensibly to help her to modernize. Yet neither Wilson nor his successor in 1921 recognized the nationalist movement led by Sun Yat-sen, one that by the early Twenties was beginning to gain leadership of the great Chinese Revolution.[91]

In trying to create a consortium to influence events in China, Lansing was following, with slight modifications, the American open door policy established at the turn of the century: maintain the territorial integrity of China and at the same time protect and expand American commercial interests there on a basis of free trade among the traditional imperial powers. When Japan tried to exclude Manchuria and Mongolia from the proposed consortium's range of activities, Lansing threatened to organize the group without Japan. After much wrangling, in May, 1920, Japan approved the consortium pretty much on the terms Lansing had originally laid down in 1918.[92] The bankers never did much; as Daniel Smith has commented, their chief signifi-

---

1921 (Pittsburgh, 1971), 161ff. Unterberger, *America's Siberian Expedition*, and White, *Siberian Intervention*, emphasize the Wilson administration's fear of Japan more than its fear of Bolshevism in Siberia.

[90] *Foreign Relations of the United States, 1918*, 169–71.

[91] Warren I. Cohen, "From Contempt to Containment: Cycles in American Attitudes toward China," in *Twentieth-Century American Foreign Policy*, ed. John Braeman *et al.* (Columbus, 1971), 521–32. Perhaps Wilson should not be faulted for failing to recognize Sun. Cohen notes that in the 1918–22 period, Sun Yat-sen "was not yet the personification of Chinese nationalism, not even to the Chinese. On the contrary, he was merely China's best-known politician, consorting with a variety of warlords in a desperate effort to capture the reins of power." But cf. William Appleman Williams, "China and Japan: A Challenge and a Choice of the Nineteen Twenties," *Pacific Historical Review*, XXVI (August, 1957), 259–79, who criticizes U.S. policy-makers for not supporting Sun in the early Twenties.

[92] Colby to Wilson, May 8, 1920, Box 3, Colby Papers.

cance was to reveal "vigorous American support of the Open Door and . . . a more cautious, moderate policy on the part of Japan."[93] Japan, moderate or not, appeared to be a greater threat to American interests in the Far East than was revolutionary China. Secretary Colby was delighted when, in 1920, the British government, equally concerned about Japan's increasing power, chose not to renew a 1902 Anglo-Japanese alliance.[94] But the very abrogation of that alliance encouraged creation of another one, since Britain was no less determined than the United States to maintain its power in the Far East. As Wilson left office in 1921, the groundwork was already being laid for the Harding administration's Washington Conference of 1921–22, out of which would come a series of treaties and naval agreements designed to protect American and British interests in the Far East, while recognizing Japan's presence there as well.[95] Whether the Washington treaties recognized the reality of the Chinese Revolution is another matter.

Woodrow Wilson's policy toward Japan, Mexico, and Russia can easily demonstrate the recent judgment of one historian who states, "One of the basic concerns of United States policy makers from 1920 to 1941 was the establishment and maintenance of a world order which would be conducive to the prosperity and peace of the United States," the prosperity in turn supposedly requiring "free access to markets, raw materials, and investment opportunities."[96] Of course, to find such a pattern or enduring theme in a multitude of events and ideas requires stress upon some facts more than others. And certainly it requires subjective judgment on the outlook and motives of American foreign policy-makers. The historical generalizations that emerge from such contemplation may be closer to metaphysics than to science, but then many historians have never claimed scientific status for their occupation. The concern among American policy-makers in 1919–20 for expanded trade and investments does, in fact, appear to be as close to verification as any historical judgment can be. The European food relief program managed by Herbert Hoover in 1919 demonstrated American generosity, but, more importantly in Hoover's view,

[93] Smith, *Aftermath of War*, 79.

[94] *Ibid.*, 79ff.

[95] Thomas H. Buckley, *The United States and the Washington Conference, 1921–1922* (Knoxville, 1970).

[96] Robert Freeman Smith, "American Foreign Relations, 1920–1942," in Barton J. Bernstein, ed., *Towards a New Past: Dissenting Essays in American History* (New York, 1968), 237–38.

it was designed to maintain agricultural prices at home by draining off surplus and at the same time was usable as a weapon against the Bolsheviks in Europe.[97] The Fifth Liberty Loan bill of 1919 provided for extension of $1.5 billion in credits to foreign governments and established the War Finance Corporation to make long-term loans to Americans engaged in the export trade.[98] Such a policy was in keeping with proposals made by Frank Vanderlip of the First National Bank, New York, who made a hasty tour of Europe in 1919 and decided that Europe needed large amounts of long-term American capital for reconstruction; the American economy could profit both from the loans and from trade with a restored European economy.[99] Vanderlip was not alone in stressing the need for American economic expansion. Carl Parrini's recent study has demonstrated that, for the most part, the Harding administration of the early Twenties continued a policy begun by Wilson: to shape the world into an economic community in which all doors stood open to trade and commerce, especially that of the United States, which must replace Britain as economic and political leader of the western world.[100]

Wilson's war to make the world safe for democracy had, it seemed, at least made the world open to American enterprise. Late in 1920, as Warren G. Harding awaited his inaugural and Woodrow Wilson prepared for retirement, the American secretary of state took stock of things. "Matters in the Department do not wear a particularly troublesome aspect at the moment, and the immediate outlook is serene."[101] Shut off from American life by illness and decline, Wilson could hardly know that the society over which he still theoretically presided vibrated with tension and turmoil.

[97] Gary Dean Best, "Food Relief as Price Support: Hoover and American Pork, January–March, 1919," *Agricultural History*, XLIV (October, 1970); Mayer, *Politics and Diplomacy of Peacemaking*, 24–28; cf. Frank M. Surface and Raymond L. Bland, *American Food in the World War and Reconstruction Period* (Stanford, 1931), which stresses the humanitarianism of the food program, as did Hoover himself in his memoirs and in *The Ordeal of Woodrow Wilson* (New York, 1958).

[98] *Annual Report of Secretary of the Treasury, 1919* (Washington, 1919), 44, 235–40.

[99] Frank A. Vanderlip, *What Happened to Europe* (New York, 1919). See also Paul P. Abrahams, "American Bankers and the Economic Tactics of Peace: 1919," *Journal of American History*, LVI (December, 1969), 572–83, for an argument that American bankers in 1919 wanted the government to take on a new financial role in Europe.

[100] Carl P. Parrini, *Heir to Empire: United States Economic Diplomacy, 1916–1923* (Pittsburgh, 1969).

[101] Colby to Wilson, November 27, 1920, Box 3b, Colby Papers.

VIII

American Society, 1920

In 1920, three hundred years after the Pilgrims came ashore in Massachusetts, the nation held a tercentenary celebration of their arrival there. It also held its fourteenth decennial census, which revealed some dimensions of the nation that had taken shape during the three centuries or so since Roanoke, Jamestown, and Plymouth. A prestigious Research Committee on Social Trends, appointed by President Hoover in 1929 to survey social changes in the country, judged population growth in America through the 1920 census to have been "one of the outstanding phenomena in world history." The committee estimated that in 1650 the total population of the seaboard colonies (excluding Indians) was 52,000.[1] In 1920 the population of the United States numbered over 106,000,000. During the American Revolution the total population was less than the population of Los Angeles and Detroit at the end of World War I. The rate of growth since the Civil War had held steady at 20 to 25 percent per decade until 1910. It dropped sharply after 1913 and reached a bottom in 1918, when the influenza pandemic of that year, along with the war, restricted growth to about 575,000. After the war, the growth rate began to shoot up again, though it would soon decline once more in the early Twenties.[2]

But head count was only one feature of the 1920 census. Demographers, economists, and other students of the subject had a wondrous array of facts at their disposal in the returns brought in and assembled by the Census Bureau. Even before the count got underway, observers marveled at the mechanics and methods of the bureau. Although pro-

[1] Warren S. Thompson and P. K. Whelpton, *Population Trends in the United States* (New York, 1933), 1. This is one of several monographs prepared under direction of the Research Committee. The committee's own report is *Recent Social Trends in the United States* (New York, 1933).

[2] Thompson and Whelpton, *Population Trends*, 1–3; Bureau of the Census, *Fourteenth Census of the United States Taken in the Year 1920* (Washington, 1921), I, 14–15.

fessional statisticians had criticized the bureau's work, the *New York Times*, in admiration, reported details on the "mechanical clerks" placed in a big emergency war building in Washington, where a "figure factory" was to handle the "great in-pouring streams of material from all over the country." These mechanical clerks could do the work of 500 human clerks, and in some cases more. Even so, there were 4,000 human employees on hand in Washington to assemble the "grist of assorted data" which would pour into the computers. Throughout the country there were 379 census supervisors, in charge of districts coextensive with congressional districts. In addition, there was a supervisor for each large city—except New York, which required four.[3]

The information that resulted from this undertaking was subject then, as it is now, to almost endless analysis. Perhaps the single most prominent item was the revelation that a majority of Americans now lived in urban areas (incorporated communities of 2,500 or more). This finding, long expected but awaited with some apprehension, generated profound discussion in the Twenties and has continually since then served to illustrate the fact that urbanization was a central feature, perhaps the most crucial one, in American life after World War I.[4] But in 1920 the urban majority was thin indeed: 54,318,032 urban dwellers to 51,390,739 in rural territories. And of course the urban population was heavily focused in several states. New York led the nation in urban inhabitants, with Pennsylvania placing second, Illinois third, Ohio fourth, and Massachusetts fifth. Rhode Island had the highest percentage of urban population (97.5). Mississippi was the most rural state in 1920 (86.6%), though North Dakota was only

[3] *New York Times*, November 23, 1919, III, 7:1. Because of the critical attitude of the American Statistical Association and the American Economic Association toward the Bureau of the Census, Secretary of Commerce William Redfield in November, 1918, asked the two associations to advise the bureau in its 1920 work. On the results, see "Report of the Joint Census Advisory Committee of the American Statistical and American Economic Association," *American Economic Review*, X (March, 1920), Supplement, 267–78. On operations of the Census Bureau, see Secretary of Commerce, *Reports of the Department of Commerce, 1920* (Washington, 1921), 47–65.

[4] Lewis Mumford, "The City," in Harold E. Stearns, ed., *Civilization in the United States* (New York, 1922), 3–20; R. D. McKenzie, "The Rise of Metropolitan Communities," in President's Research Committee, *Recent Social Trends*, 443–96; McKenzie, *The Metropolitan Community* (New York, 1933); Charles N. Glaab, "Metropolis and Suburb: The Changing American City," in *Change and Continuity in Twentieth-Century America: The 1920's*, ed. John Braeman *et al.* (Columbus, 1968), 399ff.

a fraction behind (86.4), with South Dakota next (84.0), Arkansas fourth (83.4), and South Carolina fifth (82.5). Mississippi and New York polarized the population distribution, a fact not unrelated to the cultural image that each state has projected in the twentieth century. New York in 1920 contained nearly 8,600,000 urban and 1,800,000 rural people. Mississippi had 240,000 townsmen and 1,500,000 rural inhabitants. The nation's center of population, according to the 1920 count, was in the extreme southeast corner of Owen County, Indiana. During the 1910–20 period that center had moved some ten miles west and a fraction north from Bloomington, Indiana, the center in 1910.[5]

Even though a narrow majority of Americans lived in urban communities, some 59,400,000 of them lived in places of less than 8,000.[6] In the Twenties, as the total population increased, so did the urban majority and urban concentration in that population. Political personalities and issues in the decade would reflect this increasing urban tilt. In 1921 Warren G. Harding, from Blooming Grove by way of Marion, Ohio, entered the White House. Twenty-nine months later his successor from Plymouth Notch, Vermont, took over the office, and in 1929 he gave way to a native of West Branch, Iowa. But in the meantime Al Smith of New York had made a serious bid for the Democratic presidential nomination in 1924, had gained it in 1928, and, though losing to Hoover, had once and for all brought the city, as symbol and as power, into the presidential campaign. But in 1920, both in population distribution and in its presidential choice, the nation hovered closer to the small town than to the farm or the metropolis.

Even so, as the country left World War I behind and entered the Twenties, it worried over the loss of community that presumably was the price it was paying for urban growth. By 1920 the style and pace of city life had already begun to intrude upon the countryside and the small hamlet, but for this very reason zealots of "back to the land" and advocates of community life expressed alarm at the trend.[7] One contemporary analyst admitted that such alarm was hardly new: "Xenophon complained that the Greeks loved the city rather than the

[5] *Fourteenth Census*, 32–33, 46–47; Thompson and Whelpton, *Population Trends*, Ch. 1.

[6] *Ibid.*, 20.

[7] Paul K. Conkin, *Tomorrow a New World: The New Deal Community Programs* (Ithaca, N.Y., 1959), 11–36, offers a succinct appraisal of back-to-the-land movements before and during the Twenties.

village."[8] A current song expressed part of the concern: "How 'Ya Gonna Keep 'Em Down on the Farm, after They've Seen Paree?" But alarm over urbanization went beyond farm economics. In 1630 John Winthrop told his company of fellow migrants in Puritan Massachusetts: "We must delight in each other, make each other's condition our own, rejoice together, mourn together, always having before our eyes our Communion and Community in the work, our Community as members of the same body."[9] Admittedly Winthrop was on a peculiar mission, and the community he envisioned underwent drastic change in subsequent years. But in a more secular twentieth century Americans still worried over community—and the loss of it.[10]

Before World War I some notable Progressives gave considerable thought to the idea of community.[11] During the war the Council of National Defense tried to organize community councils in every school district to help arouse support and greater efficiency for war work. "America," wrote one community enthusiast, "is the sum total of thousands upon thousands of neighborhoods, and therefore the neighborhood is the logical unit of the community center organization."[12] In the cause of national unity and victory individuals would work together—so ran a widespread sentiment—but in a community

[8] Benjamin H. Hibbard, "The Drift toward the City," in Elisha M. Friedman, ed., *America and the New Era: A Symposium on Social Reconstruction* (New York, 1920), 152.

[9] John Winthrop, "A Model of Christian Charity," in Perry Miller and Thomas H. Johnson, eds., *The Puritans* (New York, 1963), I, 198.

[10] The term "community" evidently meant many things to its users in 1919, ranging from "neighborhood" to "home town." One authority on the subject recently defined community as: "A group of people living together in some identifiable territory and sharing a set of interests embracing their lifeways. . . . Community, unlike neighborhood, implies more than geographical propinquity—it requires some identification of its members with the area and each other and some self-consciousness as a social entity." This same writer then added an observation that seems particularly relevant to the advocates of community in 1919–20: "Community, finally, is that mythical state of social wholeness in which each member has his place and in which life is regulated by cooperation rather than by competition and conflict. It has had brief and intermittent flowerings through history but always seems to be in decline at any given historical present. Thus community is that which each generation feels it must rediscover and re-create." Charles Abrams, *The Language of Cities: A Glossary of Terms* (New York, 1971), 59–61.

[11] Jean B. Quandt, *From the Small Town to the Great Community: The Social Thought of Progressive Intellectuals* (New Brunswick, N.J., 1970); see also Jackson Wilson, *In Quest of Community: Social Philosophy in the United States, 1860–1920* (New York, 1968).

[12] Ida C. Clarke, *The Little Democracy: A Text-Book on Community Organization* (New York, 1918), 4.

unit that enabled them to retain their sense of local identity and to control their own lives. This attempt to retain individual autonomy, in the face of the impersonality, bureaucracy, and homogenization brought on by urban and industrial growth, intensified after the war.[13] As the Twenties began, Americans struggled with the problem of creating the city while retaining the old sense of community and autonomy.[14] This conflict between rural and urban cultures would permeate American life in the decade.[15]

Wherever they lived in 1920, "native whites of native parentage" (the Census Bureau's term) outnumbered all other kinds of Americans, though New England and the Middle Atlantic states contained a considerable number of "foreign-born whites," as well as native-born whites whose parents were foreign-born.[16] America in 1920 was, as the cliché put it, a white man's country. The 1920 census counted some 10,500,000 blacks in the United States.[17] Between 1910 and 1920 the growth rate of the black population was less than half that of the white, but in view of the race riots of 1919, this growth rate was less important than where the black Americans had moved during the 1910–20 period. Before 1910 some 90 percent of all blacks in the United States lived in the South, where they made up nearly one-third of the region's total population. During World War I, in a spectacular migration northward, a half-million southern blacks left their tenant farms, their dilapidated schools, their marginal existence, and their caste society and moved into northern industrial cities. The number

[13] See, for example, the countless references to "community" endeavor reported in U.S. Council of National Defense, *Readjustment and Reconstruction Activities in the States*; also papers in *Proceedings of the National Conference of Social Work . . . 1919* (Chicago, 1920), 467–562.

[14] Lewis Mumford, "The City," in Stearns, ed., *Civilization in the United States*; Roy LuBove, *Community Planning in the 1920's: The Contribution of the Regional Planning Association* (Pittsburgh, 1963).

[15] A case study of this conflict is Don S. Kirschner, *City and Country: Rural Responses to Urbanization in the 1920's* (Westport, Conn., 1970). See also Paul Murphy, "Sources and Nature of Intolerance in the 1920's," *Journal of American History*, LI (June, 1964), 60–76, which applies to the rural-urban dichotomy of the decade the notion of *Gemeinschaft* vs. *Gesellschaft* developed by the German sociologist Frederick Tönnies.

[16] *Fourteenth Census of the U.S.*, II, Table 12, pp. 38–39; Thompson and Whelpton, *Population Trends*, 41–44.

[17] T. J. Woofter, Jr., "What Is the Negro Rate of Increase?" *Journal of the American Statistical Association*, XXVI, n.s. (December, 1931), 461–62; Woofter, *Races and Ethnic Groups in American Life* (New York, 1933). See also T. Lynn Smith, "The Redistribution of the Negro Population of the United States, 1910–1960," *Journal of Negro History*, LI (July, 1966), 155–73.

of blacks living outside the South almost doubled between 1910 and 1920. More than 50,000 blacks came to Chicago within an eighteen-month period in 1917–18. Detroit's black population increased from 5,700 in 1910 to 41,500 in 1920.[18]

The North hardly turned out to be the land of Canaan that migrating blacks had anticipated. Sometimes the lure of a good job materialized—in meat-packing, in automobile and truck production, in shipbuilding, on railroads, and in other industries geared for war.[19] As often as not, the migration North led to the ghetto and to an inferior job. A stone mason in the South became a coalyard laborer in Chicago; a barber became a janitor; a plasterer became a steelworker. Yet again and again these migrants said they "felt more like a man" and found "living easier" than in the South.[20] Blacks in the North soon discovered, however, that racism in the United States was not confined to the section they had left behind, and that while the war may have been a "pursuit of democracy in Europe there was a wide-spread destruction of it at home."[21]

In East Saint Louis in 1917, nine whites and forty or more blacks lost their lives in a riot that broke out over their employment in a defense plant.[22] This 1917 riot was the prelude to a ghastly time of trouble in 1919, when, between June and December, at the same time the Red Scare was sweeping to its climax, race riots erupted in some twenty towns and cities across the country from Longview, Texas, and Elaine, Arkansas, to Chicago and Washington. At least 120 people lost their lives in this carnage; meanwhile, seventy-eight blacks died at the hands of lynch mobs, an increase of fifteen such deaths over 1918 and thirty over 1917.[23]

[18] Thompson and Whelpton, *Population Trends,* 74–80; Woofter, *Races and Ethnic Groups,* 72–73; Chicago Commission on Race Relations, *The Negro in Chicago: A Study of Race Relations and a Race Riot* (Chicago, 1922), 79–80.

[19] U.S. Department of Labor, Division of Negro Economics, *The Negro at Work during the World War and during Reconstruction* (Washington, 1921); see also Emmett J. Scott, *Negro Migration during the War* (New York, 1920); Dewey H. Palmer, "Moving North: Negro Migration during World War I," *Phylon,* XXVII (Spring, 1967), 52–62; Jane Lang Scheiber and Harry N. Scheiber, "The Wilson Administration and the Wartime Mobilization of Black Americans, 1917–19," *Labor History,* X (Summer, 1969), 433–58.

[20] Chicago Commission, *Negro in Chicago,* 95, 97–103.

[21] John Hope Franklin, *From Slavery to Freedom* (New York, 1969), 474.

[22] Elliott M. Rudwick, *Race Riot at St. Louis, July 2, 1917* (Carbondale, Ill., 1964).

[23] Arthur I. Waskow, *From Race Riot to Sit-In: 1919 and the 1960's* (New York, 1966); William M. Tuttle, Jr., *Race Riot: Chicago in the Red Summer of 1919* (New

At the time they occurred, periodically since then, and especially in recent years these riots of 1919 provoked extended appraisals, ranging from guilty soul-searching to indignant polemics to bland sociology.[24] At short range, these riots precipitated by white attack upon black appear to have arisen over economic and psychic tensions brought on by the war and reconstruction. Competition for jobs, especially in the postwar reconstruction shuffle, was keen; at the same time, the black's sense of independence and dignity had been strengthened by his wartime job and his service in the army, which in turn challenged the white to reassert his own customary privilege of place, residence, and authority. In larger perspective the riots appear to have been only a tragic explosion into action of the latent racism that has permeated American history from its beginnings.[25] From far off or up close, a striking feature of the 1919 riots was the refusal of blacks to submit passively to white violence. In Washington, especially, blacks had demonstrated their ability to retaliate if not to overcome their attackers. But what blacks thought and did about their plight in America as the Twenties opened varied from utter apathy to occasional militancy, and there were many points along the ideological spectrum from accommodation on the right to protest on the left. In New York, where a galaxy of black poets and novelists and actors would provide the nucleus for the Harlem Renaissance of the Twenties,[26] Claude McKay in 1919 voiced a militancy toward the riots of that year: "If we must die, let it not be like hogs / Hunted and penned in an inglorious spot, / While round us bark the mad and hungry dogs. . . ."[27]

York, 1970); Lloyd M. Abernethy, "Washington Race War of July 1919," *Maryland Historical Magazine,* 58 (December, 1963), 309–24; Lester C. Lamon, "Tennessee Race Relations and the Knoxville Riot of 1919," *East Tennessee Historical Society Publications,* no. 41 (1969), 67–85; J. W. Butts and Dorothy James, "The Underlying Causes of the Elaine Riots of 1919," *Arkansas Historical Quarterly,* XX (Spring, 1961), 95–104; O. A. Rogers, Jr., "The Elaine Race Riots of 1919," *ibid.,* XIX (Summer, 1960), 142–50; Walter F. White, *Rope and Faggott, a Biography of Judge Lynch* (New York, 1929).

[24] See bibliographical essay.

[25] Cf. C. Vann Woodward, "White Racism and Black 'Emancipation,'" *New York Review of Books,* XII (February 27, 1969), 5–11. On racism after the war, see I. A. Newby, *Jim Crow's Defense: Anti-Negro Thought in America, 1900–1930* (Baton Rouge, 1965), 157–61, 172.

[26] Nathan I. Huggins, *Harlem Renaissance* (New York, 1971).

[27] Claude McKay, "If We Must Die," in Robert T. Kerlin, ed., *The Voice of the Negro, 1919* (New York, 1920), 183–88.

In 1919, too, the NAACP began working to gain passage of a federal anti-lynching law, though even when in the decade ahead such a bill occasionally reached the floor of Congress, it was talked to death;[28] meanwhile black critics, among them A. Philip Randolph of the monthly *Messenger,* were damning the NAACP's tactics as irrelevant to the needs of the great mass of blacks.[29] In 1919 the NAACP also began publicizing gruesome details on lynchings as they occurred, and the association, as it had done for a decade, kept up its campaign in the courts to gain for blacks the civil rights they were frequently denied.[30]

Far more dramatic and visible than the NAACP was the Universal Negro Improvement Association. Marcus Garvey, a black Jamaican who organized the UNIA in 1914, came to the United States in 1916 to establish a New York chapter. He stayed to create a national organization that for a spell in the early Twenties captured the support of several million black followers.[31] Unlike the NAACP leadership, made up of whites and blacks advocating integration, Garvey preached black pride and black capitalism—and black separatism. W. E. B. Du Bois of the NAACP denounced Garvey, who in turn belittled the NAACP and comparable integrationist and elitist stances.

Meanwhile, as the NAACP and the UNIA responded in their fashion to the race turmoil in America after the war, there were other black Americans who seemed uncommitted to either organization. Like Americans of other colors, black citizens were often preoccupied with their jobs, their families, and some modicum of recreation and

[28] Charles Flint Kellogg, *NAACP: A History of the National Association for the Advancement of Colored People,* I: *1909–1920* (Baltimore, 1967); *Tenth Annual Report of the National Association for the Advancement of Colored People, for the Year 1919* (New York, 1920), 87–91.

[29] A. Philip Randolph, "Lynching: Capitalism Its Cause; Socialism Its Cure," *The Messenger,* March, 1919, 9–12, reprinted in August Meier, Elliott Rudwick, and Francis L. Broderick, eds., *Black Protest Thought in the Twentieth Century* (Indianapolis, 1971), 58–91.

[30] Monroe N. Work, ed., *Negro Year Book, 1921–1922* (Tuskegee, Ala., 1922), 83–84.

[31] E. David Cronon, *Black Moses: The Story of Marcus Garvey and the Universal Negro Improvement Association* (Madison, 1970), 204, points out that "it is next to impossible to give an accurate estimate of the size of his following at any time" but offers several contemporary and retrospective estimates, ranging into the millions. On the Garvey movement, see also Amy Jacques Garvey, *Garvey and Garveyism* (London, 1970), and Theodore G. Vincent, *Black Power and the Garvey Movement* (Berkeley, 1971).

ease in their day to day routine—though for any black, in contrast to most whites, this required an end to second-class citizenship.[32] In 1920 a new magazine called *The Competitor* appeared. Launching their publication, its editors said they hoped to answer a pressing need among blacks for a journal "replete with matters calculated to inspire the race to its best efforts in everything American." The Negro was "beginning to see the folly of being a special American. . . . He wants to be swallowed up in the great scheme of Americanization."[33] To judge by the journal's contents, Americanization meant of course freedom from discrimination and an end to racism. But it also meant good health, attractive clothes, quality education, better income, and better "colored" baseball teams.[34] In specific response to the claim that a "New Negro" had arisen since the war, *The Competitor* editorialized: "There is no New Negro. There is a Negro with new ideals; and when he is allowed to live, to work, to develop himself into a full man, dependent upon himself rather than upon another, self-sustaining and self-respecting, he will appear as commonplace as any other American."[35] In June, 1921, soon after Harding succeeded Wilson, *The Competitor* welcomed the change and looked to better times. The "colored press," it reported, "is practically unanimous in the opinion that the out-going administration was a failure. . . . Negro leaders worked hard to elect [Harding]. The race was almost solid for the Grand Old Party, and now more than ever before the 'colored brother' [expects] a benefit for his race."[36] Shortly after its June publication, *The Competitor* ceased operations. For Black America life went on,[37] but the benefits came no more readily under Harding than under Wilson.[38]

While blacks talked of a "New Negro" emerging from the war,

[32] See *Half-Century Magazine*, VIII and IX (January–December, 1920), for suggestions of the heterogeneous interests of blacks in 1920, though cf. *Negro Year Book, 1921–22*, "Review of Events Affecting the Negro, 1919–1921," 1–109, which emphasizes lynching and other forms of racism.

[33] *The Competitor*, I (January, 1920), 2.

[34] *Ibid.*, 65–66.

[35] *Ibid.* (February, 1920), 4.

[36] *Ibid.*, III (April, 1921), 16.

[37] Blacks were not the only ethnic minority in the country in 1920. For brief reference to Mexican-Americans and others, see bibliographical essay.

[38] Randolph C. Downes, "Negro Rights and White Backlash in the Campaign of 1920," *Ohio History*, 75 (Spring–Summer, 1966), 85–107; Richard B. Sherman, "The Harding Administration and the Negro: An Opportunity Lost," *Journal of Negro History*, XLIX (July, 1964), 151–68; Sherman, "Republicans and Negroes: The Lessons of Normalcy," *Phylon*, XXVII (Spring, 1966), 63–79.

American women anticipated a new status for themselves after the war, too. Some time between 1890 and 1920 the Flapper replaced the Gibson Girl as an ideal of American womanhood, at least as she was visualized by men—in this case Charles Dana Gibson and John Held. The latter's drawings in the humor magazine *Life* portrayed for the Twenties a young girl who "bobbed her hair, concealed her forehead, flattened her chest, hid her waist, dieted away her hips and kept her legs in plain sight."[39] By the mid-Twenties one male observer was writing with appreciation of the "New Nakedness" in the "New Era of Undressing."[40] The woman that Charles Dana Gibson had depicted (his wife served as model) was a study in contrast: "long hair, high brow, thirty-six inch bust, narrow anatomically precise waist, broad hips and well-concealed legs . . . maternal and wifely [and seemingly] incapable of an immodest thought or deed."[41]

The transition from Gibson Girl to Flapper was only one element in a tumultuous women's movement that occurred between the end of the nineteenth century and the end of World War I. If the Flapper emerged from that quarter-century of agitation, so did the Nineteenth Amendment. And women who wanted to vote and exercise other civil rights were, if anything, more conspicuous between the Nineties and the Twenties than women who wanted to get away from home and bed and excess underwear. The period 1890 to 1920, notes William O'Neill, was "a kind of feminist golden age. In no other time were there so many women of heroic stature,"[42] among them Lillian Wald, Florence Kelly, Jane Addams, Charlotte Perkins Gilman, Carrie Chapman Catt, Alice Paul, Emma Goldman, and Cheryl Eastman. But these talented and outspoken women did not constitute a single cohesive movement or manifest a single ideology. Some were preoccupied with social justice, meaning such goals as abolition of child labor. Others with single-minded devotion focused on woman suffrage. Others were feminists, seeking emancipation far beyond the right to vote. They talked of equal job and educational opportunities, of birth control and an end to a moral double-standard; as

[39] Kenneth A. Yellis, "Prosperity's Child: Some Thoughts on the Flapper," *American Quarterly*, XXI (Spring, 1969), 44–64; see also G. Stanley Hall, "Flapper Americana Novissima," *Atlantic Monthly*, CXXIX (June, 1922), 771–80; and Bruce Blivin, "Flapper Jane," *New Republic*, XLIV (September 9, 1925), 65–67.

[40] Blivin, "Flapper Jane."

[41] Yellis, "Prosperity's Child."

[42] William L. O'Neill, *The Woman Movement: Feminism in the United States and England* (London, 1969), 73.

Bruce Blivin reported, they clearly meant "that in the great game of sexual selection" they would "no longer be forced to play the role, simulated or not, of helpless quarry."[43]

What Frederick Lewis Allen fearlessly called a "revolution in manners and morals" in the Twenties may not have quite measured up to a revolution, but the change that he was describing—and that the Flapper presumably personified—was underway well before 1920, and even before World War I. The "new woman" of 1920 was not entirely new. Well before 1914 cars for dating, phones for romantic (or at least personal) accommodation, and a "variety of partners at the office or the factory" were providing considerable "privacy and permissiveness between the sexes."[44] One style-watcher in 1914 wrote that the new ideal was a "slim, boy like creature."[45] By 1910, in contrast to 1900, many American women were avidly cultivating their beauty of face and form and were displaying enough of the latter to have scandalized the Gibson Girl.[46] Powder, rouge, lipstick, and eyebrow stain enjoyed wide sales by the end of World War I, partly because thousands of doughboys in France sent home duty-free parcels of Parisian perfumes and cosmetics. Rolled-down hose appeared in 1917; scarcity of wool and cotton popularized silk for stockings during the war and put the hobble-skirt and trailing dinner gown out of style.[47]

[43] Blivin, "Flapper Jane," 67; Eleanor Flexner, *Century of Struggle: The Woman's Rights Movement in the United States* (Cambridge, 1959), 248–324; Aileen Kraditor, *The Ideas of the Woman Suffrage Movement* (New York, 1965); William L. O'Neill, *Everyone Was Brave: Rise and Fall of Feminism in America* (Chicago, 1969).

[44] James R. McGovern, "The American Woman's Pre–World War I Freedom in Manners and Morals," *Journal of American History*, LV (September, 1968), 315–33.

[45] Dorothy Dix, in *Boston American*, April 7, 1910; quoted *ibid.*, 324.

[46] Much contemporary opinion reported this development, and contemporary magazines often depicted the change in attire, or the lack of it. See, for example, *Harper's Weekly*, LXI (July 10, 1915), 41; on the other hand, page after page of *Vanity Fair* and other periodicals devoted to fashion depicted the American woman swathed in material that, by the standards of the Twenties, would seem downright Victorian. The road from the hoop skirt to the miniskirt has been long and uneven.

[47] McGovern, "Pre–World War I Freedom," 327; Dixon Wecter, *When Johnny Comes Marching Home* (Cambridge, 1944), 342. The first beauty shops in the United States opened for business between 1900 and 1910. In 1859 the total value of cosmetics manufactured in the United States came to just over $1,000. Fifty years later they totaled $7,000 or so. By 1914, they reached over $16,000. During the next five years, sales soared to $59.5 million; and this figure doubled by 1925. Aytoun Ellis, *The Essence of Beauty* (New York, 1962), 120–21; cf. Wecter, *Johnny*, which lists "the annual cosmetic and perfume trade" in 1914 at $17,000,000, and in 1925 at $141,488,000.

Meanwhile, there were suffragists who, in dress and morals, were thoroughly upright and old-fashioned girls but who demonstrated and agitated and proselytized for woman suffrage alone as a necessary prerequisite to any further emancipation of women. In fact, the view of women as sex objects was precisely what some suffragists deplored. As David Kennedy has pointed out, some feminists "wanted to free women *from* sex," whereas Margaret Sanger, for one, "called upon women to develop their sexual natures."[48] The day before Woodrow Wilson's first inaugural, 5,000 women marched through the center of Washington. During the next seven years suffragists kept the pressure on Wilson, on Congress, and on state legislatures. America's entry into war in 1917 was a boon to the women's movement. It brought thousands of women out of the home into industry and government, where they frequently gained a new sense of economic independence.[49] The war supplied Wilson and other former opponents of woman suffrage the "convenient fiction that woman suffrage was a war measure," and they were able to yield to the pressure of the cause without appearing to have suffered defeat.[50] Despite the opposition to the war by several pacifistic groups of suffragists, Wilson called for woman suffrage as a war measure on January 10, 1918. In June, 1919, after intense lobbying by its supporters, the Nineteenth Amendment went to the states. In August, 1920, just in time for women to vote in the presidential election of that year, the amendment gained approval by the necessary thirty-sixth state legislature and became the law of the land.

The year 1920 was, judges one student of the subject, "the moral pinnacle of American feminism."[51] Woman suffrage was a reality. The Eighteenth Amendment had also gained the prohibition against drink that many (but by no means all) women had advocated for a quarter-century, and child labor had been declared illegal by a 1918 congressional act. But for every gain there was a loss. Many women who had gone to work during the war lost their jobs to returning

[48] David B. Kennedy, *Birth Control in America: The Career of Margaret Sanger* (New Haven, 1970). See also Mary Ware Dennett, *Birth Control Laws, Shall We Keep Them, Change Them, or Abolish Them?* (New York, 1926).

[49] Ida Clyde Clarke, *American Women and the World War* (New York, 1918); Emily Newell Blair, *The Woman's Committee: United States Council of National Defense—An Interpretative Report* (Washington, 1920); Marion Nims, *Women in the War: A Bibliography* (Washington, 1918).

[50] O'Neill, *The Woman's Movement*, 79. See also Flexner, *Century of Struggle*, 276–93, 306ff.

[51] O'Neill, *The Woman's Movement*.

veterans.[52] In keeping with their increasing enrollment in colleges during the previous two decades, women in 1920 made up 47.3 percent of all college enrollment, but that percentage would fall in the decade ahead. In 1919–20, 93 women (compared to 433 men) received Ph.D.'s, and 1,180 received M.A. degrees (compared to 1,650 men), suggesting that the old prejudice against higher education for women was dying. Yet the woman graduate then suffered job discrimination, with the better jobs and the higher salaries going to men with comparable degrees of education. And some jobs remained, as before the war, for men—or women—only. Men pretty much monopolized college and university teaching, women the elementary and secondary schools.[53]

The "new woman" of 1920 lived a different life from her female peer of 1900, but her emancipation, by any feminist's standard, was yet to come. She could vote in national elections, though this did not produce any verifiable bloc of voters who could influence candidates and their policies.[54] She had gained a modicum of economic independence during the war that the postwar readjustment did not entirely destroy, but she still suffered job and salary discrimination.[55] She found readier access to college but not to the professions that her education qualified her for. She found divorce and birth control easier to come by than before the war, but at least one feminist, while admitting that "men and women are no more to blame for being oversexed than a prize hog for being overfat," still lamented the "overdeveloped sex instinct of men, requiring more than women were willing to give."[56] And for every Fitzgerald Flapper of the Twenties,

[52] *Ibid.*; Sophonisba P. Breckinridge, *Women in the Twentieth Century: A Study of Their Political, Social and Economic Activities* (New York, 1933), 154.

[53] *Ibid.*, 199–203; Willystine Goodsell, "The Educational Opportunities of American Women—Theoretical and Actual," *Annals* of the American Academy of Political and Social Science, CXLIII (May, 1929), 1–13; Marion O. Hawthorne, "Women as College Teachers," *ibid.*, 146–53. For discussion of "the kind of work women do," covering a considerable range of occupations, see President's Research Committee, *Recent Social Trends*, 716ff.

[54] S. A. Rice and M. M. Willey, "American Women's Ineffective Use of the Vote," *Current History Magazine*, XX (1924), 641–47.

[55] Alice Rogers Hager, "Occupations and Earnings of Women in Industry," *Annals* of the American Academy of Political and Social Science, CXLIII (May, 1929), 65–73; Nellie Swartz, "The Trend in Women's Wages," *ibid.*, 104–8.

[56] Charlotte P. Gilman, "Towards Monogamy," in Freda Kirchwey, ed., *Our Changing Morality: A Symposium* (New York, 1924), 65; Kennedy, *Birth Control in America*, 72–107; Arthur Garfield Hays, "Modern Marriage and Ancient Laws," in Kirchwey, ed., *Our Changing Morality*, 19–33; Elsie Clews Parsons, "Changes in

there were countless fatigued and undernourished textile mill operators and migratory fruit-pickers and mining town and ghetto house-
wives who never knew the life of Zelda Fitzgerald.[57] The "new
woman" of 1920 was as chimerical as the "New Negro."

In comparable fashion prohibitionists, who in 1920 could talk of
a new morality, found themselves within the next decade discredited
and seemingly put to rout. On December 22, 1918, Congress submitted the Eighteenth Amendment to the states for approval; the
amendment, if ratified, would prohibit the manufacture, sale, and
transportation of intoxicating liquors in the United States. By January 16, 1919, the amendment received approval of the necessary
thirty-six states. On January 16, 1920, it went into operation, as did
the Volstead Act of October 28, 1919, which defined intoxicating
liquor as any beverage containing more than half of 1 percent
alcohol.[58]

The "noble experiment," as Herbert Hoover would label it in
1928,[59] began with unrestrained rejoicing by the Dry forces. Just
past midnight on January 17, 1920, with Prohibition a legal reality,
William Jennings Bryan spoke before a night-watch service by temperance workers and quoted Matthew 20:2—"for they are dead
which sought the young child's life." In Norfolk, Virginia, evangelist
Billy Sunday exulted: "Slums will soon be only a memory. We will
turn our prisons into factories and our jails into storehouses and
corncribs. Men will walk upright now, women will smile, and the
children will laugh. Hell will be forever for rent."[60]

Sex Relations," *ibid.*, 37–49; Beatrice M. Hinkle, "Changing Marriage," *Survey*,
LVII (December 1, 1926), 286–89.

[57] See Breckinridge, *Women in the Twentieth Century*, 99ff., including a revealing
chart of "selected occupations" on p. 140. A study of conditions in one area is Ruth
Allen, *The Labor of Women in the Production of Cotton* (Austin, Tex., 1931) ; see
also Helen Glenn Tyson, "Mothers Who Earn," *Survey*, LVII (December 1, 1926),
275–79; and Beulah Amidon, "They Must Work," *ibid.*, 311, 340–42.

[58] *Cong. Rec.*, 65 Cong., 2 sess. (December 17–18, 1918), 422–70, 477–78, 490;
David Leigh Colvin, *Prohibition in the United States: A History of the Prohibition
Party and of the Prohibition Movement* (New York, 1926) ; *Cong. Rec.*, 66 Cong.,
1 sess. (October 28, 1919), 7633–34.

[59] During the presidential campaign that year, Hoover said: "Our country has
deliberately undertaken a great social and economic experiment, noble in motive
and far-reaching in purpose." Hoover, *The Memoirs of Herbert Hoover: The Cabinet
and the Presidency* (New York, 1952), 201.

[60] Bryan quoted in Lawrence W. Levine, *Defender of the Faith, William Jennings
Bryan: The Last Decade, 1915–1925* (New York, 1965), 127. Sunday quoted in
Harry Elmer Barnes, *Prohibition versus Civilization: Analyzing the Dry Psychosis*
(New York, 1932), 68.

Such remarks point up one of the enduring myths of Prohibition —that it was a movement engineered by Fundamentalist fanatics trying to censor, if not banish to the nether regions, those temptations of the flesh being spawned by an emerging industrial and urban society. There was, of course, a powerful strain of old-time religious morality at work in the Prohibition movement, a fact emphasized ever since debate over the Eighteenth Amendment began during World War I.[61] In 1927, trying to comprehend the tensions racking American society at the time, Walter Lippmann saw Prohibition as part of a larger social struggle: "The defense of the Eighteenth Amendment . . . has become much more than a mere question of regulating the liquor traffic. It involves a test of strength between social orders. . . . The Eighteenth Amendment is the rock on which the evangelical church militant is founded, and with it are involved a whole way of life and an ancient tradition."[62] In 1962, endorsing Lippmann's interpretation while translating it into a psychological idiom, Andrew Sinclair wrote: "Prohibition was the final victory of the defenders of the American past. On the rock of the Eighteenth Amendment, village America made its last stand." When the rock crumbled with repeal, so did "rural morality," as the "old order of the country gave way to the new order of the cities."[63]

This is a plausible view. Certainly Drys tended to be strong in their Protestant faith,[64] and the proclivity of Catholics for wine, if only in church, and the abundance of speakeasies and rum-running gangsters in the city during the Twenties no doubt reinforced the rural moralist's anathema on urban living. But the correlation of Drys with rural Anglo-Protestant traditionalists, in contrast to Wet urban Catholics and sophisticates, requires some qualification. Prohibition was not a one-dimensional movement engineered by freaky Protestant moralists; rather, it was part of a design for a better society envisioned by a wide range of prewar Progressives.[65] To these reformers there were scientific, social, economic, and political as well as religious arguments for Prohibition. As Joseph Gusfield has noted, many occupational and social groups supported the drive for the

---

[61] For titles on Prohibition, see bibliographical essay.

[62] Walter Lippmann, *Men of Destiny* (New York, 1927), 30–31.

[63] Andrew Sinclair, *Prohibition: The Era of Excess* (New York, 1964), 5.

[64] Joseph R. Gusfield, "Prohibition: The Impact of Political Utopianism," in Braeman *et al.*, eds., *Change and Continuity in Twentieth-Century America*, 262–66.

[65] James H. Timberlake, *Prohibition and the Progressive Movement, 1900–1920* (Cambridge, 1963).

Eighteenth Amendment: social workers who thought it could alleviate the deep-seated poverty in industrial areas; businessmen who saw the drinking immigrant as a threat to sober and disciplined ways of life; reformers who thought the end of drinking might help to end political corruption. Drys often cited not Scripture but scientific data to bolster their claims that alcohol was debilitating; employers concerned with safety in their establishments cited drunkenness as a major cause of accidents. Still, Gusfield finds that "national prohibition sentiment" was highest "where the populations were Protestant, rural, and nativist."[66]

Prohibition in 1920 to some degree marked the temporary victory of a Protestant rural morality—as repeal in 1932 would mark an urban supremacy. But the victory, like the terms "urban" and "rural," was nebulous. The United States was a heavy-drinking society before World War I. Despite folklore to the contrary, Prohibition cut consumption to perhaps half the prewar rate, but the rate of decrease came largely from diminished beer-drinking and not from less consumption of the harder stuff, which in bootlegged fashion poured in from Cuba, Canada, and elsewhere. After repeal, alcoholic consumption did not rise appreciably.[67] Yet statistics are one thing and cultural symbols another. In 1920, and while it lasted in the decade or so ahead, Prohibition and the searing debate that it provoked did demonstrate a conflict of cultures. The dichotomy of urban-rural, Catholic-Protestant, and immigrant-nativist gained an added ingredient: Wet-Dry.

Living amidst the turmoil of demobilization and reconstruction, the panic of the Red Scare, the violence of the 1919–20 race riots, and the conflict of cultures focusing on Prohibition, Americans in 1920 were hardly in a position to rejoice over the state of their society. The very day's routine was becoming a matter of urgency and dispute, as illustrated by the discussion that broke out over daylight saving time in 1919. During the war, as a means of saving on fuel and electricity and to increase efficiency of production, Congress established daylight time, and the Interstate Commerce Commission even drew up five new time zones, altering the ones set by the railroads in

[66] Gusfield, "Prohibition," 266. But cf. Robert A. Hohner, "The Prohibitionists: Who Were They?" *South Atlantic Quarterly*, LXVIII (Autumn, 1969), 491–505, for the view that prohibition was fundamentally a middle-class rather than a rural phenomenon.

[67] Gusfield, "Prohibition."

the 1880's.[68] Beginning at 2:00 A.M. on the last Sunday in March, the clock was set ahead one hour; on the last Sunday in October, it was returned to standard time. In the spring of 1919 a bill to repeal this wartime practice came before Congress, which debated the measure at interminable length. The debate took on a distinct rural vs. urban alignment, with municipalities and city-based organizations calling for continued daylight time, and rural constituents and pressure groups demanding repeal. Finally, in August, 1919, Congress voted for repeal. Wilson vetoed the bill, claiming that daylight time in the summer months was convenient to citizens and profitable to the economy. Congress overrode his veto. A number of cities and states thereupon established daylight time for themselves and urged others to do the same. Debate over the issue moved into the Twenties.[69]

While some Americans were trying to save time, others were trying to kill it. Leisure and ways to enjoy it were commonplace by 1920. The normal work week in some American industries—though by no means in all of them—had declined some twenty hours during the preceding half-century, and especially during and just after the war; annual vacations of a week to a month were becoming common.[70] By 1920 the sports and other amusements once enjoyed by the privileged few were within reach of urban workers, now freed from at least some of their traditional lengthy work days. Too, the standard of living had risen since 1900, enough to bring on an extraordinary outlay for recreation and amusement,[71] including use of the automobile. In Decem-

[68] *Cong. Rec.*, 65 Cong., 1 sess. (March 15, 1918), 3564–84; (March 16, 1918), 3594–95; (March 20, 1919), 3756; *Decisions of the Interstate Commerce Commission of the United States, August, 1918, December, 1918* (Washington, 1919), LI, 273–86. The five zones were eastern, central, mountain, Pacific, and Alaska.

[69] *Cong. Rec.*, 66 Cong., 1 sess. (June 18, 1919), 1304–36; (July 12, 1919), 2492; (August 19, 1919), 3982; (August 20, 1919), 4008; Samuel A. Welldon, "Let Us Have Daylight Saving," *The American City*, XXI (November, 1919), 432–33; *New York Times*, December 11, 1919, 24:6; March 28, 1920, 1:4; June 13, 1920, 17:1; April 25, 1920, II, 3:4.

[70] President's Research Committee, *Recent Social Trends*, 828–29; John R. Commons *et al.*, *History of Labor in the United States*, III; Don D. Lescohier, *Working Conditions* (New York, 1935), 97–110; Solomon Fabricant, *Employment in Manufacturing, 1899–1939* (New York, 1932), 12–16, 233–43; Lazare Teper, *Hours of Labor* (Baltimore, 1932).

[71] President's Research Committee, *Recent Social Trends*, 813–21. According to one estimate, average annual real earnings of employed wage earners in 1900 were $97 (1914 = $100), in 1910 were $101, and in 1920 were $106. Jesse Frederick Steiner, *Americans at Play: Recent Trends in Recreation and Leisure Time Activities* (New York, 1933), 9–11. But see other estimates for various occupational groups in Daniel J. Ahearn, Jr., *The Wages of Farm and Factory Laborers, 1914–1944* (New York,

ber, 1919, Secretary of the Interior Franklin K. Lane drew up an inventory of certain commodities and privileges held by Americans. According to Lane's count, there were some 5,000,000 automobiles in the United States.[72] Apportioned among 25,000,000 families, this provided one family in five with a car, which most likely was a Ford. Purchasers in 1920 could choose among 266 different makes of automobiles, but Henry Ford's Model T, priced at just over $500, outsold all others by a wide margin; Ford built 750,000 of the nearly 2,000,000 motor vehicles sold in 1919. Well behind Ford in sales came the other best sellers—Dodge, Chevrolet, Buick, and Overland. Beyond these, there were makes and models of all kinds. The four-cylinder Allen touring car, out of Dayton, Ohio, sold for $1,495 and carried fifty-six rear springs to "iron out rough roads." The Apperson, built in Kokomo, Indiana, was a V-8 capable of accelerating in high gear from one to forty miles per hour in twenty seconds. Cadillacs cost $3,000 and up; nevertheless, more than 20,000 of them were sold in 1920. The Columbia Six, built in Detroit, was advertised as "the gem of the highway" and a car that "has no bolshevistic tendencies." The Franklin, out of Syracuse, sold for $2,600 and was unique in 1920 for its air-cooled engine. The Pierce-Arrow was also special, featuring right-hand drive and a clock built into the dashboard. Most of the makes available in 1920 would not survive the decade ahead, which saw the automobile work a profound revolution on the nation's economy and society but also saw the emergence of the Big Three— Ford, General Motors, and Chrysler—as dominant in the automobile industry.[73]

Even in 1920 Lane could boast, "We have more automobiles than

---

1945) ; Whitney Coombs, *The Wages of Unskilled Labor in Manufacturing Industries in the United States, 1890–1924* (New York, 1926) ; and especially the study that is commonly cited as the most reliable for the early years of the century when reliable statistics were often unobtainable, Paul Douglas, *Real Wages in the United States, 1890–1926* (Boston, 1930).

[72] *New York Times*, December 28, 1919, IV, 3:1. The total motor vehicle registration at the time was considerably higher—7,565,446 in 1919, and 9,231,941 in 1920 (as compared to 1,258,062 in 1913), but this included trucks and other motor-powered vehicles and reflected, as well, transfer of titles from one owner to another. See Department of Commerce, *Biennial Census of Manufactures, 1921* (Washington, 1924), 1034–35.

[73] Tad Burness, *Cars of the Early Twenties* (Philadelphia, 1968) ; *Facts and Figures of the Automobile Industry* (New York, 1927) ; John B. Rae, *The American Automobile* (Chicago, 1965), 87–101; Automobile Manufacturers Association, *Automobiles of America* (Detroit, 1968), 70–72; *New York Times*, January 4, 1920, VIII, Supplement.

all the rest of the world put together."[74] This abundance of automobiles created an abundance of new recreational schemes and sites: country camps for upper-middle-class and wealthier Americans; access to new hunting and fishing sites for millions; picnicking and sight-seeing in national parks and other locations along the open road, away from the growing urban sprawl.[75] In 1917 some 3,160,000 tourists visited the country's National Forests; by 1920 the number reached 4,832,671, and would leap upward in the decade ahead. In 1920 over 4,000,000 hunting licenses were issued. The Bureau of Navigation registered some 1,600 yachts of sixteen gross tons and over.[76]

Apart from trips in the country and hunting expeditions and yachting and summer tours, all of which boomed after the war, there was the phenomenal development of spectator sports. "What other country is there," asked Secretary Lane, "in which so much time is spent on sports?"[77] In 1920 baseball was unquestionably the major sport in the United States. Between 1911 and 1920 the annual World Series drew a total attendance of 1,730,900. During the Twenties attendance at the series rose to 2,455,203, an increase of 41 percent over the previous decade.[78] The Black Sox scandal of 1919 evidently did little to diminish the fans' enthusiasm for the game that since the 1880's had been the national pastime. On the other hand, in a year that saw seventy-eight blacks killed by lynching and that saw Al Capone arrive in Chicago to begin a decade of rampant criminality, the escapades of several baseball players seems to have stirred up an inordinate amount of sentiment. Reaction to the scandal merely demonstrated the prevailing dogma that baseball, as President William Howard Taft declared in 1910, was "a clean, straight game," one that "summons to its presence everybody who enjoys clean, straight athletics."[79]

[74] *New York Times*, December 28, 1919, IV, 3:1.

[75] Steiner, *Americans at Play*, 34ff.; Earl Pomeroy, *In Search of the Golden West: The Tourist in Western America* (New York, 1957), 125, 129–30, 146ff.

[76] Steiner, *Americans at Play*, 41, 49, 54; *Annual Report of the Commissioner of Navigation . . . June 30, 1920* (Washington, 1920), 241; *Annual Report of the Department of Agriculture for 1920* (Washington, 1920), 239–40.

[77] *New York Times*, December 28, 1919, IV, 3:1.

[78] Steiner, *Americans at Play*, 84–85.

[79] Harold Seymour, *Baseball: The Golden Age* (New York, 1971), 274. Given Taft's orthodoxy, it is not surprising that in 1918, during baseball's search for a new commissioner, he was a prominent nominee for the job, which he finally declined. *New York Times*, November 24, 1918, 1:2; November 25, 1918, 14:1; December 7, 1918, 12:3.

Even so, scandals and unethical behavior were abundant in baseball both before and after 1919, though the World Series that year became the most publicized affair in the game's history.

The Chicago White Sox, heavy favorites to win the series, lost to the Cincinnati Reds five games to three. After nearly a year of rumors and investigations, a Cook County grand jury in October, 1920, indicted eight White Sox players[80] and a number of gamblers for attempting to fix the series. In August, 1921, after a sensational trial, seven Chicago players gained acquittal; charges against the eighth had been dropped for lack of evidence. The new baseball commissioner, Kenesaw M. Landis, promptly banned from baseball the seven players acquitted in a court of law, as well as two others not even indicted.[81] Landis already had a reputation for severity, gained from his harsh sentencing of Bill Haywood and other Wobblies at their Chicago trial in August, 1918. His actions as baseball commissioner were in character, but the acquittal followed by the Landis excommunication points up the ambiguity in the entire Black Sox affair. Play by play accounts of the series offer little proof that games were actually thrown. The so-called Black Sox performed better than their teammates, the "Clean Sox." Harold Seymour notes that "some of the players in some of the games undoubtedly tried to lose, but there is no certainty about which games they succeeded in deliberately losing, if any, [and] which games the Cincinnati Reds won by their own efforts. After all, the opposing team must have had something to do with the results."[82] Finally, the trial itself focused on the players and not on the gamblers, none of whom was convicted.[83]

The careers of the blacklisted players ended, but the game went on, and so did football, tennis, and golf, all of which were booming in popularity by 1920 and which in the decade ahead would produce a

[80] Pitchers Ed Cicotte and Claude Williams; infielders George Weaver, Chick Gandil, Charles Risberg, and Fred McMullin; outfielders Oscar Felsch and Joe Jackson.

[81] Fred McMullin, whose indictment was dropped after the original charges were made against the eight Sox, and Joe Gedeon, an infielder for the St. Louis Browns, who had gambled on the series.

[82] Seymour, *Baseball: The Golden Age,* 332.

[83] The best account of the scandal is in Seymour's exhaustive and scholarly history of the sport. A succinct coverage is David Q. Voigt, "The Chicago Black Sox and the Myth of Baseball's Single Sin," *Journal of the Illinois State Historical Society,* LXII (Autumn, 1969), 293–306. Victor Luhrs, *The Great Baseball Mystery: The 1919 World Series* (South Brunswick, N.J., 1966), contains a reprint of the official play-by-play description of the 1919 Series.

quartet of folk heroes: Babe Ruth, Red Grange, Bill Tilden, and Bob Jones (his fans called him "Bobby," a name he hated).[84] The other great sports celebrity of the Twenties, Jack Dempsey, suffered a momentary period of unpopularity in 1919, the year he was crowned heavyweight boxing champion. Dempsey had sat out the war, gaining deferment because of his job in war industry. In February, 1920, he was indicted for draft evasion. Though he gained acquittal in June, he underwent a lot of criticism, especially from American Legion posts. While Dempsey was being acquitted, Jack Johnson, great black heavyweight under indictment for violation of the Mann Act and living in Cuban exile, volunteered to come home, faced trial, was sentenced, and entered Leavenworth prison in September, 1920. White supremacists had tried for years to raise a White Hope to dethrone Johnson, who, when well past his prime, finally lost his heavyweight title to Jess Willard (white) in 1915 in a twenty-six-round bout in Havana. Leavenworth was one more blow against a black champion who had beaten white fighters and had married three white women in quick succession, and after prison would marry a fourth.[85]

When for their recreation they were not playing games or watching their heroes, Americans in 1920 were likely to be at the movies. Six hundred million times that year Americans laid down the price of admission to movie houses, some of them rococo piles of lush and lavish stone and furnishings, spread out in villages and cities all over the country. By the end of World War I, the American film industry dominated the world market. Studio stocks were listed on Wall Street, and movie-making was the fifth-largest industry in the country. By 1919 Hollywood studios were spending some $20,000,000 a year on salaries and $12,000,000 more for other film costs. Cecil B. DeMille, already a noted director who tried to keep in step with what he thought

[84] Roderick Nash, *The Nervous Generation: American Thought, 1917–1930* (Chicago, 1970), 128–30; Frank Litsky, "Star of a Golden Age," *New York Times,* December 19, 1971, 1:4, 61:1–6.

[85] *New York Times,* January 14, 1920, 10:8; January 21, 1920, 8:5; January 30, 1920, 16:3; February 26, 1920, 1:2; June 9, 1920, 16:4; June 16, 1920, 17:4; June 17, 1920, 32:3; July 10, 1920, 5:2; July 21, 1920, 16:6; July 26, 1920, 11:5; September 15, 1920, 17:5; September 21, 1920, 16:3; "War Record of Dempsey," *Literary Digest,* 64 (February 14, 1920), 122–24; "The Return of Jack Johnson," *The Competitor,* II (July, 1920), 71–72; John Lardner, *White Hopes and Other Tigers* (Philadelphia, 1947), 34–35, 56–57; Finis Farr, *Black Champion: The Life and Times of Jack Johnson* (New York, 1968).

was public taste (however gross it may have been), began production in 1919 of a series of modern comedies about the fabulously rich, leading off with *Male and Female*. For another kind of comedy, the great Charles Chaplin built a new studio in Los Angeles, from which some brilliant films would issue in the decade ahead. In fact, slapstick comedies, along with Westerns, were perhaps the outstanding and certainly the most indigenous films produced in Hollywood in the Twenties.[86] With whatever it produced, Hollywood would profoundly influence American manners and perhaps morals as well in the years to come. Meanwhile, the written and spoken words continued to work their acculturation, too.

Church membership and school attendance, at least, registered a continuing devotion to faith and to learning. Between 1906 and 1926 church membership grew at virtually the same rate as the nation's population; four years before 1920, as well as six years after that date, 55 percent of the American people thirteen years of age and over were church members.[87] Between 1916 and 1926, however, membership growth differed strikingly from one denomination to another. The African Methodist Episcopal Zion Church, for one, grew at a startling rate (77.6 percent), but the overall concentration of population remained in a few traditional denominations, such as Methodist Episcopal, Southern Baptist, and Catholic. Whatever their sect, the majority of American church members—five out of eight—were Protestant.[88]

The war seems to have had no measurable effect on church membership, though churches had gone to war with zeal, and numerous church organizations after the war called for U.S. entrance into the League

[86] Arthur Knight, *The Liveliest Art* (New York, 1959), 107ff. Lewis Jacobs, *The Rise of the American Film* (New York, 1939); Benjamin B. Hampton, *A History of the Movies* (New York, 1931); "The Motion Picture in Its Economic and Social Aspects," *Annals* of American Academy of Political and Social Science, CXXVIII (November, 1926), 1–175.

[87] President's Research Committee, *Recent Social Trends*, 1020; Bureau of the Census, *Religious Bodies, 1916* (Washington, 1919), I, 19ff.; Bureau of the Census, *Religious Bodies, 1926* (Washington, 1930), I, 15–18. See also *World Survey: Interchurch World Movement of North America* (New York, 1920), 206–7. While growth in church membership kept pace with population growth, construction of churches did not. Due to concentration of people in the city and due to denominational mergers, churches by 1920 were growing fewer while memberships in them grew larger. President's Research Committee, *Recent Social Trends*, 1019–20; Bureau of the Census, *Religious Bodies, 1926*, 46–51.

[88] Bureau of the Census, *Religious Bodies, 1916*; *Religious Bodies, 1926*.

of Nations and looked forward to a world of peace, brotherhood, and Christian successes.[89] Also, as a result of the war, an Interchurch World Movement got underway in 1919, based, as one of its organizers recalled, on "the vision of a united church uniting a divided world."[90] The Interchurch Movement never got off the ground. As one scholar summarized its difficulties, "The long-developing pattern of a rising urban, non-Protestant, non-Puritan secularized American population, which had caused increasing alarm to Protestant leaders since the Civil War, had begun to come of age after World War I."[91] In contrast, the war gave a real impetus to the organization and growth of socioreligious organizations such as the YMCA, YWCA, Knights of Columbus, and Jewish Welfare Board. These organizations collected huge funds during the war for use overseas; at the Armistice they still had money on hand and promptly began spending it on reconstruction schemes such as education for veterans and foreign relief programs.[92]

Americans who attended church in 1920 ranged in creed from bedrock Fundamentalism to modernism—and some no doubt to realms beyond any faith at all. The Twenties would produce a dramatic struggle by the Fundamentalists to hold fast to their faith before the challenge of modern times, represented to the Fundamentalist by science, the city, and the school.[93] The war had deeply influenced the Fundamentalists. It intensified their anxiety over the sinfulness of man, it made them more chauvinistic than before, and it gave them in the German enemy another reason for rejecting the higher criticism of the Scripture that had come out of Germany in the nineteenth century and that had helped to undermine the "literal inerrancy" of the Holy Word. The Fundamentalist regarded the postwar Inter-Church Movement as the rankest apostasy. In 1920 the Fundamental-

[89] John F. Piper, Jr., "The American Churches in World War I," *Journal of the American Academy of Religion*, XXXVIII (1970), 147–55; Ray H. Abrams, *Preachers Present Arms: A Study of Wartime Attitudes and Activities of the Churches and the Clergy in the United States, 1914–1918* (New York, 1933); Robert T. Handy, *A Christian America* (New York, 1971), 184–86.

[90] William Adams Brown, *The Church in America* (New York, 1922), 119.

[91] Eldon G. Ernst, "The Interchurch World Movement of North America, 1919–1920," (Ph.D. thesis, Yale University, 1968), 374, quoted in Handy, *A Christian America*, 196.

[92] C. Howard Hopkins, *History of the YMCA in North America* (New York, 1951), 577–78; Mary S. Sims, *The Natural History of a Social Institution, the Young Woman's Christian Association* (New York, 1936), 188–91; *Recent Social Trends*, 1038–39.

[93] For titles on Fundamentalism, see bibliographical essay.

ists stood ready to do battle, choosing the school as their primary battleground and the teaching of science as the first stronghold to capture. Fundamentalists would lose their battle to control the teaching of science in the schools, but Fundamentalism itself hardly died away. Alongside it, another element in Protestant theology expressed a comparable pessimism (though not a comparable obscurantism) over the nature and future of man. As one religious thinker put it, "the outbreak of the war . . . shattered all optimism." Reinhold Niebuhr and other Protestant theologians later recalled the sobering impact of the war upon their thinking. In 1924 prominent liberal clergyman Harry Emerson Fosdick wrote about the need for "a fresh sense of personal and social sin." The neo-orthodoxy that later became so widespread in American religious circles was evidenced as early as 1920 for those who chose to find it.[94] In the meantime, the Social Gospel and other rationales led church members into examining and coping with a great range of day-to-day matters, such as working conditions, race riots, and reconstruction.[95]

Churches inclined to influence American society in 1920 had the means to do so. In 1916 church expenditures totaled around $329,000,000; by 1926 that total reached $817,000,000. Churches spent much of their money on schooling. In 1920 there were about 1,500 private high schools in the country under denominational control or at least enjoying denominational support. However, public high schools outnumbered them nearly fourteen to one. Public secondary high schools and academies in 1920 contained some 2,187,000 students, located in about 200,000 local districts.[96] Their curricula, as well as ones in colleges and universities, had been deeply affected by the war.

Even before the war, under pressure from John Dewey and other supporters of progressive education, school curricula had begun to

[94] William R. Hutchison, "Liberal Protestantism and the 'End of Innocence,' " *American Quarterly*, XV (Summer, 1963), 126–38; William Lee Miller, "The Rise of Neo-Orthodoxy," in Arthur M. Schlesinger, Jr., and Morton White, eds., *Paths of American Thought* (Boston, 1963), 326–44.

[95] John A. Ryan, *Social Reconstruction* (New York, 1920); Interchurch World Movement, Commission of Inquiry, *Report on the Steel Strike of 1919* (New York, 1920); Eldon G. Ernst, "The Interchurch World Movement and the Great Steel Strike of 1919–1920," *Church History*, XXXIX (June, 1970), 212–13.

[96] President's Research Committee, *Recent Social Trends*, 1028–29; U.S. Bureau of Education, *Biennial Survey of Education, 1918–20* (Washington, 1923), 497, 538; Lawrence A. Cremin, *The Transformation of the Schools: Progressivism in American Education, 1876–1957* (New York, 1961), 275.

change. Such traditional subjects as Latin, Greek, algebra, and rhetoric had begun to decline in enrollment, and new subjects such as manual training, typing, and civics appeared. On the college and university level, enrollment in classics and mathematics declined conspicuously between 1910 and 1920, while classes in law and commerce rose sharply. Practical and applied courses, designed to prepare students for life as citizens and workers, came to characterize much of American education. At Columbia, Stanford, and the University of Chicago the dissertation lists showed an acceleration of interest in scientific topics. The exigencies of war—the need for skilled engineers and chemists and industrial innovators, as well as the drive for "100% American" citizens—intensified the trend toward education for technology and conformity. Yet by war's end any number of tensions and disputes over the nature and the potential of education had arisen among educators and among pundits of the academic life.[97]

Intelligence and aptitude tests became a subject of great controversy. In 1917 the American Psychological Association constructed group intelligence tests and began to administer them to thousands of army recruits. After the war a number of writers began citing data from these tests as evidence that the average mental age of Americans was fourteen, and that therefore most Americans were uneducable beyond high school. Controversy over testing was high in 1920 and went on intermittently for the next two decades. Meanwhile, Freudian psychology also began to enter the dialogue of pedagogy. Soon after the Armistice *The Child's Unconscious Mind* and comparable titles appeared from the hands of several zealous teachers. As Lawrence Cremin has noted, "Teachers were urged to recognize the *unconscious* as the real source of motivation and behavior in themselves and their students. The essential task of education was seen as one of *sublimating* the child's *repressed* emotions into socially useful channels."[98]

In the universities, advocates of high intellectual life disagreed with educators and administrators wanting to see colleges and universities develop "the whole person." The former thought that uni-

---

[97] President's Research Committee, *Recent Social Trends*, 330ff.; Cremin, *Transformation of Schools*, 179ff.; R. L. Finney, "Education and the Reconstruction," *School and Society*, VIII (July 6, 1918), 11–17; F. J. Teggart, "University Reconstruction," *Public*, XXI (November 9, 1918), 1382–84; Edgar Dawson, "A Conspicuous Educational Failure," *Historical Outlook*, X (February, 1919), 77–79.

[98] Cremin, *Transformation of the Schools*, 209. On the army tests, see *ibid.*, 187–92; Daniel J. Kelves, "Testing the Army's Intelligence: Psychologists and the Military in World War I," *Journal of American History*, LV (December, 1968), 565–81.

versities should be devoted exclusively to higher learning, in the German tradition; the latter wanted students to study but also to elect beauty queens, field football teams, and join fraternities and student government associations. Even in the camp of the scholars, schisms developed between those vaguely categorized as humanists and those more confidently labeled social scientists.[99] In 1919 ten American learned societies—those of philosophers, economists, historians, and sociologists among them—organized the American Council of Learned Societies Devoted to Humanistic Studies. In theory, the ACLS was to promote research and liaison among its constituent disciplines. Instead, the membership promptly fragmented, as the humanists and social scientists parted company, each group tending to ignore and denigrate the other.[100] The Twenties would be a richly productive period in belles lettres, science, and social studies, and the existence of numerous learned societies, a dozen or more of which came into existence in 1919–20,[101] would testify to the avid pursuit of learning going on in the decade. By the early Twenties most national learned societies were members of one or more of four councils, each of which was national in scope and which together covered all branches of learning. Each of these four—the American Council on Education, the National Academy of Sciences–National Research Council, the American Council of Learned Societies, and the Social Science Research Council—were "to a greater or lesser degree . . . an outgrowth of World War I."[102] Still, as the Twenties began, the social sciences and the humanities were already displaying a rivalry and a separation of outlook and goals that made for a "schism in American scholarship,"[103] the counterpart to tensions in the society outside the classroom and the library.

[99] William Osler, *The Old Humanities and the New Science* (London, 1919); Andrew F. West, "The Humanities after the War," *Educational Review*, LVII (February, 1919); John Higham, "The Schism in American Scholarship," *American Historical Review*, LXXII (October, 1966), 1–21; Frederick Rudolph, *The American College and University: A History* (New York, 1962), 450–61.

[100] Waldo G. Leland, "The American Council of Learned Societies," *American Historical Review*, XXV (April, 1920), 440–47; Leland, "The Organization of the International Union of Academies and of the American Council of Learned Societies," *ACLS Bulletin*, October, 1920; Higham, "Schism in American Scholarship."

[101] Among them the Agricultural History Society, the American Geophysical Union, the American Meteorological Society, the American Catholic Historical Association, the American Society of Mammalogists, and the Society of Economic Geologists. See *The World of Learning* (London, 1972).

[102] Joseph C. Kiger, *American Learned Societies* (Washington, 1963), 120–31.

[103] Higham, "Schism in American Scholarship."

Perhaps as much as any other subject, history sought to bridge that schism. In the name of general education, Columbia University in 1919 adapted to peacetime use a "war issues" course which it had offered, renaming it a course in "contemporary civilization." It affirmed that "there is a certain minimum of [the Western] intellectual and spiritual tradition that a man must experience and understand if he is to be called educated." Heavily oriented to history, the Columbia course deeply influenced college history courses and college undergraduate requirements during the next quarter-century.[104] History books even appeared on the best-seller lists of the postwar period, though these lists reflected escape from the war or curiosity about it more than anything else.[105] In fact, as the schisms and tensions in American life in 1919–20 demonstrated, the Great War had spawned a troubled society, which is probably why Americans in 1920 by a huge majority voted for a change of political parties in Washington. The election of 1920 reflected the traits of the society that had moved from the exhilaration of Armistice, 1918, through the sobering and bewildering years of 1919–20.

[104] Rudolph, *The American College and University,* 455–56; Daniel Bell, *The Reforming of General Education: The Columbia College Experience in Its National Setting* (Garden City, N.Y., 1968), 14–15, *passim.*

[105] The best-selling novel of 1919 was *The Four Horsemen of the Apocalypse,* by V. Blasco Ibañez. The best-selling nonfiction title was Henry Adams, *The Education of Henry Adams,* followed by several titles dealing with contemporary affairs, such as *Belgium,* by Brand Whitlock, novelist and Progressive who was minister to that country, and *Bolshevism,* by John Spargo, an old Socialist turned rightward. In 1920 virtually every one of the top ten fiction sellers was a pot-boiler, such as Zane Gray's *The Man of the Forest,* or *The River's End* by James Oliver Curwood. Nonfiction continued to register interest in the war—or the peace—with Philip Gibbs, *Now It Can Be Told,* and John Maynard Keynes, *The Economic Consequences of the Peace,* heading the list. See Alice Payne Hackett, *Fifty Years of Best Sellers, 1895–1945* (New York, 1945), 39–43.

IX

Remnants of Progressivism

More than twenty-six million Americans went to the polls in November, 1920. The techniques of quantitative history, or of "prospography,"[1] may ultimately lead to some comprehensive understanding of the American voter's behavior in that election. Short of such an enormous undertaking, an examination of a handful of politically conscious men may at least suggest the varied attitudes that Americans brought to the election of 1920. By appraising the position of William J. Ghent, Amos Pinchot, Ray Stannard Baker, William Gibbs McAdoo, Donald Richberg, and William E. Borah, one can locate several points along the political spectrum from left to about the center. At that point, Warren G. Harding and his supporters can, for the most part, represent the remainder of the spectrum as it moves rightward.

William J. Ghent, though a distinctive and independent thinker, neatly illustrates the general course that one segment of the Socialist Party of America took between the prewar and postwar period.[2] His position by 1920 points up the distaste for reformers that some old activists (such as Ghent) by then were manifesting. William James Ghent, born in Frankfort, Indiana, on April 29, 1866, had by his late twenties served as a tramp printer in the Rocky Mountain West and finally gravitated to New York. There, during the two decades before World War I, he was an active and articulate figure in the SPA, more precisely in the center faction led by Algernon Lee, Morris Hillquit, and himself. A regular contributor to socialist journals, secre-

[1] The technique of collective biography, whereby the age, education, occupation, religion, status, mobility, and other data on a considerable number of party members (or of other groups) is studied and, at best, correlated to reveal the characteristics of the party (or group). See Lawrence Stone, "Prospography," *Daedalus*, 100 (Winter, 1971), 46–89.

[2] Lawrence Goldman, "W. J. Ghent and the Left," *Studies on the Left*, III (Summer, 1963), 21–40, is virtually the only published study of Ghent, though his name is prominent in most histories of American Socialism.

179

tary and then for two years president of the Rand School in New York, and author of two unduly neglected books portraying what he labeled "the Morganization" of American society (one economically stratified into six functioning economic classes and incipiently fascist), Ghent by World War I had proved himself a gifted if sometimes contentious writer and party intellectual.[3]

World War I was for Ghent, as it was for the entire Socialist movement in the United States, a trauma. The SPA, never monolithic, had always contained a mixture of various regional, ideological, and occupational elements. America's entry into the war added a new divisive force to the party. After Wilson asked Congress for war in April, 1917, the SPA held a National Emergency Convention in Saint Louis on April 7–14, where an overwhelming majority of the delegates declared their opposition to the war. But Ghent, along with a crucial minority of party intellectuals,[4] opted to support the war and to oppose the party's antiwar stand. In fact, Ghent had already broken with the party over the war issue. In 1914 he had moved to Los Angeles, where he became editor of the *California Outlook*. In the fall of 1915 the Socialist National Executive Committee held a referendum on a proposal to expel from party membership any Socialist official voting money for naval or military purposes. The referendum

[3] Ghent to Jay E. House, April 8, 1934, Ghent Papers, Box 3, Division of Manuscripts, Library of Congress; Ghent to Joan London, August 27, 1937, copy, Box 4, Ghent Papers; Algernon Lee to Ghent, March 29, 1931, Box 1, Ghent Papers; Lillian Symes and Travers Clement, *Rebel America* (New York, 1934), 204; Ira Kipnis, *American Socialist Movement* (New York, 1952), 37, 257–59.

Ghent was a prolific and confident but extremely careful worker. Evidence of his diligent care for detail and accuracy appears in almost all of his letters. See, for example, Ghent to Carl D. Thompson, January 11, 1913, Box 3, and April 10, 1913, Box 5, Socialist Party Papers, Duke University. Ghent's two major publications before World War I were *Our Benevolent Feudalism* (New York, 1902) and *Mass and Class: A Survey of Social Divisions* (New York, 1905). When the SPA Information Department in Chicago drew up a list of "The Twelve Best" and the "Second Twelve Best Books on Socialism," it included *Mass and Class* in the latter—along with Marx's *Das Kapital*. See broadside (1915?), Socialist Party Papers.

[4] Defections from the party over the war issue were numerically small, but they included an impressive list of figures, among them Ghent, Charles Edward Russell, William English Walling, John Spargo, Algie M. Simons, Allan Benson, Upton Sinclair, and Gustavus Myers. See David A. Shannon, *The Socialist Party of America* (New York, 1955), 99–100, and Daniel Bell, *Marxian Socialism in the United States* (Princeton, 1967), 312–13, for discussion of the impact these defections had. But cf. James Weinstein, *The Decline of American Socialism, 1912–1924* (New York, 1967), for the claim that the SPA suffered a fatal blow not during the war but shortly afterward, in the factional struggle with American Communists.

carried by a whopping majority. Ghent, in disgust, publicly challenged the majority's decision. "This war," he wrote, "has taught us . . . that there are some things worse than war. . . . It has taught the existence of a racial and national fanaticism held by the great majority of persons of German blood. . . . I know of nothing in the world worse than this." As a member of the SPA, Ghent favored a "reasonable degree of military preparedness" and denied "the right of the majority to commit me to the blithering idiocy expressed in the referendum." Ghent later recalled that "for me, it was virtually the end of my connection with the party." He soon afterward stopped paying his party dues, "thus ending my membership."[5]

If Ghent's prowar (or anti-German) position separated him from the majority of his SPA brethren, the party's role during the war and the transformation of one faction into the Communist Party of America after the Russian Revolution totally alienated him. For some ten years after his break with the party, Ghent continued to write pieces critical of its policies, and in 1923 he published *The Reds Bring Reaction*, a book in which he argued that Communists, by their extremism, merely incited reactionary repression against progressives, liberals—and genuine Socialists. Years earlier, in 1905, Ghent had expressed fears over the newly organized IWW, declaring that it was "misguided" and would "divide and disrupt the present organization of labor." In 1912 he reaffirmed this, arguing that Bill Haywood of the Wobblies was encouraging reaction by creating dissension in the Socialist party. With the Bolshevik Revolution and the emergence of a Communist party in the United States, drawn in part from the SPA ranks, Ghent began to attack the "fanatical outbursts of Bolshevik disciples in America," and to declare that "the *old* order" was "infinitely preferable to the thing offered by the professed harbingers of the new day." Ghent, who had been a stalwart and respected voice in the prewar Socialist movement, found the glory of that movement "dimmed forever by the fanatical adulation given by American Socialists . . . to the reign of violence in Russia."[6]

Disenchanted by 1920, Ghent began to turn more and more to the

---

[5] Memo, "The Socialist Referendum, 1915," (1937?), Box 4, Ghent Papers.

[6] W. J. Ghent, *The Reds Bring Reaction* (Princeton, 1923) ; Ghent to Charles O. Sherman, general president, IWW, November 7, 1905, Box 6, Ghent Papers; *National Socialist*, January 18, 1912; Ghent to Harry W. Laidler (March, 1928?), copy, Box 3, Ghent Papers; Shannon, *Socialist Party of America*, 284.

past for study and for income. By the late Twenties he was deep into frontier history and, until he died in 1942, he wrote competent books and articles on the subject. In 1927 he joined the staff of the new *Dictionary of American Biography*, for which he wrote 175 essays on Western figures such as Charles Bent and John Chisum, and on Socialists such as Daniel DeLeon and Eugene Debs. For the young tramp printer who had come East and joined the Socialist movement in its burgeoning, World War I had been a decisive moment, all but bisecting his life. It led him away from his first career as Socialist in the urban East and turned him westward and backward to a second career as frontier historian. His support for war in 1917, his contempt for the Bolsheviks, and his growing appreciation for the American past and the old order (as compared to what he thought American Socialists had to offer) set him apart from thousands of his former Socialist comrades by 1920. On the other hand, Harding's normalcy was hardly an anchor and a refuge for him, either. In his peculiar fashion Ghent entered the Twenties as alienated as any of the country's newly rising radical intelligentsia, a type he frequently scorned.[7]

In contrast to Ghent, Amos Pinchot entered the 1920 election year chock-full of reform enthusiasm and far more critical of the status quo than Ghent. But Pinchot was also a far more mercurial personality, one who by the late Thirties would have orbited somewhere to the right of the New Deal—a not uncommon experience for old prewar Progressives.[8] In 1920 Pinchot was by his own analysis a "radical," though the noun seems incongruous in light of Pinchot's wealth and his practice of corporate law in New York. Brother of Gifford Pinchot, self-styled leader of the conservation movement in the United States, younger Amos was, like his brother, a patrician figure of enduring social consciousness. Yet unlike Gifford, who labeled himself a "Roosevelt Republican" both during and after that great Progressive's tenure in the White House, Amos Pinchot was an unanchored maverick. In 1912 he was a Bull Moose Republican, but then he went with Wilson in 1916. In the 1918 off-year election he supported the Socialist ticket. The previous year he helped to put up bail for Bill

[7] Ghent to Isabel Putnam, *New York Herald Tribune*, January(?), 1925; Ghent to *Jewish Daily Forward*, New York, May(?), 1926, Box 3, Ghent Papers. On Ghent's relationship with the *D.A.B.*, see series of letters between Ghent and Allen Johnson and Ghent and Dumas Malone, 1926–32, Box 2, Ghent Papers.

[8] On Pinchot's reaction to the New Deal, see Otis L. Graham, Jr., *An Encore for Reform: The Old Progressives and the New Deal* (New York, 1967), 43, 49, 74–78.

Haywood when the Wobbly leader was jailed; he also contributed to a *Masses* defense fund, raised to help that Greenwich Village journal through its trial for sedition in 1918.[9] And in June, 1920, he wrote a blistering and sarcastic open letter to the Senate Overman Committee investigating Bolshevism in the United States. The committee, charged Pinchot, busied itself publishing catalogs of traitors and shouting boo at witnesses, when there was far more "social dynamite in the statistics of child mortality in our slums and steel towns, in jails full of men convicted for their opinions, or in the gouging of the public by profiteering trusts and monopolies . . . than in the total propaganda of all the revolutionary minded persons in the country."[10]

Just after the Armistice, Pinchot began talking about the need for a new political party in the United States. Both major parties were "in the hands of reaction." "Take Wilson out of the Democratic Party," he declared, "and what is left? Take a little minority of fairly progressive politicians out of the Republican Party and you are in darkest Egypt."[11] Once Wilson had come home from Paris and gone on his cross-country tour in defense of the League, Pinchot was finding even the President and the "fairly progressive" Republicans unfit to govern. Wrote Pinchot to Robert La Follette: "The public is inclined to think Mr. Wilson a wise person. As a matter of fact, he does not know much, hates to digest anything and trusts to his brilliancy and tact to carry him through." If the public could only realize "how ignorant" Wilson was of current events, and "how utterly sloppy, according to his own account, was his preparation for the great struggle with European diplomacy . . . they would perhaps begin to say, 'This man is either a liar or an ass.' "[12] Neither Hiram Johnson nor William E. Borah was attacking Wilson hard enough to satisfy Pinchot. They should "shout the truth . . . that he spent his time at Paris standing in the corner with a dunce cap and that he came home so

[9] G. V. Newton, deputy commissioner of internal revenue, to Amos Pinchot, June 22, 1920, Box 40; Sumner Gerard to Pinchot, February 19, 1919, and May 8, 1919, Box 39; George Foster Peabody to Pinchot, December 12, 1918, Box 36; Amos Pinchot to William Bross Lloyd, February 11, 1918, Box 37; Albert DeSilver to Pinchot, December 24, 1918, Box 35; Pinchot to DeSilver, December 28, 1918, Box 35; Crystal Eastman to Pinchot, February 17, 1919, Box 39, Amos Pinchot Papers, Division of Manuscripts, Library of Congress; Graham, *Encore for Reform*, 75.

[10] Amos Pinchot to Overman Committee, published in a New Jersey Catholic weekly, *The Monitor*, June 19, 1920, copy in Subject File no. 57, Pinchot Papers.

[11] Pinchot to George Foster Peabody, December 19, 1918, Box 37, *ibid.*

[12] Pinchot to La Follette, September 22, 1919, Box 38, *ibid.*

thoroughly spanked that he had to run around the country because he could not sit down."[13]

This tirade against Wilson and the treaty was, for Pinchot, unexceptionable, since he was an opinionated critic of most public figures and issues. It did indicate his disenchantment with Wilson, but more revealing was his evident attempt to spur La Follette into greater action. For by September, 1919, Pinchot was a key figure in a newly emerging third-party movement, the Committee of Forty-eight, and La Follette was its most likely presidential candidate. The Committee emerged from "a gathering of men and women interested in public affairs held in New York City in January, 1919."[14] The party's name, selected at a subsequent gathering in February, was supposed to reflect the nationwide representation in the party, though in fact the committee throughout its existence was clustered at 15 East 40th Street, New York. Its roster was suggestive of an intellectual and upper class Who's Who in eastern seaboard society.[15] The chairman of the executive committee (and primary financial backer) was J. A. H. Hopkins. Pinchot was treasurer of the executive committee.

Following its organization in New York, the committee launched a publicity and mailing campaign to solicit membership, gained an encouraging response, and in September issued a call for a National Conference in Saint Louis in December, to draw up a platform. Despite opposition by Saint Louis American Legionnaires, the committee met and formulated a platform. It called for public ownership of transportation, various public utilities, and natural resources; it advocated that "no land and no patents be held out of use"; and it proposed "equal economic, political, and legal rights for all, irrespective of sex or color."[16] In addition, the committee resolved that current government ownership of the railroads should continue for at least two years under existing conditions, that Congress not be empowered to declare war without a prior national referendum, and

[13] *Ibid.*

[14] "Platform of the Committee of Forty-eight, adopted at the First National Conference, Saint Louis, Missouri, Dec. 2–12, 1919," Subject File no. 11, Pinchot Papers.

[15] Some of the original subcommittees of the party included philosopher Horace M. Kallen, historian Will Durant, journalist Lincoln Colcord, editor Albert Jay Nock, writer Harold Stearns, and other well-known figures. See list of contributors in J. A. H. Hopkins to Amos Pinchot, February 15, 1919, Box 39, *ibid.*

[16] *Facts*, National Conference Number, issued by Committee of Forty-eight, Saint Louis, December 12, 1919, Subject File no. 10; Pinchot memo, Subject File no. 11, *ibid.*

that all American troops currently in Russia be brought home.[17]

By mid-1920 Pinchot and the committee had begun to suffer numerous trials and frustrations. Hightly articulate, educated, and well to do, the Forty-eighters had organized with hope and enthusiasm. Their very existence demonstrated that the war had not stifled all reform. But they soon learned the difficulties of translating enthusiasm into organized and successful power. In June both the Forty-eighters and the Labor party held a national convention in Chicago, where the committee hoped to unite with the Labor party behind a "presidential ticket and platform."[18] But the two groups were unable to agree on so much as the name for a new organization. The Labor representatives insisted on retaining the name Labor, while the Forty-eighters held out for a more comprehensive label. According to the committee's analysis, when the Labor crowd refused to surrender its "class" distinction, La Follette refused the presidential nomination that could have been his. The committee decided to spend the remainder of the 1920 campaign year working for "selected nominees."[19]

By August, Pinchot and his friend George Record, veteran New Jersey Progressive active in the committee, were becoming impatient with (to them) Hopkins's inept leadership of the committee. Record also had concluded that "nobody has understood our platform." Socialists "in the West," for instance, took it to be socialist "because they identify government ownership with socialism."[20] Record suggested that the Committee of Forty-eight "mark time and hold expenses down" until after the election, and then completely reorganize. If, as he expected, the Republicans were "overwhelmingly victorious" in 1920, the committee could pick up a host of recruits from the Democrats.[21] Even executive chairman Hopkins was narrowing his vision by August. He proposed that in New York the committee concentrate on the 19th Congressional District, where the Forty-eighters

[17] *Facts*, National Conference daily edition, December 12, 1919, Subject File no. 10, *ibid.*

[18] *Chicago Tribune*, June 15, 1920, clipping, Box 40, *ibid.* The Labor party was an attempt to merge labor party movements that had developed in several states in 1919, especially in Illinois and Iowa. Including a good many ex-Socialists, the Party gained support neither from the AFL nor from the SPA.

[19] Pamphlet, "Facts about the Chicago Convention," Subject File no. 11, Pinchot Papers.

[20] George Record to Amos Pinchot, August 25, 1920; George Record to Amos Pinchot, August 27, 1920, Box 40, *ibid.*

[21] *Ibid.*

were well established. Hopkins wanted Pinchot himself to stand for the congressional seat there.[22] But Pinchot, far from campaigning as a Forty-eighter, chose to resign from the organization.

Pinchot felt that the committee—at least the current leadership—no longer expressed his views. To Pinchot, an economic movement could not proceed when the intellectual leadership was deficient in economics. Pinchot, confident that he understood the country's needs, felt that he and Record were outnumbered on the Forty-eighter's executive committee by men who simply did not understand what they were doing. A. W. Ricker, financial editor of the *Christian Science Monitor* and assistant treasurer of the executive committee, recognized a split in the membership but did not think it irreconcilable. He urged Pinchot and Record to come back into the committee and help write a new platform and try for a referendum on it from the entire committee membership.[23] Ricker, writing just after Harding's election in November, looked to the future and hoped to keep the committee alive but with a less radical program. The country had shown its distaste for the Socialists and the Farmer-Labor party, as well as the committee's own planks, some of which were "ridiculously too strong."[24] Meanwhile, following the election, J. A. H. Hopkins announced that he and other Forty-eighters would continue to work for a new third party.[25] With this sentiment, if not Ricker's, Pinchot could have agreed, for he spent the rest of his life (he died in 1944) criticizing the party in power—whichever it was.

Unlike Ghent and some other prowar Socialists, Pinchot and the Forty-eighters had entered the postwar period with their zeal for reform unabated. But their experience in 1919–20 left them, like Ghent, defeated. Their third-party movement had disintegrated. The country's fate lay with the two major parties and their leaders. And in 1920 Ray Stannard Baker saw little to differentiate them, except that Harding and the Republicans were worse than the Democrats.

The two years following the war were difficult for Baker. Between the Armistice and Harding's election Baker moved from guarded optimism to doubt and despair to philosophical acceptance of his world and a qualified renewal of faith in "what we liberals have to

[22] J. A. H. Hopkins to Pinchot, August 21, 1920, *ibid.*

[23] A. W. Ricker to Arthur Wrey, December 14, 1920; Ricker to Allen McCurdey, December 13, 1920, copy; Ricker to Record, December 16, 1920, copy, *ibid.*

[24] Ricker to Arthur Wray, December 14, 1920, copy; Ricker to George Record, December 16, 1920, copy, *ibid.*

[25] *New York Times*, November 15, 1920, 10:1.

do."[26] It was not the war but Wilson's failures with Congress over treaty ratification, plus the Red Scare and other turmoil at home in 1919–20, that caused him to flounder for a while in depression.

Before the war Baker had been a conspicuous figure among muckraking journalists and had developed a consciousness and concern over racism, poverty, and other social ills that he never lost.[27] When war came to the United States in 1917, Baker went along with the Wilsonian rhetoric. By early 1918 he was at work in Europe as a special agent of the State Department, filing reports on public opinion in England. He traveled widely, interviewed numerous public figures, and began to develop doubts about the possibility of a "democratic peace" emerging from the war.[28] In December, 1918, at Wilson's request Baker became head of the American Press Bureau at Versailles.[29] As early as January, 1919, he began to appreciate the difficulties that Wilson faced at Paris—and the limitations of the President's vision. Baker talked to Herbert Hoover, Walter Lippmann, and other Americans in the peace delegation who were pessimistic about Wilson's inability to realize the enormous difficulties he faced. Wilson needed to "get away from generalities and vague expressions of idealistic purpose."[30] As the conference went on, Baker showed increasing pessimism, though he kept hoping that Wilson would salvage some portion of his peace program, for the President was a "very wise and a very great man."[31]

With the conclusion of the peace conference Baker returned home, unhappy with the treaty but defending it as the best settlement available. "I took up the work at Paris," he wrote, "full of the warmest anticipations of some settlement that would realize liberal ideals. I saw the reaction [in Paris] from the War and I realized . . . the enormous strength of the old imperialistic and military systems." Though not sure that Wilson "got all that he could have gotten without breaking up the conference," Baker was convinced that the treaty was "very much better than it would have been if [Wilson] had not

26 Baker Notebook, Christmas(?), 1920, Box 125, Ray Stannard Baker Papers, Division of Manuscripts, Library of Congress.

27 Two biographical studies of Baker are John Semonche, *Ray Stannard Baker: A Quest for Democracy in Modern America, 1870–1918* (Chapel Hill, 1969), and Robert C. Bannister, Jr., *Ray Stannard Baker: The Mind and Thought of a Progressive* (New Haven, 1966).

28 Baker to Colonel Edward House, November 1, 1918, Container 96, Baker Papers.

29 Bannister, *Baker*, 168–83.

30 Baker Notebook, January 6, 1919, Container 124, Baker Papers.

31 Baker Notebook, March 8, 1919, *ibid.*

been there." Rejection of the treaty and the League would only "contribute to anarchy and further disorganization."[32]

Chastened by the peace conference and its results, Baker's gloom deepened in the months after his return to the United States. "The world," he wrote in October, 1919, "was never in such a state of disorganization and demoralization." America was experiencing strikes and race riots, Italy was witnessing the "lawless" escapades of the "patriot" Gabriele D'Annunzio and his followers, and Britain was suffering a great railroad strike. "Everyone is preaching rights rather than duties."[33] By November, Baker was lamenting the want of leadership in America and in Europe. "No one here seems to do any thinking, take any responsibility except Wilson—and he is in bed, ill. . . . It seems only possible to get prohibition, oppositions, negative actions, out of our leaders. They abolish liquor, they legislate against and enjoin workmen, they hold endless futile inquiries, they [fight] the treaty and the President to no good purpose whatever." Meanwhile, the government was "raiding, beating up, and arresting alleged radicals—and spreading the fires of radicalism" by creating martyrs. "It looks black in America these days."[34]

Early in 1920 Baker began to speculate on the upcoming presidential election and found himself "eagerly, wistfully [turning] to some savior of the nation," though Baker wondered why he did so. "Three times before I thought the salvation of the country depended upon the election of certain men: two of them, Roosevelt and Wilson, were elected: La Follette was rejected. I have seen them dragged in the mud and trampled under by swine . . . and nothing much changed." For the moment Baker was attracted to Herbert Hoover as that potential savior and even voted for him in the Massachusetts primary in April, though Baker had "little interest one way or the other, save . . . to help Hoover and defeat Senator Lodge."[35] When the Republican convention in June chose Warren G. Harding and Calvin Coolidge, Baker deplored the result. The convention had brought forth "a hopeless platform and even more hopeless candidates."[36] But then in July, when the Democrats nominated James M. Cox and Franklin D. Roose-

[32] Baker to Elizabeth G. Evans, August 7, 1920, copy, *ibid.*
[33] Baker Notebook, October 1, 1919, Box 125, *ibid.*
[34] Baker Notebook, November 10, 1919, *ibid.*
[35] Baker Notebook, March 25 and 31, 1920; April 27, 1920, *ibid.*
[36] Baker Notebook, June 13, 1920, *ibid.*

velt, Baker was little more pleased. Cox was a "doubtful candidate," and his platform was superior to the Republican only because the latter was "zero." Cox was a better man than Harding, but, Baker lamented, "that is saying little." In fact, both the vice-presidential candidates were, to Baker, better than their running mates. Baker wondered what "independent liberals" like himself should do. Third-party options were little, if any, better: they were "mostly the parties of extremists or else led by unwise men." "We are," Baker concluded, "in the political doldrums."[37]

If not the country, Baker himself was in the doldrums and struggling to come out. He brooded over his malaise. "I have had a hard time getting over this war," he wrote. "My old world died; I have had trouble [creating] my new one." He finally decided that "the securities [and] hopes of the new world were to be found exactly where the old ones [were]—in *me*, working in my garden at Amherst." He had been "terribly serious, borne down by the Problems of the World." And then he learned to laugh at this "absurdity" that "I [and] most other people . . . had been . . . trying to regulate the lives of other people and had stopped trying to regulate our own lives."[38] Still depressed, however, over the Senate's rejection of the League and over the events in the nation in 1919–20, Baker mustered little enthusiasm for the political process in 1920. Even Hoover, who earlier seemed to be a potential savior, had proved to "lack the necessary vision." Baker decided to vote Democratic because the party supported the League. Baker did not expect Cox to win: "The reaction from the war, the present unpopularity of Mr. Wilson [and] the rampant appeal to the narrowest and most provincial spirit in our national life" were all helping Harding. "The grim old school master in Washington" still held power in the land, but he was "about the only unmoveable thing left."[39]

During the Christmas season, just after Harding's election, William Allen White wrote to Baker: "What a God damned world this is! I trust you will realize that I am not swearing; merely trying to express in the mildest terms what I think of the conditions that exist. . . . All this in response to your Christmas card." When he received White's letter, Baker jotted in his notebook: "I've *been through* that stage—

[37] Baker Notebook, July 7, 1920, *ibid.*
[38] Baker Notebook, July 17, 1920, *ibid.*
[39] Baker to Brand Whitlock, August 11, 1920, copy, *ibid.*

all this last summer and fall, [but now] I have a new outlook." With all "former silly illusions" shattered, Baker was "now ready to begin at the bottom."[40]

Ray Stannard Baker, man of letters, introspective journalist, and Wilson disciple, had taken a tortuous route from Armistice to normalcy. Although he supported the Democratic candidate in 1920, Baker's political interests thereafter lay more in the past than in the present, and he lived out his life writing and editing volumes in defense of the "grim old school master" who left the White House in March, 1921.[41]

William Gibbs McAdoo, Wilsonian Democrat, moved through 1919–20 on a more positive (and ambitious) tack and never seemed to suffer the despair that Baker felt, though he, too, experienced personal distress of a sort. In 1920 McAdoo wanted the Democratic presidential nomination, had abundant support for it, and might have won it except for one overwhelming obstacle—the silence of Woodrow Wilson. When McAdoo resigned from the Wilson cabinet just after the war, he said he needed to make money for his family. He denied having a desire "for any political office, not even for the presidency."[42] He took a California vacation, opened a law office in New York, and for lucrative fees became counsel to several large corporations.[43] One of these firms was Edward L. Doheny's Pan-American Petroleum Company, which had large oil holdings in Mexico. McAdoo denied that his job as counsel for Doheny implied any position on U.S. policy toward the Mexican Revolution, though he admitted that if he ever ran for political office his political enemies might try to exploit his association with Doheny.[44]

[40] Baker Notebook, Christmas (?), 1920, Box 125, *ibid.*

[41] On Baker's activities from 1920 until his death in 1946, see Bannister, *Baker,* 200–311. On his relative detachment from the New Deal, see Graham, *Encore for Reform,* 167, 172.

[42] McAdoo to N. Brucker, December 14, 1918, Letterbook 64, Container 500; McAdoo to Colonel E. M. House, November 29, 1918, Letterbook 66, Container 500, William Gibbs McAdoo Papers, Division of Manuscripts, Library of Congress.

[43] McAdoo to Franklin K. Lane, January 31, 1919, Container 217, *ibid.*; see Containers 217 and 218 for correspondence with General Electric, National Surety, United Artists, and other firms.

[44] McAdoo to Joseph P. Tumulty, November 21, 1919, Container 226, *ibid.* McAdoo could not anticipate how damaging that association with Doheny would prove to be. In 1924, while he was making a strong run for the Democratic presidential nomination, McAdoo's connection with Doheny came to light shortly after Doheny's dubious relationship with Secretary of Interior Albert B. Fall had been revealed by a Senate subcommittee exploring the Teapot Dome affair. Though not himself im-

McAdoo had—or anticipated having—political enemies because he had political ambitions. Despite his disclaimers to office, he never retired from partisan political activity. Early in 1919 he began nudging his way toward the 1920 presidential nomination. He expressed constant concern over the leadership and makeup of the Democratic national committee. He deplored some of Wilson's cabinet changes, which did not "strengthen the Cabinet politically."[45] Either out of loyalty or conviction, he never directly criticized Wilson for spending time at Paris and totally neglecting affairs at home, but he did declare in the early spring of 1919 that the party and the country needed more "militant leadership."[46] When friends began asking him to provide this missing quality, McAdoo parried their remarks in the timeless language of presidential aspirants: "The whole situation," he said to one correspondent in August, "is in such a state of flux that the path of duty is not at all clear. I feel that it is premature to discuss 1920 until certain things are cleared away."[47] This was circumspect language to describe a dilemma that McAdoo faced. He clearly had ambitions for the nomination, and he had evidence of substantial support from well-heeled and otherwise influential Democrats.[48] But unless or until Woodrow Wilson declared himself out of contention for renomination, or called for an open and competitive race by other candidates, or (at best) gave his blessings to his son-in-law's candidacy, McAdoo could make no overt move toward the nomination.

---

plicated in the Teapot Dome scandal, McAdoo's candidacy suffered immeasurable harm. See Burl Noggle, *Teapot Dome: Oil and Politics in the 1920's* (Baton Rouge, 1962), 100–164; David H. Stratton, "Splattered with Oil: William G. McAdoo and the Presidential Nomination," *Southwestern Social Science Quarterly*, XLIV (June, 1963), 62–75.

[45] McAdoo to Colonel E. M. House, January 15, 1919; McAdoo to Daniel C. Roper, January 15, 1919, Container 217, McAdoo Papers.

McAdoo was especially bothered by the appointment of A. Mitchell Palmer as attorney general replacing Thomas Gregory. McAdoo's objection, however, registered no prescience about Palmer's behavior during the forthcoming Red Scare. Rather, Palmer came from a "hopeslessl/ Republican state." Pennsylvania was already represented with Secretary of Labor Wilson, and New York with Secretary of State Lansing and Secretary of Commerce Redfield. Wilson ought "not to bunch his cabinet any longer." McAdoo to Colonel House, January 15, 1919, *ibid.*

[46] McAdoo to Bernard Baruch, March 22, 1919, Container 218, *ibid.*

[47] McAdoo to Jouett Shouse, August 31, 1919, Container 223, *ibid.*

[48] Claude G. Bowers to McAdoo, June 13, 1919, Container 223; Clarence Poe to McAdoo, December 20, 1919, Container 227; Jesse H. Jones to McAdoo, June 13, 1919, Container 221; Jouett Shouse to McAdoo, August 12, 1919, Container 223; Joseph H. O'Neil to McAdoo, November 18, 1919, Container 225, *ibid.*

While a member of Wilson's cabinet, McAdoo had married Wilson's daughter Eleanor. The sobriquet "crown prince," quickly born, expressed the favoritism that McAdoo supposedly enjoyed as political heir to Wilson's party leadership. His undoubted competence as secretary of the treasury and as director general of the railroads during the war gave some substance to his qualifications. Yet his very association with Wilson contributed to his dilemma in 1920. McAdoo felt both loyalty to Wilson ("the greatest leader of liberal thought in the world today"[49]) and reluctance to declare himself available for the nomination unless Wilson took himself out of contention. This the president refused to do; he neither avowed nor disavowed his wish to be renominated. As long as Wilson remained silent, McAdoo was trapped. Some of his supporters recognized this. In December, 1919, McAdoo turned down an invitation to speak to the annual Jackson Day gathering of Democrats, since "it will be assumed that every man who speaks at this gathering is an avowed candidate." McAdoo did not want to be "put in that position." Thomas Gregory, former attorney general, commiserated: "I understand the embarrassment you must feel growing out of the President's condition and the fact that no definite statement has yet been made by him in regard to the next campaign." Still, Gregory hoped that McAdoo would speak, since failure to do so would be tantamount to "an announcement that you will not [run]."[50]

Wanting to run, McAdoo was stymied at every turn. The primaries raised the same problem for him that the Jackson Day invitation created. He wrote to a key supporter, Thomas Love of Dallas, "I do not want to enter these primaries and I am greatly puzzled about them. If I refuse to allow my name to be used it will be assumed that I would, in no circumstances, go into the race, [and yet] I am not prepared to eliminate myself completely." McAdoo wanted to "wait until conditions are clearer."[51]

But those conditions never became clearer. As of February, 1920, McAdoo was confident that in November the Republicans would receive "one of the finest lickings they ever got,"[52] but his optimism

[49] McAdoo to John B. Elliott, August 5, 1919, Container 223, *ibid.*

[50] McAdoo to W. D. Jamison, finance director, Democratic National Committee, December 19, 1919, Container 227; Thomas Gregory to McAdoo, December 9, 1919, Container 226, *ibid.*

[51] McAdoo to Thomas B. Love, January 26, 1920, Letterbook 11, Container 503, *ibid.*

[52] McAdoo to Frank C. Jordan, February 10, 1920, Container 229, *ibid.* This

over a Democratic victory only made his position as would-be candidate even more painful. In February, evidently convinced that Wilson was not going to "clarify" the issue, McAdoo adopted a new strategy. When supporters proposed his name in the Georgia primary, McAdoo telegraphed to one of them, asking that his name not be entered: "I cannot consistently enter the primary in any state when it is my earnest conviction that the delegate from every state should go to the Convention without instruction."[53] McAdoo needed a draft from an open convention, in order to overcome the roadblock that Wilson's silence had raised. As he explained to his ardent supporter Love, "I have gone further in this telegram than ever before—saying, in effect, that it would be my duty to accept the nomination if it came to me unsolicited. This is, as I understand it, the thing that you and all my friends wanted me to say."[54]

McAdoo's Georgia telegram, which he promptly copied and began to circulate all over the country, had been a carefully planned move. One of his publicity agents congratulated him on it. "You have greatly improved this . . . since its . . . first writing. . . . The dignified tone will greatly strengthen you. . . . Your statement received a very good play through the press, [and] I am arranging [comment from] some of the boys who write semi-editorial stories."[55]

McAdoo's strategy was to avoid the appearance of a campaign, quietly sustain the strength he already had, try to build on it, and hope for a draft at the convention scheduled to open at San Francisco on June 28, 1920. As strategy this was hardly unique in American politics. Yet it turned into a strange campaign. His friends went to work, creating a convention organization while trying to avoid the appearance of doing so. And then on June 18, ten days before the convention was to open, McAdoo announced that he would not allow his name to be placed before the convention; he could not, he explained, afford the campaign expense.[56] Some of his supporters took his statement at face value and went to work for another candidate.

---

naive judgment was typical enough for McAdoo. Most of his correspondence is bereft of comment on world or national affairs, except for an occasional bland reference in favor of the League and in criticism of "stand pat" Republicans (his prose was full of such clichés). If McAdoo ever formulated any clear ideas about the ills plaguing the United States in 1910–20, his correspondence does not reveal them.

[53] McAdoo to Miller S. Ball, February 17, 1920, Container 228, *ibid.*
[54] McAdoo to Thomas Love, February 19, 1920, Letterbook 12, Container 504, *ibid.*
[55] Lambert St. Clair to McAdoo, February 18, 1920, Container 229, *ibid.*
[56] *New York Times*, June 19, 1920, 1:8.

Others did not and continued to work for his nomination. As the convention began, McAdoo promised to make no more withdrawal statements and appeared ready to accept a draft. For a while that draft appeared quite possible, if not imminent. McAdoo, a candidate who had inexplicably withdrawn only to return to contention, led from the first through the eleventh ballot. After twenty-two ballots, he was a close second behind James M. Cox, regained the lead on the twenty-ninth round, and held it for several roll calls. He then began to slip downward. Cox gained the nomination on the forty-fourth ballot.[57]

Handicapped by a reluctant candidate and by their inability to build up delegate strength before the convention, McAdoo's managers had performed well. Without those handicaps they might have won the nomination for McAdoo, and thus a Wilsonian Progressive would have made the run against Harding in November. Harding would still have won. The Wilsonian coalition that in 1916 reelected Wilson (a minority president in his 1912 victory) had begun to come apart as early as the off-year election in 1918.[58] In any case, McAdoo's image as Wilson's heir in 1920 was not entirely an asset. The president's failure to force the League through the Senate had revealed the strength of his opposition as well as his own infirmities. Government policies of 1919–20—either in coping with incidents such as the coal and steel strike, or in helping to intensify them, as during the Red Scare—hardly built up confidence in the Wilson administration. As for that nebulous label "Progressive," the months after the Armistice had taken their toll among people of that persuasion. Some prewar Progressives, such as Amos Pinchot and other Forty-eighters, had come out of the war with their reform enthusiasm intact, even intensified, but had dissipated it in third-party futilities. Others, such as Ray Stannard Baker, looked in vain for a leader to overcome the strife and tension of 1919–20, and in resignation opted for the least reactionary of the two major candidates in 1920. Perhaps McAdoo would have attracted more of such voters than Cox did, but hardly enough to have overcome Harding's commanding majority.

Donald Richberg, worrying through the year 1920, showed one

[57] *Official Report of the Proceedings of the Democratic National Convention Held in San Francisco, California, June 28, 29, 30, July 1, 2, 3, 5, 6, 1920* (Indianapolis, 1920).

[58] David Burner, "The Breakup of the Wilson Coalition of 1916," *Mid-America*, 45 (January, 1963), 18–35.

variation on the travail that Progressives suffered in moving toward normalcy. Richberg was a Bull Mooser with Theodore Roosevelt in 1912, and a New Dealer with Franklin D. Roosevelt in the early Thirties (he later recanted). A look at his career and outlook between these two periods is a study in what has become a standard conundrum for historians of the postwar years: what happened to Progressivism in the Twenties?[59] The question presents all kinds of difficulties, among them the definition of terms. The "Progressive movement" is a historian's construct, a label applied in retrospect to the years from the turn of the twentieth century to World War I, and of late both the noun and the adjective have come to be challenged.[60] Nevertheless, the fifteen-odd years before the war were years of reform, when men and women, full of concern over what they regarded as social problems, sought to correct or overcome them. As William Allen White observed in 1910: "For ten years there has been a distinct movement among the American people. . . . It is called variously: Reform, the Moral Awakening, the New Idea, the Square Deal, the Uplift, Insurgency, and by other local cognomens; but it is one current in the thought of the people."[61] Whatever motivated this movement and however it may be categorized in the nomenclature of American political ideology, it did occur. But by the early Twenties some of its participants were beginning to wonder: "Where are the pre-war radicals?"[62] Historians have tended to agree with the question's implication that Progressivism died some time around World War I. And, again depending on the definition of terms, they have seen it reborn with the New Deal. This kind of historiography therefore blocks out the period from World War I to about 1933 as one bereft of Progressive reform, or at least sorely deficient in it. Students of the Twenties, however, have lately found more reform in the decade

[59] Cf. Arthur S. Link, "What Happened to the Progressive Movement in the 1920's?" *American Historical Review*, LXXIV (April, 1959), 1205–20; Herbert Margulies, "Recent Opinion on the Decline of the Progressive Movement," *Mid-America*, XLV (October, 1963), 250–68; Richard T. Ruetten, "Senator Burton K. Wheeler and Insurgency in the 1920's," in *The American West: A Reorientation*, ed. Gene M. Gressley (Laramie, 1966), 111–31, 164–72.

[60] Peter G. Filene, "An Obituary for 'The Progressive Movement,'" *American Quarterly*, XXII (Spring, 1970), 20–34; Gabriel Kolko, *The Triumph of Conservatism: A Reinterpretation of American History, 1900–1916* (Glencoe, Ill., 1963); James Weinstein, *The Corporate Ideal in the Liberal State, 1900–1918* (Boston, 1968).

[61] William Allen White, *The Old Order Changeth* (New York, 1910), 29–31.

[62] "Where Are the Pre-War Radicals? A Symposium," *Survey*, LV (February, 1926), 556–66.

195

than did an earlier generation of historians, who tended to denigrate the decade as a shallow period of frivolity and reaction.[63]

Richberg is an example of a prewar radical whose Progressivism survived the war, though not without modification. In 1912, when in Richberg's phrase "T. R. located Armageddon and the band played marching hymns," Richberg was one of the army that "put on shining armor and went out to battle for the Lord."[64] Richberg preferred the Rooseveltian brand of social justice to the kind advocated by Wilson, Bryan, or La Follette. In 1912, as Richberg later remembered, Roosevelt Progressivism drew a clear line between right and wrong, assumed that people would vote right if given the chance, and believed that if public officials only responded to public opinion they would do the right thing. Some experience in the realities of party politics between 1912 and 1916 began to weaken Richberg's faith in this creed, and then the "terrible lessons of World War I" seriously undermined his faith.[65] The brutal war in Europe, the death of his friends, the greed of American businessmen profiting from the war, and the ruthless repression of dissent at home all left Richberg haunted by the war's terrible impact. With the end of the war and the death in 1919 of Theodore Roosevelt, Richberg judged the country to have reached "the end of an era," partly because T.R., Wilson, Bryan, and La Follette were either dead, discredited, or engaged in their "twilight activities." The progressivism which had "inspired my generation," wrote Richberg about 1930, "ceased at the end of the World War when the first of its four great leaders died."[66]

But Richberg himself hardly retired into seclusion or shrank back in alienation from public conflict. In 1915 he had become special counsel for the city of Chicago, and in 1918 "special counsel in gas matters." In his job Richberg, by his own account, fought "against

[63] Link, "What Happened to the Progressive Movement in the 1920's?"; Ruetten, "Wheeler and Insurgency in the 1920's"; Jackson K. Putnam, "The Persistence of Progressivism in the 1920's: The Case of California," *Pacific Historical Review*, XXXV (November, 1966), 395–411; Paul W. Glad, "Progressives and the Business Culture of the 1920's," *Journal of American History*, LIII (June, 1966), 75–89. An important book on reform in the Twenties is Clarke A. Chambers, *Seedtime of Reform: American Social Service and Social Action, 1918–1933* (Minneapolis, 1963).

[64] Donald Richberg, *Tents of the Mighty* (New York, 1930), 32; Richberg, *My Hero: The Indiscreet Memoirs of an Eventful but Unheroic Life* (New York, 1954).

[65] Richberg, *Tents of the Mighty*, 34–35; *My Hero*, 51–59.

[66] Richberg, *Tents of the Mighty*, 98.

the control of government by public utilities in pursuit of private profit."[67] In 1920 he took on an additional job representing railroad labor in Interstate Commerce Commission hearings. By 1926, when he helped write the Railway Labor Act, Richberg had developed a reputation as an expert on railroad labor organizations.[68] Meanwhile, in 1919 and 1920 he bitterly criticized the "weakness of present industrial leaders" for their anti-labor policies. When Elbert H. Gary of U.S. Steel, along with other industrialists, filled the public ear with "clamor against radicals and bolshevists," their "baby talk" impressed ill-informed people, but to Richberg it was simply industry's excuse for its own failure to establish good relations with labor. Business executives, he said, should not manage an industry solely for the benefit of the capital invested; they should also benefit the workers. Richberg wanted to see competition between labor and capital ended, in favor of joint control and equal sharing of industry's profits. "An industrial corporation should not," he said, "be an enemy to society. It should be a servant of society." Anticipating criticism, Richberg distinguished his idea "from what is commonly described as bolshevism." His plan did not contemplate the elimination of capital or the rights of capitalists. He merely wanted to eliminate "the autocratic domination of capital contributors in an institution whose success or failure depends upon obtaining the voluntary and whole-hearted support of labor contributors."[69]

Richberg had only ridicule for Harding and Coolidge in 1920. Some notable Republican spokesmen were not entirely pleased with the ticket themselves—William E. Borah, for one. But then Borah was never a conventional party man, though he insisted that the true partisan served his party best by denouncing it when he thought it wrong. "The savior," said Borah, "could not choose even twelve men all of whom would prove true against corruption. How shall it be expected that politics will always be clear of individual betrayers?" To close "your eyes to the demands of privilege because they happen

---

[67] *Ibid.*, 109; see also Richberg, *My Hero*, 102–11.

[68] Richberg, *My Hero*, 112–33; Robert Zeiger, "From Hostility to Moderation: Railroad Labor Policy in the 1920's," *Labor History*, IX (Winter, 1968), 23–38.

[69] Memorandum, "Industrial Failure and a Remedy," 1920(?), Box 5, Article File; see also Richberg to Ogdon Armour, December 3 and 14, 1917, Container 1; "Making Illinois Safe for Democracy: A Farce in Several Acts," Box 1, General Correspondence, 1914–18, Donald Richberg Papers, Division of Manuscripts, Library of Congress.

in your own party," he said, "is not true partisanship. . . . It is a betrayal of party."[70]

This was not entirely pious rhetoric. Borah did, in fact, manage to remain well within party lines and to rise to seniority and chairmanship on Senate committees, while at the same time he developed a public position on the Progressive fringe of the party.[71] In 1920 several of his fellow Progressives asked him to overcome some of the party's supposed deficiencies. Soon after Harding's nomination in June, 1920, party worker Judson Welliver, who would eventually become a Harding speechwriter, wrote to Borah begging him to supply the leadership that Harding could not provide. "Harding," said Welliver, "is pathetically without color, atmosphere, ideas, or knowledge about affairs generally." In fact, to Welliver he was "an ignoramus, a sonorous fraud, a sounding brass. . . . He's awful." Welliver wanted Borah to guide and moderate his fellow Progressive Republicans in 1920–21, much as Jonathon Dolliver had guided "prima donnas such as Beveridge and La Follette" in the 1909 tariff fight. Against the "background of reaction" that would appear if Harding won, Borah and other progressives would "have a wonderful chance" to make their program clear. Welliver suggested the terms of that program: an excess profits tax, a stiffer income tax, an inheritance tax "of a sort not yet dreamed of," and government ownership of railroads, mines, oil, and stockyards. Welliver called Borah the "inevitable leader" for this program. Borah replied: "I agree with your letter as to what ought to be done and I am willing to . . . do whatever I can."[72]

In the presidential campaign, however, Borah's single-minded concern seemed to be denunciation of the League of Nations.[73] His

[70] Borah speech, Idaho Falls, October 7, 1924; text in Box 97, William E. Borah Papers, Division of Manuscripts, Library of Congress.

[71] Borah's identification as a Progressive was durable enough; witness, for example, his inclusion among the "Sons of Wild Jackasses" by Senator George Moses of New Hampshire, who coined the term as a characterization of Borah and several other Progressives in Congress. See Ray Tucker and Frederick R. Barkley, *Sons of the Wild Jackass* (Boston, 1932). The degree of Borah's Progressivism and its relationship to the prewar movement are open to conjecture, however. See Ruetten, "Wheeler and Insurgency in the 1920's," and Leroy Ashby, *The Spearless Leader: Senator Borah and the Progressive Movement in the 1920's* (Urbana, Ill., 1972).

[72] Judson Welliver to Borah, July 1, 1920, Box 199; Borah to Welliver, July 8, 1920, Borah Papers.

[73] "I do not care who gets the nomination, the party or man who sidesteps the great question . . . will not get my support." Borah to J. E. Clinton, December 22, 1919, *ibid.*

attitude toward Harding—now favorable, now critical—turned purely upon Harding's opposition to the League.[74] Apart from this immovable antipathy to the League (at a time when Harding was trying to take a flexible stand that would alienate the fewest voters), Borah in 1920 appeared to be entirely the regular Republican. He made no overt move to lead or even to stimulate a Progressive ferment in the party.

William J. Ghent's weary withdrawal into the past, Amos Pinchot's naive third-party flirtation, Ray Stannard Baker's resigned acceptance of a mediocre Democratic candidate, William G. McAdoo's handicapped thrust for the nomination, and William E. Borah's preoccupation with the single League issue demonstrate several features of American politics on the eve of the presidential race in 1920: the fragmentation of old reform elements, and in the Wilsonian Democracy a shortage of leaders able to articulate a program or to project an image that would gain majority support in November. For eight years the Democratic party had been directed by Woodrow Wilson's heady oratory, his Calvinist sense of destiny, and his indomitable will. In 1920 he was shattered and close to death. It is a measure of Wilson's dominance that the efficient but colorless McAdoo was, if partly in jest, dubbed crown prince and heir apparent— and he played Hamlet while a bevy of mediocrities competed for the Democratic nomination. The confusion of the Democrats encouraged a number of Republicans to make a determined bid for their party's nomination. Yet the Republicans in their own proceedings haggled for days between a jingoist general and a competent governor and finally chose a senator of marginal distinction. No one else of notable record, charisma, or talent offered his services to the nation in 1920 except Eugene V. Debs, and he was in the Atlanta penitentiary.

Between May, 1919, when the first postwar Congress (the 66th) convened,[75] and election day in November, 1920, the achievements of the Democratic administration and the Republican-controlled Congress matched the qualifications of the two 1920 candidates: they were modest, at best. The economy was the one overriding problem in 1919–20 for both the White House and the Congress. After the

[74] Robert K. Murray, *The Harding Era: Warren G. Harding and His Administration* (Minneapolis, 1969), 58–59; Robert James Maddox, *William E. Borah and American Foreign Policy* (Baton Rouge, 1969), 79–82.

[75] The Congress that assembled on December 2, 1918, and adjourned on March 4, 1919, was the lame duck holdover from the wartime 65th Congress.

war, despite the abrupt cancellation of many war contracts and the release of army and navy personnel onto the job market, the country managed to avoid an immediate postwar recession. Production fell sharply in late 1918 and early 1919, and unemployment shot upward, but by early spring of 1919 a boom was underway that lasted well into 1920 before it finally collapsed. Students of the subject have identified four or five causes for this brief prosperity. Government spending continued after the Armistice in payment for the numerous war contracts that were not cancelled. Both the government and private bankers made substantial reconstruction loans to Europeans, who promptly spent much of the money in the United States. The Federal Reserve Board launched an easy credit policy, one that among other things allowed bondholders to put up their war bonds as collateral for loans from banks. Finally, to a limited degree, a building boom set in just after the war, especially in housing.[76]

Yet even during the postwar boom signs of trouble appeared. Prices climbed rapidly throughout 1919 and 1920.[77] In 1919 the cost of living was 77 percent above that of 1914 and rose to 105 percent above it in 1920.[78] In the spring of 1920 a fad for wearing overalls suddenly developed as a protest against the high cost of clothing. Congressman William D. Upshaw of Georgia appeared on the floor of Congress dressed in a four-dollar suit of blue overalls. He said he wore it as president of the "Congress Overall and Old Clothes Club." In Cleveland a judge sat on the bench clad in blue denim. Employees of a watch factory in Elgin, Illinois, organized an overalls club. Another group appeared in Hannibal, Missouri, led by the mayor. The thirty members of the Cheese Club in New York jogged into Times

[76] Paul A. Samuelson and Everett E. Hagen, *After the War—1918–1920: Military and Economic Demobilization of the United States* (Washington, 1943) ; George Soule, *Prosperity Decade: From War to Depression, 1917–1929* (New York, 1947) ; Carl P. Parrini, *Heir to Empire United States Economic Diplomacy, 1916–1923* (Pittsburgh, 1969) ; Wilson F. Payne, "Business Behavior, 1919–1922," *Journal of Business of the University of Chicago*, XV (July and October, 1942), vii–215; Elmus R. Wicker, *Federal Reserve Monetary Policy, 1917–1933* (New York, 1966) ; Paul P. Abrahams, "American Bankers and the Economic Tactics of Peace, 1919," *Journal of American History*, LVI (December, 1969), 572–83.

[77] The wholesale price index (with 1913 = 100) in 1918 stood at 195.7. It averaged 203.4 for 1919, and 227.9 for 1920. See Soule, *Prosperity Decade*, 84; U.S. Bureau of Labor Statistics, Bulletin no. 300, *Retail Prices, 1913 to December 1920* (Washington, 1920) ; National Industrial Conference Board, *Changes in the Cost of Living, July 1914–March, 1922* (New York, 1922).

[78] "Prices and Cost of Living," *Monthly Labor Review*, XII (March, 1921), 21–63.

Square one afternoon dressed in overalls, to demonstrate their support for the movement. Several New York restaurants bought denim for their waiters. But what began as a practical gesture against high prices quickly caught the fancy of the affluent and the fashionable. Showman Billy Rose promenaded down Chicago's Michigan Avenue clad in trousers and jumper of blue denim but set off with a neat pin stripe of white. In his breast pocket he wore a two-dollar handkerchief, and a twenty-dollar silk shirt was visible above the collar of the denim jacket. In New York a dress designer explained how rugged denim could be made into a costly garment by the use of heavy silk lining and trim of platinum rivets. In the meantime, war surplus overalls that the War Department had sold for sixteen cents a pair began to bring three dollars each in Hoboken, New Jersey.[79]

Protest against the price of clothing was not the only evidence of discontent with the economy. More than 3,600 strikes broke out in 1919, among them the great strike that failed against U.S. Steel, the city-wide general strike in Seattle which all but closed down the city for five days, a strike by cigar workers in Tampa, one by automobile workers at Willys-Overland in Ohio, and a dreary and debilitating strike in coal that dragged on for months in 1919 and into 1920.[80]

Economic unrest increased in the spring of 1920, when the postwar boom suddenly turned into a postwar depression. The wholesale price index fell from 227.9 to 150.6 in 1921 (1913=100). The gross national product dropped from $40.1 billion in 1920 to $37.6 billion in 1921. Some 4,754,000 Americans went without jobs in 1921, more than 100,000 bankruptcies occurred, and 453,000 farmers lost their farms.[81] One authority judges that the fiscal policy of the federal government was "the most fundamental influence of all in the deflation." The government, which during and after the war had been spending billions more than it received, suddenly reversed the process in the last quarter of 1919.[82] But federal fiscal policy alone did not

[79] *New York Times*, April 18, 1920, 1:5; April 25, 1920, 1:4.

[80] David Brody, *Labor in Crisis*; Interchurch World Movement, Commission of Inquiry, *Report on the Steel Strike of 1919* (New York, 1920); Robert L. Friedheim, *The Seattle General Strike*, (Seattle, 1965); Durward Long, "The Open-Closed Shop Battle in Tampa's Cigar Industry, 1919–1921," *Florida Historical Quarterly*, XLVII (October, 1968), 101–21; David A. McMurray, "The Willys-Overland Strike, 1919," *Northwest Ohio Quarterly* (Autumn, 1964); *Report of the Department of Labor, 1920* (Washington, 1921), 103–15.

[81] Soule, *Prosperity Decade*, 96; Bureau of Labor Statistics, Bulletin no. 300, *Retail Prices, 1913 to December, 1920*.

[82] Soule, *Prosperity Decade*, 97. For discussion of federal fiscal policy, see Elmus

cause the depression. The demand for exports, especially farm products, fell rapidly in 1920. Farmers who had expanded their output during the war, with its heavy demand for farm goods, by 1920 found themselves with a huge surplus on hand, as European farmers resumed much of their prewar production and ships freed from war use began carrying farm goods from Argentina, Australia, and other agricultural regions. During the last six months of 1920 the average price of the ten major crops dropped 57 percent. Net farm income in 1919 was 219 (1914=100); in 1920 it was 185; and in 1921 it was down to 84.[83]

While farmers worried over their surplus in 1920, American businessmen faced a comparable difficulty. As prices at home rose through 1919 and 1920, consumers bought less and less of what business was producing. Businessmen began to cancel orders for goods and to lower prices on existing inventories. Manufacturers, in turn, cut back sharply on production, and unemployment rose accordingly. Neither stockholders nor laborers suffered as much from the depression as farmers did. Industrial profits had become so huge that corporations were able to continue paying dividends and interest with little trouble. Labor (except for the unemployed, who numbered some 4,754,000 in the winter of 1920–21) took a reduction in wages during the depression, but a steep decline in the cost of living at the time gave workers more real purchasing power than they had before the downturn. Farmers, on the other hand, entered the Twenties suffering from an agricultural depression that lasted all through the decade and of course worsened after the 1929 crash.[84]

All of these economic troubles—high prices, costs of living, strikes, production rates, agricultural surpluses, and unemployment—gained attention of a sort from the administration and from Congress. Wilson himself did virtually nothing but hang onto his flickering life, how-

R. Wicker, "A Reconsideration of Federal Reserve Policy during the 1920–1921 Depression," *Journal of Economic History*, XXVI (June, 1966), 223–38; Milton Friedman and Anna Jacobson Schwartz, *A Monetary History of the United States, 1867–1960* (Princeton, 1963).

[83] James H. Shideler, *Farm Crisis, 1919–1923* (Berkeley, 1957); Secretary of Agriculture, *Annual Reports of the Department of Agriculture . . . 1920* (Washington, 1921), 3–27.

[84] Shideler, *Farm Crisis;* Soule, *Prosperity Decade,* 96ff.; National Industrial Conference Board, *Changes in the Cost of Living, July, 1914–March, 1922;* U.S. Bureau of Labor Statistics, Bulletin no. 310, *Industrial Unemployment: A Statistical Study of Its Extent and Causes* (Washington, 1922).

ever, while his cabinet worked at cross purposes and Congress for the most part floundered toward the 1920 election.

Between Armistice and normalcy Wilson's cabinet played a game of musical chairs. In December, 1918, Senator Carter Glass of Virginia replaced McAdoo as secretary of the treasury. In March, 1919, A. Mitchell Palmer of Pennsylvania replaced Thomas Gregory of Texas as attorney general. The Senate confirmed Palmer's nomination in August, some five months after he took office; during those five months Palmer busied himself reorganizing the Justice Department and joining the pursuit of American Reds. In December, 1919, Joshua W. Alexander, a Missouri congressman, succeeded W. C. Redfield as secretary of commerce. In November, 1919, Glass, after less than a year in office, resigned the treasury post (effective January 1, 1920) and, through appointment by the governor of Virginia, returned to the Senate. David Houston of Texas, who had served as secretary of agriculture since 1913, replaced Glass at the treasury. Edwin T. Meredith, an Iowa banker and publisher, in February, 1920, moved into Houston's old post as secretary of agriculture. Also in February, 1920, Franklin K. Lane resigned as interior secretary, replaced in March by John Barton Payne, wartime general counsel of the Emergency Fleet Corporation.[85] Finally, in February, 1920, Robert Lansing resigned as secretary of state. Though fundamental differences between him and Wilson over foreign policy lay behind Lansing's resignation, the precipitating issue was Lansing's decision as senior cabinet officer to call cabinet meetings without Wilson's prior approval. Lansing felt that, despite the President's illness, affairs of state must go on. Wilson found this action intolerable, if only because it confirmed his own incapacity to act—and evidently a feature of Wilson's illness was his literal inability to accept his infirmity. Bainbridge Colby, a New York lawyer who served on the Shipping Board during the war, replaced Lansing at the State Department.[86]

Thus within a space of fourteen months (December, 1918, to Feb-

[85] *New York Times,* December 6, 1918, 15:3; December 15, 1918, III, 10:1–7; March 6, 1919, 10:7; April 18, 1919, 1:3; November 16, 1919, 1:4; December 17, 1919, 16:7; December 18, 1919, 17:4; February 3, 1920, 10:1; March 16, 1920, 23:5.

[86] Daniel M. Smith, "Lansing and the Wilson Interregnum," *Historian,* XXI (February, 1959), 135–61; Edwin A. Weinstein, "Woodrow Wilson's Neurological Illness," *Journal of American History,* LVII (September, 1970), 324–51; Daniel M. Smith, *Aftermath of War: Bainbridge Colby and Wilsonian Diplomacy, 1920–1921* (Philadelphia, 1970), 7–10.

ruary, 1920) Wilson made six cabinet changes and came under pressure to make at least one more when critics of Postmaster General Albert Burleson in 1919 began to demand he resign because of his heavy-handed censorship during the war and his denial of mailing privileges to radical publications after the war.[87] The only wartime cabinet members who remained in office for the twenty-eight months of Wilson's tenure after the war were Burleson, Josephus Daniels (Navy), Newton D. Baker (War), and William B. Wilson (Labor).

Some cabinet turnover is normal enough, but the constant shifting of secretaries that occurred after the war added to the turmoil of reconstruction and compounded the lack of executive stability and direction arising from Wilson's illness and his obsession with the League. Among all of Wilson's cabinet members after the war, only Lansing and Glass seemed to make any positive thrust toward formulating policy or initiating significant legislation—and Glass quickly retired, while Lansing was fired. Palmer seemed preoccupied with Reds and with his own presidential ambitions. Colby, handicapped by a short tenure, followed or established several policies that his Republican successors would build on in the Twenties but otherwise left the department as unobtrusively as he entered it.[88]

A more forceful administration would no doubt have suffered even greater opposition than Wilson did receive (even so, he vetoed a considerable number of bills[89]), since Congress was controlled by an obstructionist Republican majority, elected in November, 1918, and convening for the first time in May, 1919. The first session of the 66th Congress (May 19–November 19, 1919) passed some necessary appropriations bills, repealed daylight saving time, submitted the Nineteenth Amendment to the states, and provided for enforcement of the new Eighteenth Amendment by passing the Volstead Act. Beyond this, the Congress wrangled over Wilson's peace treaty and his illness, and occasionally investigated labor conditions and the wave of strikes plaguing the country.[90] As for the second session

[87] Donald Johnson, *The Challenge to American Freedoms: World War I and the Rise of the American Civil Liberties Union* (Lexington, Ky., 1962), 81–82.

[88] Stanley Coben, *A. Mitchell Palmer* (New York, 1963) ; and Smith, *Aftermath of War.*

[89] Carleton Jackson, *Presidential Vetoes, 1792–1945* (Athens, Ga., 1967), 181–86.

[90] A convenient and often acerbic survey of congressional activity during 1919 is Lindsay Rogers, "American Government and Politics: The Special Session of Congress," *American Political Science Review*, XIV (February, 1920), 74–92. "Problems left unsolved rather than measures which were passed" were the "noteworthy features" of this session to Rogers.

(December 1, 1919–June, 1920), political scientist Lindsay Rogers found the dominant *motif* to have been "partisanship and hostility to the President."[91] The session did, among other things, pass the 1920 Railway Act, the Army Reorganization Act, a Merchant Marine act, a coal and oil leasing act, a water power act, and a civil service retirement act. Yet this cluster of laws hardly balanced off the anti-radical inquiries, the hysterical oratory, the interminable and partisan haggling over the Treaty of Versailles, and the failure of Congress to cope with the steel and coal strikes, or to provide an employment service and other agencies to effect a better reconstruction program. But only a harmonious and united body, driven by a strong and energetic president, could have coped with the country's needs after the war. Wilson was physically beyond such leadership, while Congress was well shy of harmony or a disposition to receive executive direction. Robert Murray has neatly capsuled the legacy that Harding acquired in March, 1921: "From Wilson he received a disintegrating presidency, a confused and rebellious Congress, a foreign policy in chaos, a domestic economy in shambles, a society sundered with hatreds and turmoil." As Colonel Edmund W. Starling, chief of the White House secret service, later recalled, "the country was in a mess."[92]

That any man would want to take over from Woodrow Wilson in 1921 is, if nothing else, a testimony to human ambition. Yet not one but at least three major candidates and a half-dozen dark horses and favorite sons tried for the Democratic nomination.[93] And apparently so did Woodrow Wilson. As early as January, 1918, talk was common that Wilson and Theodore Roosevelt would once more compete for the presidency, each trying for a third term. In January, 1919, Roosevelt died. In February, 1919, even while Wilson was bedridden and all but sealed off from anyone but the closest family and advisers, his staff denied a rumor that he had decided not to try for the nomination. Wilson never issued a statement taking himself out of contention, and there is evidence that he was striving, or at least hoping, for the nomination up to the final hours of the convention itself—that from his White House solitude he kept in touch with the proceedings

[91] Lindsay Rogers, "American Government and Politics: The Second Session of the 66th Congress," *American Political Science Review*, XIV (November, 1920), 660.
[92] Murray, *Harding Era*, 91–92; Sterling quoted, p. 92.
[93] Wesley M. Bagby, *Road to Normalcy: The Presidential Campaign and Election of 1920* (Baltimore, 1962); Donald R. McCoy, "Election of 1920," in *History of American Presidential Elections, 1789–1968*, ed. Arthur M. Schlesinger, Jr., *et al.* (New York, 1971), III, 2349–56.

through his friends, waiting for the call that must come after the delegates had found him to be the only man they could unite around. Although he never formally asked for renomination, Wilson tried to determine the issue in the campaign. In February, 1920, he wrote a letter to the Jackson Day dinner, demanding that the country make the election a "great and solemn referendum" on the League.[94]

Wilson's refusal to deny his own candidacy sorely handicapped any other Democratic contender for the nomination. McAdoo, as already noted, was hurt badly by Wilson's behavior. On the other hand, A. Mitchell Palmer showed scant regard for his chief's aspirations and made a bold and open bid for the nomination. Building his candidacy on the anti-Red hysteria of 1919–20, Palmer's chances, which were never strong, evaporated when the Scare fizzled in the spring of 1920.[95] The old three-time loser, William Jennings Bryan, did not make a formal entry into the race but said he would consider accepting the nomination if the party demanded it.[96]

The campaign of Governor James M. Cox of Ohio, who eventually received the nomination, was low-key and for a while all but obscured by the other campaigns. Though he eventually accepted Wilson's dictum to make the League the central issue, Cox at first focused on a proposal to liberalize the new Prohibition amendment—he favored sale of light wines and beer. His stand gained him support from some big city Democratic bosses who felt that the party had little chance for the presidency in 1920 but realized that a Wet candidate could help to carry their home city vote in November. Less associated with Wilson than any other serious candidate, Cox had a mildly progressive record, yet he was not saddled with a Wilsonian identity. And as governor of a pivotal state with a large electoral vote, Cox operated from a strong political base. By the time the Democratic convention

[94] Wesley M. Bagby, "Woodrow Wilson, a Third Term, and the Solemn Referendum," *American Historical Review*, LX (April, 1955), 567–75; Kurt Wimer, "Woodrow Wilson and a Third Term," *Pennsylvania History*, XXIX (April, 1962), 193–211; Richard L. Merritt, "Woodrow Wilson and the 'Great and Solemn Referendum,'" *Review of Politics*, XXVII (January, 1965), 78–104; McCoy, "Election of 1920," 2353–54, 2364–65.

[95] Coben, *Palmer*, 246–67; McCoy, "Election of 1920," 2354.

[96] Bryan was pessimistic about the party's chances in 1920, had few illusions about gaining the nomination himself, and was most intent upon shaping the party platform and influencing selection of the candidate. See Lawrence W. Levine, *Defender of the Faith, William Jennings Bryan: The Last Decade, 1915–1925* (New York, 1965), 157; and Louis W. Koenig, *Bryan: A Political Biography of William Jennings Bryan* (New York, 1971), 584–85.

opened in June, Cox was one of the front runners. Harding's nomination, already achieved by the Republicans earlier at Chicago, strengthened Cox, since Harding was also from Ohio. Nomination of Cox might hold Ohio for the Democrats.[97] Cox placed third behind McAdoo and Palmer on the first ballot, held his position through six more rounds, and on the seventh ballot climbed to second place behind McAdoo. He passed McAdoo on the twelfth ballot but was still far from victory. The convention underwent some interminable maneuverings and even a weekend adjournment before it finally chose Cox on the forty-fourth ballot. It then quickly chose Franklin D. Roosevelt as vice-presidential running mate.[98]

The 1920 Democratic convention in San Francisco was in several ways a prelude to the suicidal brawl that occurred four years later at the party convention in New York. In 1924, rural and small town Drys, mostly Protestant and often Fundamentalists in their faith, and strongest in the South and the West, would stand behind McAdoo for over a hundred ballots. With equal fervor, Democrats predominantly from the Northeast who were urban, Wets, and Catholics (or less than rigid Fundamentalists) would stand fast for Al Smith of New York. This dichotomy of the Twenties, this conflict between an older rural and a newly emerging urban culture, permeated American life in the Twenties. Glimmers of the conflict appeared at the 1920 convention. Bryan, who would spend his last years fighting Demon Rum and religious modernism, pleaded for a strong Prohibition plank. He lost because southern and western delegates were less united behind the Dry standard than they would be in 1924. Cox drew most of his votes from the Wet, urban delegates. McAdoo, an avowed Dry, gained their animus.[99]

Warren G. Harding earned no man's animus, and therein lay a key to his nomination and his election. From his early years in Ohio politics to his brief presidential career, and during the years since his death, political anecdotes and myths derogating Harding have abounded. He has been ridiculed more than any other president. His

[97] Bagby, *Road to Normalcy*, 73–76; Frank Freidel, *Franklin D. Roosevelt: The Ordeal* (Boston, 1954), 62, 65; James M. Cox, *Journey through My Years* (New York, 1946), 225ff.; David Burner, *Politics of Provincialism*, 62–63; "Final Standings of the Democratic Candidates," *Literary Digest*, LXV (June 12, 1920), 20.

[98] *Official Report of the Proceedings of the Democratic National Convention Held in San Francisco* (Indianapolis, n.d.) ; Freidel, *Ordeal*, 50–69; Bagby, *Road to Normalcy*, 102–22; McCoy, "Election of 1920," 2361–66.

[99] Burner, *Politics of Provincialism*, 3–27; Levine, *Defender of the Faith*, 161–68.

character and his administration have all but become the standard measurement for what a president should not be.[100]

Yet Robert Murray's recent biography,[101] copious in detail and solidly footnoted, bluntly challenges much of this traditional image of Harding that historians and journalists have sustained for over half a century. Theodore Roosevelt's daughter, Alice Roosevelt Longworth, who ruled over Washington society during Harding's presidency and cared little for either Florence Harding or her husband, once said, "Harding was not a bad man. He was just a slob."[102] Murray portrays another Harding, though he does not, as revisionists often do, reverse the image and make of Harding a paragon of civic and moral virtue. (Harding was obviously nothing of the kind.)

In 1899 Harding ran for an Ohio Senate seat and won his first elective office. In "an age of wide-scale corruption," writes Murray, Harding "made a mark by being reasonably honest." He quickly became the mediator, the advocate of party harmony, a man who "somehow retained the good will of both reformers and standpatters."[103] As editor of the prospering *Marion Star*, as a genial, outgoing personality with a wide circle of friends, and as an avid participant in community affairs, Harding easily advanced up the Ohio hierarchy, reaching the U.S. Senate in 1914. He arrived there with the firm conviction that "conciliation and harmony were superior political weapons to obstruction and strife."[104] His career as senator was undistinguished, and on the record alone he deserved the Republican nomination in 1920 less than did one or two of his competitors. Yet just as he discounts the sensational "Negro blood" stories that followed Harding throughout his career,[105] Murray also deflates other ancient myths: that Harding's nomination in 1920 resulted from purchase by tainted oil money, or that he was handpicked in a deal

[100] Murray, *Harding Era*, 513–37; Gary M. Maranell, "The Evaluation of Presidents: An Extension of the Schlesinger Polls," *Journal of American History*, LVII (June, 1970), 104–13; Burl Noggle, "The New Harding," *Reviews in American History*, I (Spring, 1973).

[101] See also Randolph C. Downes, *The Rise of Warren Gamaliel Harding, 1865–1920* (Columbus, 1970), for a deeply researched and detailed study.

[102] Alice Roosevelt Longworth, *Crowded Hours* (New York, 1933), 325.

[103] Murray, *Harding*, 10.

[104] *Ibid.*, 11.

[105] Francis Russell, *The Shadow of Blooming Grove: Warren G. Harding and His Times* (New York, 1968), emphasizes the supposed "shadow" of race that hung over Harding throughout his life. For a more skeptical evaluation of Harding's supposed ancestry, see Randolph C. Downes, "Negro Rights and White Backlash in the Campaign of 1920," *Ohio History*, 75 (Spring and Summer, 1966), 85–107.

by a senatorial cabal in the Blackstone Hotel the night before his nomination, or, finally, that Mrs. Harding (the Duchess) forced and browbeat Warren into running for the presidency. Florence Harding was no beauty, and her husband did, in truth, have more than one extramarital affair, but the Duchess was a competent business associate in Harding's newspaper office and actually opposed his running for the presidency, at least until he gained the nomination.[106]

Harry M. Daugherty, Harding's campaign manager, claimed that he made Harding president. Yet from the beginning of their relationship in Ohio politics around 1900 it was clear, says Murray, that "Daugherty always needed Harding more than Harding needed Daugherty."[107] Harding had several other boosters in Ohio and elsewhere around the country, though Daugherty was of course an aggressive and ebullient manager. But Harding himself worked harder than Daugherty or anyone else in his campaign. He had lots of friends but little money (before the nomination). The two leading contenders as the Republican convention neared were Colonel Leonard Wood and former Governor Frank Lowden of Illinois. Both of them (and especially Wood) had far more financial support than Harding. Harry Sinclair, the oil man who supposedly contributed to Harding's campaign and cashed in later during the Teapot Dome affair, thought Harding "did not stand a Chinaman's chance" and actually supported Wood.[108] Besides Wood and Lowden, there were several lesser contenders for the nomination—Herbert Hoover, Charles Evans Hughes, and Calvin Coolidge among them—but Senator Hiram Johnson of California was probably the strongest. Johnson was the most "progressive" candidate in the party. Wood claimed to be Theodore Roosevelt's successor, but the only valid comparison between the Red-baiting general and the sophisticated Roosevelt was their mutual concern for military preparedness, and even then Roosevelt had a better

[106] Murray, Harding, 9, 23, 36–39, 40; cf. Downes, Rise of Harding, ch. 18, on the 1920 convention, and pp. 18–19 on Florence Harding's work on the Star.

[107] Murray, Harding, 19. Daugherty's dubious claims are registered in Harry M. Daugherty and Thomas Dixon, Inside Story of the Harding Tragedy (New York, 1932). A typical version of the 1920 campaign that perpetuates the Daugherty view is Mark Sullivan's old classic, Our Times: The Twenties (New York, 1935). For criticism of Daugherty's self-enobling role, see Nicholas Murray Butler to Mark Sullivan, March 22, 1935, Box 17, James Wadsworth Papers, Division of Manuscripts, Library of Congress; and Charles D. Hilles to Sullivan, March 2, 1935, ibid. More appreciative of Daugherty is James W. Wadsworth to Sullivan, March 5, 1935, ibid.

[108] Murray, Harding, 28; but cf. J. Leonard Bates, The Origins of Teapot Dome: Progressives, Parties, and Petroleum, 1909–1921 (Urbana, Ill., 1963), 209.

appreciation of restraint in the use of power. Lowden had a good record as governor of Illinois but lacked flair or magnetism.[109]

As the Republican convention opened in Chicago in June, Harding seemed to have little chance for the nomination. After four ballots the two leaders, Wood and Lowden, were deadlocked. Late in the evening of Friday, June 11, and into the early morning hours of Saturday, June 12, a series of conferences did in fact take place in the rooms and corridors of the Blackstone Hotel, headquarters of the Chicago convention. But Harding was not handpicked Friday night by a senatorial clique and foisted upon the next day's convention (another legend that Harry Daugherty contributed to and that contemporary reporters helped to sustain). Many of the delegates, prominent senators among them, were simply confused and wondered what to do. The convention appeared to be at an impasse. The summer heat was almost unbearable. The weekend was approaching, and both the patience and the funds of many delegates were approaching exhaustion. Harding did win the nomination on Saturday, but not due to senatorial machinations in a "smoke-filled room." Sixteen senators were delegates to the convention; thirteen of them voted against Harding on the first four ballots taken Saturday morning. During a noon recess on Saturday several senators, including Henry Cabot Lodge, tried to launch a Stop Harding movement. Harding won because he was, in the classic political phrase, the most available man. A genial, unprepossessing man from the heartland of America (at least from a pivotal state), he had political experience and had alienated none of the other candidates. The Wood, Lowden, and Johnson forces had embittered each other so much that they could agree only on a fourth nominee, Harding, who had few if any enemies and lots of friends at the convention. They chose him as the compromise solution to a deadlocked convention, not a controlled one. Calvin Coolidge's nomination for the vice-presidency was an even more spontaneous, unpremeditated decision. When the Old Guard managers tried to nominate Senator Irvine L. Lenroot of Wisconsin, support for Coolidge suddenly developed, and he won on the first ballot. The convention, wrote Coolidge later, broke away from the "coterie of . . . Senators" and "literally stampeded to me."[110]

[109] Gary Dean Best, "The Hoover-for-President Boom of 1920," *Mid-America*, 53 (October, 1971), 227–44; Bagby, *Road to Normalcy*, 25–35; William T. Hutchinson, *Lowden of Illinois* (Chicago, 1957), II, 383–469; McCoy, "Election of 1920," 2351–53.
[110] Wesley M. Bagby, "The 'Smoke-Filled Room' and the Nomination of Warren

Between the convention and the November election Harding did what a candidate normally must do, but with considerable skill: he pacified and united the various factions in the party. For most of his front porch campaign he remained at home in Marion, where to droves of visitors he made homely little speeches both on the porch and inside his comfortable green house with the white trim. Meanwhile he kept in close touch with party leaders all over the country. Harding had a campaign manager (Daugherty), a gifted publicist (Albert Lasker), and a national party chairman (Will Hays) to help expend funds and map strategy, but Marion, Ohio, was the real campaign headquarters.[111] Harding was, writes Murray, "completely in charge." He initiated the "primary thrust of the campaign," namely an emphasis "on pacification, on conciliation, on restoration, and on harmony." The money he had lacked before his nomination now was available. Albert Lasker flooded the country with bands and billboards and photographs. The Chicago Cubs came to Marion and played a local team; Harding pitched the first three balls, after which Grover Cleveland Alexander took over. Al Jolson, Eddie Foy, Ethel Barrymore, and other entertainment celebrities came to Marion and shook hands with the candidate. Obviously, as Donald McCoy has pointed out, Harding's objective was "more to win the election by projecting an image than through discussion of the issues."[112]

G. Harding," *Mississippi Valley Historical Review*, XLI (March, 1955), 657–74; Murray, *Harding*, 3–42; Downes, *Rise of Harding*, 406–26; McCoy, "Election of 1920," 2357–60; Calvin Coolidge, *The Autobiography of Calvin Coolidge* (New York, 1929), 148. See also a series of letters to Mark Sullivan by men who had attended the 1920 convention and were in 1935 criticizing Sullivan's account of the Harding nomination in *Our Times: The Twenties* — Nicholas Murray Butler to Sullivan, March 22, 1935; Charles D. Hilles to Sullivan, March 2, 1935; James W. Wadsworth to Sullivan, March 5, 1935, Box 17, Wadsworth Papers.

George Sutherland, a supporter whom Harding subsequently appointed to the Supreme Court, showed some prescience in his analysis of Harding's chances as of April, 1920. "The political situation," he wrote to an acquaintance, "is very much complicated. . . . [The] aggressive candidates are killing one another off. The fight between the Wood and Johnson forces has been so bitter that the followers of neither will support the other when the break comes in the Convention. Of the avowed candidates, I should not be surprised if Harding has the best of the situation. He and his managers have been very discreet in the conduct of his campaign. They have antagonized none of the other candidates and he is quite sure . . . to get support from all the other forces when it is discovered that none of them has sufficient strength to win." Sutherland to Henry M. Bates, April 26, 1920, Box 3, George Sutherland Papers, Division of Manuscripts, Library of Congress.

[111] Downes, *Rise of Harding*, 452ff.

[112] Murray, *Harding*, 49, 67; Downes, *Rise of Harding*, 452ff.; McCoy, "Election of 1920," 2372.

Harding, forever the conciliator, refused to make Wilson the central campaign target. "I will never," said Harding, "go to the White House over the broken body of Woodrow Wilson."[113] Even on the League issue (which was the only issue to Wilson) Harding equivocated, trying above all to harmonize the party. On election day, which was also his birthday, Harding received 16,152,200 votes. Cox gained 9,147,353. Debs, in Atlanta penitentiary, picked up 919,799 on the Socialist ticket. Harding carried thirty-seven states for a total of 404 electoral votes. The Republicans held onto every Senate seat contested in 1920 and gained ten more from the Democrats.[114]

To say that this lopsided victory reflected opposition to the League would be a distortion. Neither Cox nor Harding had taken a distinctive position on the League, though Cox more clearly supported it than Harding opposed it. Harding was deliberately ambiguous on the issue. Some Republican spokesmen, such as Taft, were outspoken advocates of the League; others, such as Borah, were vehement opponents of it. A Republican vote was as likely to have registered support for one as for the other of these Republican views.[115] Yet if the election was not the solemn referendum that he had hoped for, it was to a considerable degree a cruel referendum on Woodrow Wilson. Some five weeks before Harding's election Herbert Hoover wrote to a friend: "Since the Armistice, the present administration has made a failure by all the tests that we can apply. It has obstinately held up the peace of the world for eighteen months. . . . It has woefully neglected and failed upon great reconstruction and administrative measures that are critically necessary as the aftermath of the war.

[113] Murray, *Harding.*

[114] Edgar Eugene Robinson, *The Presidential Vote, 1896–1932* (Stanford, 1934) ; Svend Petersen, *A Statistical History of the American Presidential Elections* (New York, 1963), 83; McCoy, "Election of 1920," 2456. The popular vote figures for 1920 vary slightly from source to source. I have used the count listed in McCoy.

[115] Bagby, "Woodrow Wilson, a Third Term, and the Solemn Referendum"; Merritt, "Woodrow Wilson and the 'Great and Solemn Referendum' "; Murray, *Harding,* 68; Downes, *Rise of Harding,* 568–70.

It may well be that historians have stressed the League as an issue (and the 1920 vote as supposedly ratifying a "retreat to isolationism") far more than did the voters themselves in 1920. See William Appleman Williams, "The Legend of Isolationism in the 1920's," *Science and Society,* XVIII (Winter, 1954) ; cf. Elihu Root's statement in 1920: ". . . it is very desirable to have the public understand both in this Country and in Europe that the Senate's refusal to ratify the Treaty of Versailles does not mean a policy of isolation." Root to Ansley Wilcox, March 26, 1920, Box 138, Elihu Root Papers, Division of Manuscripts, Library of Congress.

. . . The responsibilities of government should now, therefore, be transferred."[116]

On March 4, 1921, Wilson and Harding rode together down Pennsylvania Avenue to the inauguration of normalcy. The responsibilities of government were now transferred. The Democracy of Woodrow Wilson, which had laid the foundation, gave way to the Republican Twenties. It was now Harding's turn—and after him Coolidge, then Hoover—to demonstrate responsibilities of government.

[116] Hoover cited in Murray, *Harding,* 68–69. McCoy, "Election of 1920," 2384–85, offers a succinct summary of the Harding appeal in 1920—and of the antipathy for the party of Woodrow Wilson.

Bibliographical Essay

This essay includes some of the titles already cited in the footnotes to the text, but it is primarily a discussion of additional books, articles, and other items useful to anyone pursuing the topics I have covered.

GENERAL

During World War II, E. Jay Howenstine, Jr., published a series of articles that, taken together, provide a broad view of public policy after the Armistice. I have used and cited these essays, but they are worth listing again here: "Demobilization after the First World War," *Quarterly Journal of Economics*, LVIII (November, 1943), 91–105; "The Industrial Board, Precursor of the N.R.A.: The Price-Reduction Movement after World War I," *Journal of Political Economy*, LI (June, 1943), 235–50; "Public Works Programs after World War I," *ibid.* (December, 1943), 523–37; "Lessons of World War I," *Annals* of the American Academy of Political and Social Science, CCXXXVIII (March, 1945), 180–87. A fundamental guide to wartime agencies is Waldo G. Leland and Newton D. Mereness, comps., *Introduction to the American Official Sources for the Economic and Social History of the World War* (New Haven, 1926). An early and exhaustive work by the former director of the U.S. Council of National Defense is Grosvenor B. Clarkson, *Industrial America in the World War: The Strategy behind the Line, 1917–1918* (Boston, 1923). An important recent appraisal is Paul A. C. Koistinen, "The 'Industrial-Military Complex' in Historical Perspective: World War I," *Business History Review*, XLI (Winter, 1967), 378–403. A perceptive little survey of American life just after the war is David Burner, "1919: Prelude to Normalcy," in John Braeman *et al.*, eds., *Change and Continuity in Twentieth-Century America: The 1920's* (Columbus, 1968), 3–32.

DEMOBILIZATION

The military history of World War I has received far less attention than have the problems of the war's origins and the war's effects. An official history, *The United States Army in the World War, 1917–1919* (Washington, 1948), consists of seventeen volumes of documents (with an occasional narrative essay), selected from the AEF records by the army's historical division. The compilers believed these to be "essential to a critical study of the history of the war"—a history not yet produced. (In contrast, the Army Department's *United States Army in World War II*, which began to appear two years after the end of the war, has already reached nearly eighty volumes.) Volume X of the World War I series, *The Armistice Agreement and Related Documents*, is a hefty and useful body of source materials. A unique source on army life is *Stars and Stripes*. Written, edited, and published by AEF enlisted men, the first number appeared on February 8, 1918, and regularly every Friday thereafter until June 13, 1919, when it ceased publication. Skillfully edited and full of information (Private Harold W. Ross, who would establish *The New Yorker* in 1925, became editor of *Stars and Stripes* about the third issue), the paper provides a revealing glimpse of the American doughboy in Europe. An indispensable set of documents is John J. Pershing's *Final Report, American Expeditionary Force* (Washington, 1920). This is available also in *War Department Annual Report, 1919* (Washington, 1920), I, pt. 1, pp. 547–642; it is reprinted in *U.S. Army in the World War, 1917–1919*, XII.

The one military history that I found most useful on demobilization is Edward M. Coffman, *The War to End All Wars: The American Military Experience in World War I* (New York, 1968). Coffman was concerned primarily with the war itself. Among books focusing on demobilization, the earliest to reach publication is still the most detailed and useful volume yet written on the subject—Benedict Crowell and Robert Forrest Wilson, *Demobilization: Our Industrial and Military Demobilization after the Armistice, 1918–1920* (New Haven, 1921). The authors wrote from firsthand acquaintance with the facts, but, more important, they utilized an abundance of information from government agencies and personnel, information that might otherwise have been buried in neglected piles of government archives or have died unrecorded with the men who experienced demobilization. The book stops short, however, with the physical dissolution of the army and the disposal of contracts and material of war. To follow the doughboy home as he looks for work, to see the nation attempt a reconversion and readjustment of the economy and the society to peace, one must read elsewhere. Dixon Wecter, *When Johnny Comes Marching Home* (Cambridge, 1944), covers three of the nation's demobilizations: after the Revolution, the Civil War, and the World War. The book is an admirable mixture of documented fact and insightful, artful evocation and evaluation. James R. Mock and Evangeline Thurber, *Report on Demobilization* (Norman, Okla., 1944), contains a mass of data not readily available elsewhere, but it is not footnoted, is disorganized and repetitious, and is also a case of special pleading. Written during World War II as a study of what went wrong after World War

I, it attempts to draw numerous lessons for the demobilization to come after the second war. Wecter, of course, sought to do the same thing but with more judiciousness and perspective.

A series of contemporary views on rehabilitation of the returning doughboy is "Rehabilitation of the Wounded," *Annals* of the American Academy of Political and Social Science, LXXX (November, 1918). An impassioned appraisal of the results by the early Thirties is Katherine Mayo, *Soldiers What Next?* (Boston, 1934). A good brief discussion of the American Legion's activities during the Twenties and Thirties in behalf of World War I veterans is in Davis R. B. Ross, *Preparing for Ulysses: Politics and Veterans during World War II* (New York, 1969). A solid survey of its subject is William Pyrle Dillingham, *Federal Aid to Veterans 1917–1941* (Gainesville, Fla., 1952).

RECONSTRUCTION

Bibliographies on reconstruction, their very existence indicating the extent of concern about the subject, appeared soon after the war. See, for example, V. B. Turner, "List of References on Reconstruction," *Monthly Labor Review*, VII (December, 1918), 1529–61. Estella T. Weeks, *Reconstruction Programs* (New York, 1919), contains summaries or reprints of fifty or more reconstruction proposals made at or near the end of the war. A good set of readings is *Study Outline in the Problems of the Reconstruction Period* (New York, 1918). Beginning in November, 1918, and thereafter for most of the next year, *Monthly Labor Review* offered summaries of various reconstruction programs and bills introduced in Congress. The Reconstruction Research Division of the U.S. Council of National Defense published a *Daily Digest of Reconstruction News* from December 12, 1918, to February 17, 1921. The most useful government document, however, is the Reconstruction Research Division's *Readjustment and Reconstruction Activities in the States* (Washington, 1919).

As they do for demobilization, the volumes by Dixon Wecter and by Mock and Larson touch on most of the fundamental problems dealing with reconstruction. Two essays which I discovered only after I had finished my manuscript and which deal with several of the themes I developed concerning reconstruction are Stanley Shapiro, "The Twilight of Reform: Advanced Progressives after the Armistice," *The Historian*, XXXIII (May, 1971), 349–64; and "The Great War and Reform: Liberals and Labor, 1917–19," *Labor History*, VII (Summer, 1971), 323–44.

LABOR

Labor merits much more attention than I have given it. A separate book on the subject would hardly be adequate to cover the 3,600 or more strikes that occurred in 1919 alone. For a sampling of sources and guides, see the entire issue of *Annals* of the American Academy of Political and Social Science, LXXXI (January, 1919), devoted to "A Reconstruction Labor Policy"; National Industrial Conference Board, Report no. 49, *Changes in the Cost of Living, July 1914–March 1922* (New York, 1922); Daniel J. Ahearn, Jr., *The Wages of Farm and Factory Laborers, 1914–1944* (New York, 1945); Florence Peterson, *Strikes in the United States, 1880–1936* (Washington, 1938); and Interchurch World Movement, Commission of Inquiry, *Report on the Steel Strike of 1919* (New York, 1920). John S. Smith, "Organized Labor and Government in the Wilson Era, 1913–1921, Some Conclusions," *Labor History*, III (Fall, 1962), 265–86, offers extensive bibliographical commentary. But see also David Montgomery, "The Conventional Wisdom: A Review Essay," *Labor History*, 13 (Winter, 1972); and Robert H. Zieger, "Workers and Scholars: Recent Trends in American Labor Historiography," *ibid.* (Spring, 1972).

RAILROADS

A useful contemporary appraisal is *Annals* of the American Academy of Political and Social Science, LXXXVI (November, 1919), devoted to "The Railroad Problem: A Discussion of Current Railway Issues." Two basic books are Walker D. Hines, *War History of American Railroads* (New Haven, 1928), and K. Austin Kerr, *American Railroad Politics, 1914–1920* (Pittsburgh, 1968). A fascinating item is Rogers MacVeagh, *The Transportation Act of 1920: Its Sources, History, and Text, Together with Its Amendments to the Interstate Commerce Act Explained, Analyzed, and Compared; Comprising Extracts from Reports and Debates in Congress, Rulings, Interpretations, and Decisions of the Interstate Commerce Commission, Opinions of the United States Supreme Court, Prescribed Forms, and Complete Texts of Related Acts, Including the Federal Control Act, Merchant Marine Act, 1920 and Interstate Commerce Act, All as Amended to and Including August 18, 1922* (New York, 1923). As its title suggests, this is a potpourri on the subject but a useful one. For example, it contains an elaborate chart, facing p. 8, that shows and compares various parts of nine railroad plans or bills circulating in 1919–20.

AMERICANS AND UN-AMERICANS

On wartime censorship, conformity, and violence, H. C. Peterson and Gilbert C. Fite, *Opponents of War, 1917–18* (Madison, 1957), is a pioneering survey that is full of information, anecdotes, and examples of suppression but that is formless, almost chaotic, in presentation. William

Preston, Jr., *Aliens and Dissenters: Federal Suppression of Radicals, 1903–33* (Cambridge, 1963), a book I drew much from, focuses on the crusade by state and federal officials to destroy the IWW, especially during and just after the war. James Weinstein, *The Decline of American Socialism, 1912–1924* (New York, 1967), attempts to challenge the conventional view that the election of 1912 was the peak of Socialist party activity in the United States; cf. Daniel Bell, *Marxian Socialism in the United States* (Princeton, 1967). Donald Johnson, *The Challenge to American Freedoms: World War I and the Rise of the American Civil Liberties Union* (Lexington, Ky., 1962), is admirable, both in its substance and in the author's restraint from unnecessary moralizing. A book that itself reflects the witless hysteria of the war period is Emerson Hough, *The Web* (Chicago, 1919), an "authorized history of the American Protective League . . . a vast, silent, volunteer army organized with the approval and operated under the direction of the United States Department of Justice, Bureau of Investigation."

Walter Guest Kellogg, *The Conscientious Objector* (New York, 1919), is a recollection and appraisal of American CO's during the war, written by a member of the board of inquiry appointed by Secretary of War Newton D. Baker on July 1, 1918, to "inquire into and to determine the sincerity of conscientious objectors." Beginning with the war period itself, CO's have continued to state their case, to recall their incarceration, and to keep the subject alive. See, for example, Evan Thomas, "Disciplinary Barracks: The Experience of a Military Prisoner at Fort Leavenworth," *Survey*, XLI (February 1, 1919), 625–29; Jacob C. Meyer, "Reflections of a Conscientious Objector in World War I," *Mennonite Quarterly Review*, XLI (January, 1967). For excerpts from reports on file in army camps and for statements by army personnel and by conscientious objectors, see *Cong. Rec.*, 65 Cong., 3 sess. (February 12, 1919), 3233–40. A fine study that appeared after I had completed my chapter on CO's is Charles Chatfield, *For Peace and Justice: Pacifism in America, 1914–1941* (Knoxville, Tenn., 1971).

A critical view of the literature on the Wobblies is William Preston, Jr., "Shall This Be All? U.S. Historians Versus William D. Haywood, et al.," *Labor History*, XII (Summer, 1971), 435–53. On Socialism in America, a fundamental work is *Socialism and American Life*, ed. Donald D. Egbert and Stow Persons (Princeton, 1952), 2 vols. A standard history of the SPA is David A. Shannon, *The Socialist Party of America* (New York, 1955). For a critical survey of Socialist historiography, see Bryan Strong, "Historians and American Socialism, 1900–1920," *Science and Society*, XXXIV (Winter, 1970), 387–97. On World War I, see Sally M. Miller, "Socialist Party Decline and World War I: Bibliography and Interpretation," *ibid.*, 398–411. A provocative and extensive review of the literature is D. H. Leon, "Whatever Happened to an American Socialist Party? A Critical Survey of the Spectrum of Interpretations," *American Quarterly*, XXIII (May, 1971), 236–58.

A summary of the Lusk Committee's work is in Lawrence H. Chamberlain, *Loyalty and Legislative Action: A Survey of Activity by the New York State Legislature, 1919–1949* (Ithaca, N.Y., 1951), 9–52. Among the items contemporary with the Red Scare, Zechariah Chafee, *Freedom of Speech* (New York, 1920), is classic.

WILSON AND THE WORLD

For the emphasis on Wilson's anti-Bolshevism, one should start with William Appleman Williams's early study, *American-Russian Relations, 1781–1947* (New York, 1952), but then note especially his sustained essay, *The Tragedy of American Diplomacy* (Cleveland, 1959: rev. ed., New York, 1972), and a two-part article, "American Intervention in Russia 1917–1920," *Studies on the Left*, III (Fall, 1963), 24–48; IV (Winter, 1964), 39–57. Arno J. Mayer's *Politics and Diplomacy of Peacemaking: Containment and Counterrevolution at Versailles, 1918–1919* (New York, 1967), is an exhaustive study that spells out in elaborate and sometimes interminable detail the themes more succinctly stated by Williams—though Mayer does many other things, too, his book attempting to relate domestic to foreign policy not only in the United States but in Britain, France, Germany, Italy, Hungary, and Russia as well. On Russia and the West in 1919, see also (besides the titles cited in Ch. 7) John Bradley, *Allied Intervention in Russia, 1917–1920* (New York, 1968); Beatrice Farnsworth, *William C. Bullitt and the Soviet Union* (Bloomington, Ind., 1967); Christopher Lasch, *The American Liberals and the Russian Revolution* (New York, 1962). For Soviet appraisals of the subject, see George F. Kennan, "Soviet Historiography and America's Role in the Intervention," *American Historical Review*, LXV (January, 1960), 302–22.

The two major studies of the Senate's fight with Wilson over the League are D. F. Fleming, *The United States and the League of Nations, 1918–1920* (New York, 1932), and Thomas A. Bailey, *Woodrow Wilson and the Great Betrayal* (New York, 1947). Each book, Fleming's done in the early Thirties and Bailey's just after World War II, exudes support for the League and deplores the Senate's failure to ratify the treaty—"one of the supreme tragedies of human history," wrote Bailey. A good recent monograph focusing on one group of treaty opponents and written with more detachment is Ralph Stone, *The Irreconcilables: The Fight against the League of Nations* (Lexington, Ky., 1970). Stone's book also contains a bibliographical essay which can lead the student into some of the more recent literature on Wilson, the treaty, and the League fight.

AMERICAN SOCIETY, 1919–20

Forty years after its publication, the fundamental work on American society in the decade after the war is the report of the President's Research Committee, *Recent Social Trends in the United States* (New York, 1933). On the methods and findings of this great committee, see *Survey Graphic*, XXII (January, 1933); and Barry D. Karl, "Presidential Planning and Social Science Research: Mr. Hoover's Excerpts," *Perspectives in American History* (Cambridge, 1969), III, 347–409.

For reaction to the growing urbanization of the period, a representative item is Ralph Borsodi, *Flight from the City: The Story of a New Way to Family Security* (New York, 1933), which describes the author's move from New York in 1920 to a place in the country. The episode led Borsodi to some influential proselytizing in the Twenties and Thirties. See William H. Issell, "Ralph Borsodi and the Agrarian Response to Modern America," *Agricultural History*, XLI (April, 1961). On a related theme of the Twenties, the wilderness movement, see Roderick Nash, *Wilderness and the American Mind* (New Haven, 1967), 182ff. On the attempt of sociologists to come to terms with urbanization (both as fact and as a field of study), see Maurice R. Stein, *The Eclipse of Community* (Princeton, 1960), and Park Dixon Goist, "City and 'Community': The Urban Theory of Robert Park," *American Quarterly*, XXIII (Spring, 1971), 46–59.

Robert T. Kerlin, ed., *The Voice of the Negro, 1919* (New York, 1920), is, in Kerlin's words, "a compilation from the colored press of America for the four months immediately succeeding the Washington riot. It is designed to show the Negro's reaction to that and to like events following, and to the World War and the . . . Treaty." A massive study, one inviting comparison in scope and futility with those done in the late 1960's, is *The Negro in Chicago*, by the Chicago Commission on Race Relations. Arthur I. Waskow, *From Race Riot to Sit-In* (New York, 1966), draws comparisons between 1919 and the 1960's. William M. Tuttle, Jr., *Race Riot: Chicago in the Red Summer of 1919* (New York, 1970), is a fresh, careful study of the most studied riot of 1919.

Mexican-Americans were a conspicuous group suffering from low status and low income in 1920. In that year there were some 725,000 of them in the United States. Most of them lived in the Southwest (including southern California) and engaged in hard agricultural labor, though some had migrated to Detroit, Chicago, and other midwestern industrial centers. On their plight and their growth after 1920, see Manuel Gamio, *Mexican Immigration to the United States* (Chicago, 1930); Paul S. Taylor, *Mexi-*

can Labor in the United States (Berkeley, 1928–34), I–III; John H. Burma, *Spanish-speaking Groups in the United States* (Durham, 1954); Cary McWilliams, *North from Mexico: The Spanish-speaking People of the United States* (Philadelphia, 1949); Stanley Steiner, *La Raza: The Mexican American* (New York, 1970).

On Japanese-Americans and their trials at the hands of nativists who wanted to bar further immigration, see Roger Daniels, *The Politics of Prejudice: The Anti-Japanese Movement in California and the Struggle for Japanese Exclusion* (New York, 1968).

There are numerous other studies of ethnic and linguistic groups of Americans, each demonstrating the endurance of minority status and the diversity of cultures (sometimes voluntarily and determinedly maintained) in the United States of 1920. See, for example, Humbert S. Nelli, *Italians in Chicago, 1880–1930: A Study in Ethnic Mobility* (New York, 1970); Arthur A. Goren, *New York Jews and the Quest for Community: The Kehillah Experiment, 1908–1922* (New York, 1970); Joshua A. Fishman *et al.*, *Language Loyalty in the United States: The Maintenance and Perpetuation of Non-English Mother Tongues by American Ethnic and Religious Groups* (The Hague, 1966).

On the suffrage movement, see Eleanor Flexner, *Century of Struggle: The Woman's Rights Movement in the United States* (Cambridge, 1959); Aileen Kraditor, *The Ideas of the Woman Suffrage Movement* (New York, 1965); David Morgan, *Suffragists and Democrats: The Politics of Woman Suffrage in America* (East Lansing, Mich., 1972). On the broader— or at least parallel—movement that sometimes included, but in any case went beyond, suffrage, see William L. O'Neill, *Everyone Was Brave: Rise and Fall of Feminism in America* (Chicago, 1969); Anne Firor Scott, *The Southern Lady: From Pedestal to Politics, 1830–1930* (Chicago, 1970). Among contemporary essays, a positive view of women's contribution to politics in the Twenties is Marguerite M. Wells, "Some Effects of Woman Suffrage," *Annals* of the American Academy of Political and Social Science, CXLIII (May, 1929), 207–16; less defensive and more critical of women's inaction is Emily Newell Blair, "Women in the Political Parties," *ibid.*, 217–19.

Two guides to early studies of Prohibition are Social Science Research Council, *Sources of Information Concerning the Operation of the Eighteenth Amendment* (New York, 1928), and D. C. Nicholson and R. P. Graves, *Selective Bibliography on the Operation of the Eighteenth Amendment* (Berkeley, 1931). Charles Merz, *The Dry Decade* (Garden City, N.Y., 1931), was for many years the standard study, but fresh material and new perspectives are in Andrew Sinclair, *Prohibition: The Era of Excess* (New York, 1964); James H. Timberlake, *Prohibition and the Progressive Movement, 1900–1920* (Cambridge, 1963); Joseph Gusfield,

Symbolic Crusade: Status Politics and the American Temperance Movement (Urbana, Ill., 1963); Norman Clark, *The Dry Years: Prohibition and Social Change in Washington* (Seattle, 1965); Jimmie Lewis Franklin, *Born Sober: Prohibition in Oklahoma, 1907–1959* (Norman, Okla., 1971).

The literature on Fundamentalism is large. Two recent studies of importance are Ernest R. Sandeen, *The Roots of Fundamentalism: British and American Millenarianism, 1800–1930* (Chicago, 1970), and Willard B. Gatewood, Jr., ed., *Controversy in the Twenties: Fundamentalism, Modernism, and Evolution* (Nashville, 1969). The latter contains a useful bibliography. A perceptive essay is Paul A. Carter, "The Fundamentalist Defense of the Faith," in John Braeman *et al.*, eds., *Change and Continuity in Twentieth-Century America: The 1920's* (Columbus, 1968), 179–214.

REMNANTS OF PROGRESSIVISM

Herbert Margulies, "Recent Opinion on the Decline of the Progressive Movement," *Mid-America*, XLV (October, 1963), 250–68, shows a general agreement among historians a decade ago that "the Progressive Movement was over by 1920." But meanwhile Arthur S. Link, in "What Happened to the Progressive Movement in the 1920's?" *American Historical Review*, LXXIV (April, 1959), 1205–20, had published an influential essay that argued for the survival of reform in the postwar decade. More recent studies that show varying degrees of survival are Richard T. Ruetten, "Senator Burton K. Wheeler and Insurgency in the 1920's," in *The American West: A Reorientation*, ed. Gene M. Gressley (Laramie, 1966), 111–31, 164–72; Jackson K. Putnam, "The Persistence of Progressivism in the 1920's: The Case of California," *Pacific Historical Review* XXXV (November, 1966), 395–411; J. Stanley Lemons, "The Sheppard-Towner Act: Progressivism in the 1920's," *Journal of American History*, LV (March, 1969), 776–86; Anne Firor Scott, "After Suffrage: Southern Women in the Twenties," *Journal of Southern History*, XXX (August, 1964), 298–318. Among monographs that show the survival of reform after the war, an outstanding title is Clarke A. Chambers, *Seedtime of Reform: American Social Service and Social Action, 1918–1933* (Minneapolis, 1963).

On the election of 1920, Wesley M. Bagby, *Road to Normalcy: The Presidential Campaign and Election of 1920* (Baltimore, 1962), is a virtual handbook on candidates, conventions, and campaigns. Donald R. McCoy, "Election of 1920," in *History of American Presidential Elections, 1789–1968*, ed. Arthur M. Schlesinger, Jr., *et al.*, (New York, 1971), III, 2349–56, provides a very useful thirty-six-page essay, along with the party platforms, several articles by and about the candidates themselves, and a state-by-state breakdown of the presidential vote. Mc-Coy's own judicious analysis, a neat summary of the essentials, is written with admirable clarity. Robert K. Murray, *The Harding Era: Warren G. Harding and His Administration* (Minneapolis, 1969), 513–37, contains some valuable commentary on Harding historiography. For comment on Murray and other recent items, see Burl Noggle, "The New Harding," *Reviews in American History*, I (March, 1973).

Index

225